The voluntary sector in th

362

Johns Hopkins Nonprofit Sector Series

edited by Lester M. Salamon and Helmut K. Anheier
Institute for Policy Studies, The Johns Hopkins University

Manchester University Press is proud to be publishing this important new series, the product of the most comprehensive comparative analysis of the global nonprofit sector ever undertaken. The growth of the sector between the public and the private, known variously as the nonprofit, voluntary or third sector, is one of the most significant contemporary developments in societies throughout the world. The books will cover the development and role of the sector in a broad cross-section of nations, and also provide comparative, cross-country analyses.

Johns Hopkins Nonprofit Sector Series 8

THE VOLUNTARY SECTOR IN THE UNITED KINGDOM

Jeremy Kendall
and
Martin Knapp

Manchester University Press

Manchester and New York

distributed exclusively in the United States by St. Martin's Press

Published by Manchester University Press
Oxford Road, Manchester M13 9NR, UK
and Room 400, 175 Fifth Avenue, New York, NY 10010, USA

Distributed exclusively in the USA
by St. Martin's Press Inc., 175 Fifth Avenue,
New York, NY 10010, USA

British Library Cataloguing-in-Publication Data
A catalogue record for this book is available from the British Library

Library of Congress Cataloging-in-Publication Data applied for

ISBN   0 7190 5037 5 hardback
          0 7190 5038 3 paperback

First published 1996

00 99   10 9 8 7 6 5 4 3 2

Typeset by Jane Dennett at the PSSRU
University of Kent at Canterbury

Printed in Great Britain
by Bell & Bain Ltd, Glasgow

Contents

List of tables, boxes and figures

Boxes

Figures

SERIES EDITORS' FOREWORD

This book is one in a series of monographs on the voluntary or non-pro sector throughout the world that have resulted from the Johns Hopk Comparative Nonprofit Sector Project, a major inquiry into the sco structure, history, legal position and role of the non-profit sector i broad cross-section of nations.

Launched in May 1990, this project has sought to close the glaring g in knowledge that have long existed about the thousands of schools, ho itals, clinics, community organizations, advocacy groups, day care cent relief organizations, nursing homes, homeless shelters, family counsell agencies, environmental groups and others that comprise this import sector. Though known by different names in different places, th organizations are present almost everywhere, albeit to widely differ extents. More than that, there is significant evidence that they are grow massively in both scope and scale as faith in the capability of governm to cope on its own with the interrelated challenges of persistent pove environmental degradation and social change has declined. Indeed, seem to be in the midst of a global "associational revolution" that is open new opportunities for organized private action and placing new deman and responsibilities on private not-for-profit groups. As a result, it become increasingly important to understand what the scope and conto of this non-profit sector really are, and what its potentials are for should ing the new demands being placed upon it.

The Johns Hopkins Comparative Nonprofit Sector Project w conceived as a way to meet this need, to document the scope, structu revenue base and background of the non-profit sector, and to do so i way that not only yielded solid and objective information about individ countries, but also made it possible to undertake cross-national comp isons in a systematic way. For this purpose, we identified thirteen countr representing different religious and historical traditions, different regic of the world, and different levels of economic development. Included w seven advanced industrial societies (the US, UK, France, Germany, Ita Sweden and Japan), five "developing" societies (Brazil, Ghana, Egy Thailand and India), and one former Soviet bloc country (Hungary). each of these countries we recruited a local associate and undertoo similar set of information-gathering activities guided by a common def ition, a common classification scheme, and a common set of data-gatheri

viii

:ms and instructions. The result, we believe, is the first systematic at-
:npt to put the non-profit sector on the social and economic map of the
:rld in a solid and empirical way.

The present volume reports on the results of this work in the United
:ngdom. Compared to many other countries in the study, prior to the
:earch undertaken in this part of the project, it is fair to say that the UK
:d a relatively strong research tradition in this field. This has embraced
:th academic perspectives, with small but dedicated groups of historians,
:al scholars, social policy analysts and management scientists increas-
:ly turning their attention towards the topic in the 1980s and 1990s; and
:actical work and action research involving practitioners within the vol-
:tary and statutory sectors.

However, while the existence of this research in many ways provided
: UK with a head start, in a sense it also made the tasks of synthesis and
:velopment more challenging. At the most fundamental empirical level,
:isting estimates of the basic human and financial parameters of the sector
:re found to be hard to reconcile with each other because of differing
:thodologies and definitions; yet the research reported here still attempts
:build upon these to maximum effect, rather than to start from scratch.
:the conceptual level, the task is similarly problematic because of a lack
:shared understandings about what the phenomenon under study con-
:ts of, let alone the nature of the questions that should be asked, or the
:ticipated answers to them. To give but one obvious example which dem-
:strates this difficulty: opinions differ widely on whether the examination
:d analysis of the huge education field in the UK legitimately belongs
:thin the ambit of research on the "voluntary sector". In our view, the
:swer — in the context of this study — is yes, as a cursory glance at the
:ntents of this book will show; but while including the field, the authors
:ve tried to ensure that the reader is fully aware of the extent to which
: question is both controversial in research terms, and politically highly
:arged.

The book is unique in the UK context in a number of ways, but perhaps
:ee deserve particular mention. First, it provides the first ever fully com-
:ehensive, consolidated and detailed account of the scope and scale of
: UK voluntary sector, both generally and at the field or "industry" level.
:cond, the book explores in some detail how and why this current com-
:sition has arisen, particularly by tracing the sector's historical develop-
:nt, legal treatment, and the attitude towards it of the institutions of the
:te. Third, for the first time it brings together in one volume ' 'hetic,
:used accounts of the development and role of the sector in th'   's
:which its presence has been most evident: education and pe
:vices.

From its outset, the Johns Hopkins Comparative N'

Project has been a collaborative effort among an extraordinary group
scholars with support from a wide array of funders and advisers. The te
of local associates — Martin Knapp and Jeremy Kendall in the UK, Ed
Archambault in France, Paolo Barbetta and Pippo Ranci in Italy, Helm
Anheier, Eckhard Priller and Wolfgang Seibel in Germany, Éva Kuti
Hungary, Tadashi Yamamoto and Takayoshi Amenomori in Japan, Lei
Landim in Brazil, Lawrence Atingdui and Emmanuel Laryea in Gha
Amani Kandil in Egypt, Amara Pongsapich in Thailand, Sven-Erik Sj
trand, Filip Wijkström and Thomas Lundström in Sweden — has work
together at every stage to perfect the information-gathering forms, devel
the basic definitions and classification scheme, and interpret the resu
To all of them we owe a deep debt of gratitude.

Thanks are also due to the numerous individuals who served on
International Advisory Committee to this project, to the members of
national advisory committees we formed to oversee the work, to Richa
Purslow, formerly of Manchester University Press, for the crucial enco
agement he provided in bringing this work to publication, and to the fo
dations, corporations and government agencies throughout the world t
provided support to make this work possible. In the case of the Uni
Kingdom, special thanks are due to the coalition of organizations w
funded the research: the Joseph Rowntree Foundation, the Charities A
Foundation and the Home Office. There was also a good deal of cro
subsidy for the research from internal funds held at the PSSRU.

It was more than 150 years ago that Alexis de Toqueville identified
"art of associating together" as the mother of all science. Today we app
to be in the middle of an extraordinary explosion of associational activ
as new forms of organized citizen action are taking shape and expandi
their role in widely disparate parts of the world. Our hope is that the ser
of monographs of which this volume is an important part will help ma
this process of change more visible and more understandable, and there
contribute to its success. We are convinced that important values hir
critically on this result.

Lester M. Salamon and Helmut K. Anhe
Baltimore, Maryl
April 1

PREFACE

Over recent years, there has been a noticeable upsurge in interest in the UK in organizations which occupy an intermediate position between the state and the market — agencies that in this country are typically referred to comprising a "voluntary sector". The introduction of the national lottery has sparked renewed interest from the general public, as vast sums of money are distributed by quangos to a confusing array of "good causes". Politicians of all persuasions have been quick to be seen to applaud and promote the contribution of most of these organizations, from self-help groups to the largest national charities, and from groups dedicated to the promotion of arts and culture to pre-school playgroups and youth development agencies. However, not all bodies operating neither primarily for monetary gain, nor within the public sector, have been so quick to receive automatic approval. The tax breaks and other advantages afforded to exclusive fee-paying schools by virtue of their charitable status, and whether the direct financial support from the state is a legitimate use of public funds, continue to be highly controversial issues.

At the same time, the world of academe has begun to take the study of this group of organizations more seriously — a phenomenon reflected by the research reported in this book. The recent formation of new scholarly societies, from the UK-based Voluntary Action History Society to the purposefully multidisciplinary International Society of Third Sector Researchers, and the consolidation and foundation of new journals, including *Voluntas* and *Nonprofit Studies*, are symptomatic of this development.

This book provides the first systematic account of this sector's development and current position in the UK. This has been possible through this country's participation in the first major comparative study of the "nonprofit sector" (to use United Nations terminology), led by Lester Salamon and Helmut Anheier of the Johns Hopkins University Institute for Policy Studies, Baltimore. Other books in the series report on how this set of organizations has fared in France, Germany, Italy, Sweden, the United States, Japan and Hungary, as well as pulling these diverse data together in overview volumes. The UK leg of this research was jointly funded by the Joseph Rowntree Foundation, Charities Aid Foundation and the Home Office, whom the authors would like to thank for their diligence and patience — particularly in the light of the fact that the project was first

xi

initiated in 1990. It was given strategic guidance by an advisory gro
which, at various times, included (noting institutional affiliation at the ti
of their participation in the group): Janet Lewis and Richard Best (Jose
Rowntree Foundation); Michael Brophy and Susan Saxon-Harrold (Ch
ities Aid Foundation); Roger Watkins and Geoffrey Biddulph (Volunta
Services Unit, the Home Office); Robin Guthrie, David Forrest and El
abeth Shaw (Charity Commission); Perri 6 and Janet Morrison (NCV(
and David Shawyer and Joanne Penn (Central Statistical Office). Spe(
thanks are extended to Sir Reay Geddes who chaired the group and p
vided unstinting enthusiasm and support throughout.

We would also like to offer our gratitude to all those employees
volunteers in voluntary organizations who took time out from their of(
hectic work schedules to complete questionnaires which, although sh(
were demanding in terms of the level of detail requested; to the la
number of voluntary sector intermediary or umbrella bodies and gove
ment agencies who shared their specialist databases and experiences w
us; and those from the voluntary sector and outside it who spared the ti
to allow us to interrogate them for an hour or so on various aspects of (
policy environment in which voluntary organizations are currently op
ating. Perri 6 and Anita Randon, then at the National Council for Volunta
Organisations, helped us to conduct these fascinating interviews, and Pe
also contributed directly to drafts of UK material submitted to the int
national project core staff. Marilyn Taylor and Geraint Thomas were me(
ulous co-authors of chapters of this book (Chapters 2 and 3 respectivel
and tolerant of our initial lack of familiarity with their disciplinary wo
views! Michelle Asbury, Jason Pinner and Phil Shore provided able a
cheerful research assistance in the statistical mapping of the sector that I
at the heart of this project. Other co-researchers at the Personal Soc
Services Research Unit, University of Kent, who provided support a
advice at various stages of this aspect of the study were Steve Cart
Andrew Fenyo, Jules Forder, Diane French, David Peters, Louise Priestl
Chris Ring and Justine Schneider. Tony Rees at the Centre for Health S(
vice Studies, University of Kent, entered many of the survey data. Ba
Knight of CENTRIS very helpfully provided us with access to the local
data compiled during his major study of voluntary action.

We benefited enormously from sharing thoughts and problems with t
other national researchers who participated in this cross-national stu(
particularly Edith Archambault in France, Éva Kuti in Hungary, and Pa
Barbetta in Italy, sight of whose finished manuscripts spurred us on
completion. Of course, none of this research would have been possi
without the intellectual and practical leadership, and phenomenal o
anizing and coordinating skills of Lester Salamon and Helmut Anhe
(who took the helm on the European aspects of the project), with t

ministrative support of Diana Schaub and Wojtek Sokolowski at Johns
pkins University. Early drafts of project material also benefited from
e comments of interviewees and others, with predictably insightful com-
ents coming from Nicholas Deakin, Marilyn Taylor, Peter Halfpenny and
rri 6. Ted Tapper provided detailed specific comments on a draft of
apter 6. Brian Salter offered a general micropolitical analysis of the wor-
ngs of the project (as well as life in general) over several pints of Spitfire
a regular basis, and Jeremy is grateful to him for allowing him to keep
e whole thing in perspective.

Finally, throughout the lifetime of the project, Maureen Weir has con-
buted continuously by providing sustained secretarial support, often
orking to imminent deadlines with barely legible manuscripts in the
ntext of a heavy overall workload. Jane Dennett not only typeset the
ok and helped bring it to a closure with maximum speed, but also offered
luable comments on each of the draft chapters, and copy-edited the book
erall.

Jeremy Kendall and Martin Knapp
Canterbury
April 1996

To our parents

Chapter 1

INTRODUCTION

Voluntary organizations have been at the heart of social action in the UK throughout the country's history. Service provision, mutual aid, campaigning and advocacy in all forms have evolved here, and people in the UK are often particularly proud of both charitable and solidaristic impulses that have found expression under voluntary sector auspices. Indeed, it is impossible to chart the development of UK society without frequent allusions to the pivotal role that voluntary organizations have played in changing ideologies, values, responsibilities and policies. At the same time, they have also been reactive vessels for the perpetuation of existing ideologies, attitudes and patterns of privilege and power, and they have acted as mechanisms for social control, not always of the benign variety.

The preamble of a Statute of 1601 listing contemporary examples of philanthropy is often cited in order to illustrate the longevity of voluntary action, but the roots of formally organized voluntary action stretch back much further. For example, mutual aid and friendly societies have been active in the UK at least since the first century AD, and what may be one of the oldest schools in the world — the King's School, Canterbury — was founded by St Augustine in the 6th century as an integral part of his Christian mission. To this day, religion has remained at the heart of much voluntary action, not only in the education field, but also providing the initial and continuing impetus for activities ranging from small-scale parish-based social and health services to major international emergency relief and development efforts.

The enduring freedom to form and operate voluntary associations flows naturally from the UK's relatively stable liberal tradition, with its support for tolerance, autonomy and diversity stretching back to the 18th century and before. Moreover, the state has been keen to encourage the application of private resources proactively for what have been deemed "public purposes". It has done so partly by promoting an enabling legal and fiscal framework which gives special privileges to many of the organizations that operate between public authorities and the commercial, profit-oriented market place. The concept of charity and charitable purposes, organically developed through case law in a fashion unique in Europe to the British Isles, has been central, although, as we shall see, this has been a complex, controversial and politically charged subject.

The relationship between the state and key parts of the voluntary sector has always been essentially symbiotic, and characterized by mutual dependence. Furthermore, the sector's apparently subservient role as a "junior partner" in the delivery of formal welfare services is a purely 20th century phenomenon, and the state did not displace the voluntary sector as the primary vehicle for social expenditures until the Liberal reforms of the early 20th century. Even at a time when enthusiasm for and faith in the capabilities and potential of the state were highest — the aftermath of the Second World War — the continued need for voluntary organizations was acknowledged by decision-makers and opinion-formers. In the late 1940s, for example, both pragmatic and ideological considerations lay behind the transfer of ownership of the nation's vast existing network of charity hospitals from voluntary auspices to central government control, representing a massive shift of resources to the public sector. The "agency relationship" between the state and friendly societies in the provision of insurance was also replaced with direct state provision in the aftermath of war.

Yet in another major field — education — great care was taken to negotiate a continuing major role for voluntary bodies. Furthermore, *Voluntary Action*, written in the mid-1940s by Lord Beveridge, one of the architects of the post-war welfare state, posited a general belief in the importance of voluntary activity for the healthy functioning of society despite the ongoing expansion of state control and direction. The sector was to prove remarkably robust and adaptable in reacting to the challenges imposed by an enlarged government sector, at both national and local levels. The 1978 Wolfenden report, *The Future of Voluntary Organisations*, was also a landmark of recognition, although it failed to anticipate the anti-state and pro *laissez-faire* ideology which was to challenge the *status quo* during the years of the Thatcher and Major governments.

1.1 Growth in public interest in the voluntary sector

Despite the long tradition of acknowledgement of the voluntary sector's many roles, its contributions appear to have been redis-covered over the last few years by the public at large and the media. There has also been a notable quickening in the pace of the rhetoric of "partnership" with the sector from across the polit-ical spectrum; an all-party parliamentary committee on charities has been convened and, within government, new initiatives have been launched by the Home Office's Voluntary Services Unit. What has brought about this new wave of attention? Three themes help explain the higher profile of the voluntary sector.

Dissatisfaction with the *status quo*

The government and business sectors dominate most people's thinking about the production, organization and delivery of goods and services. Government departments and agencies set public policy frameworks, provide a wide range of essential utilities and social and other services, redistribute resources to reflect collective needs and priorities, and finance some of the activities of other sectors. Business enterprises produce most of the country's tan-gible goods and services, usually in the pursuit of material gain and/or a larger market share.

These high-profile sectors and organizations do many things very well, but it is now widely understood that they are poorly placed to meet *every* social or individual need. Interest in the voluntary sector has grown with recognition of, and dissatis-faction or disillusionment with, the cumulative failures of the institutional and political *status quo* represented by government and business organizations. The general public — and their com-munity, political or media representatives — have become more critical of the consequences for cost, quality and effectiveness of heavy reliance on government or the market to solve many of the social and developmental problems of our time. Can a combination of market forces and state action alone be relied upon to allocate housing, family support or community care fairly and efficiently, or to protect a country's artistic assets and cultural heritage? Who is really best placed to meet the needs of religious or ethnic minorities, or to support those people and communities whose problems and vulnerabilities themselves may appear to stem in part from the limitations of government? Do governments have either the far-sightedness to address the world's environmental problems, or the political detachment to intervene in support of people affected by natural, social or political disasters? These shortcomings may range from a lack of understanding, knowledge and insight, through incompetence to brazen short-termism and expediency, or from fiscal constraints to partiality and wilful neglect.

At the same time, the voluntary sector itself has not been immune from public disillusionment and suspicion. At one level, the media have recently become noticeably more critical of some features of voluntary action, fuelled by stories of fraud and charity incompetence, as evidenced, for example, by the publicity surrounding scandals relating to Humana, the British Legion and Scope (formerly the Spastics Society). Furthermore, many members of the general public now appear to hold significant reservations about the probity and efficiency of some charities, with considerable numbers taking the view that too many exist, and that they often spend "too much" on administration (Fenton et al., 1993; Saxon Harrold, 1993). Moreover, fewer people than 50 years ago are now active in political parties, traditional churches and women's organizations, friendly societies and trade unions. Neither Lord Beveridge's celebration of voluntary action nor the Wolfenden Committee's more recent report could have foreseen the enormous changes in the second half of the 20th century that would be experienced by those organizational vehicles for collective social action which had been so dominant in the first half of the century.

Yet these symptoms of suspicion and decline in the sector have to be set against wider evidence that the sector continues to thrive. Most obviously, the number of registered charities in England and Wales (accounting for around two-fifths of all voluntary organizations in the UK) has grown considerably since 1970 (see Table 1.1).[1] It is probably not unreasonable to speculate

Table 1.1

Numbers of registered charities in England and Wales

Year	Number of charities newly registered	Number of charities removed from register	Net increase	Total at end of year[a]
1970	2374	na	na	76648
1971	1967	na	na	78600
1972	2219	na	na	80834
1973	2527+11140[b]	na	na	94501
1974	3110	na	na	na
1975	2858	na	na	119978
1976	2988	na	na	122750
1977	3598	405	3193	125908
1978	3506	202	3304	129212
1979	3299	208	3091	132303
1980	3955	210	3745	136048
1981	3495	254	3241	139289
1982	4057	196	3861	143150
1983	3804	190	3614	146764
1984	3873	126	3747	150511
1985	3790	166	3624	154135
1986	3942	175	3767	157902
1987	3672	198	3474	161376
1988	3609	451	3158	164534
1989	4119	483	3716	168170
1990	4013	749	3264	171434
1991	4042	1168[c]	2874[c]	166503[c]
1992	1681	4546[c]	135[c]	170357[c]
1993	12559	6050[c]	6509[c]	170932[c]

Source: Alan Polak, Charity Commission, personal communication, 1994.
a Includes subsidiary and connected charities; and see caveat in the text.
b The second figure represents educational charities transferred from DES to Charity Commission supervision.
c Figures in these years and disparities between them are partly a reflection of data-cleaning activities, including removal of duplicates and amalgamated charities.
  'na' indicates not available.

that, so far, and notwithstanding these and related criticisms, the sector emerges *relatively* unscathed in comparison with the institutions of the state and the world of business. For example, the vast bulk of media attention still tends to focus on more positive images including descriptions of the work of charities, their responses to government initiatives, and fundraising efforts. Only one in 20 "events" reported in a recent detailed analysis of printed news media concerned allegations of charity misconduct (Fenton et al., 1993; Deacon et al., 1995).

Support for pluralism and diversity

Another reason for the sector's higher profile in recent years has been increased awareness of the added value inherent both in political pluralism and service variety. Notwithstanding Beveridge's *Voluntary Action*, in the rush to equate state action with social progress, a somewhat dismissive view emerged in the mid-20th century of voluntary organizations, and charity in particular, as something associated with the failures and injustices of the past. Particularly for those on the political left, charities were regarded as creatures of the "bad old days" responsible for freezing social inequalities, contributing to the subservience and powerlessness of the disadvantaged, and making them "beholden" to those fortunate enough to be in a position to give. Charity was at best to be regarded as a residual, the domain of amateurism and inappropriate social control, to be superceded by state-led professional expertise and expanded social rights.

While the traditional concept of charity still has its critics, more positive thinking has re-emerged, rediscovering voluntary groups' important political and service provision roles in the context of recognition that the state and its professional employees cannot and should not be omnipotent nor omniscient. The numerous benefits cited by observers of the sector have included its political role in enriching civil society and providing a voice for otherwise excluded disadvantaged groups, providing a basis for countervailing power to both the state and the market, and offering developmental opportunities for political participation and control (Ware, 1989c). It has also been associated with the enhancement of flexibility, responsiveness, choice, innovation and user control in service delivery (Knapp et al., 1990). Furthermore, voluntary organizations have been promoted as enhancing social cohesion, vital to and perhaps even representative of the essence of "community".

Pursuit of political and ideological goals

Modern governments of all political complexions have appealed to the capacity and resource potential of the voluntary sector in general as a way to legitimize constraints on, or even cuts in, public social expenditures at times of fiscal austerity (Brenton, 1985). But, historically, different styles of voluntary action have chimed with different political viewpoints. For the traditional Conservative right, charities, particularly Church-based, had always been regarded approvingly as organically developed and natural microcosms of the wider society in which they were located. Hierarchically organized by the elite, and reflecting the collective wisdom of the communities in which they emerged, they were thought to render unnecessary any "interference" from the "artificial" state. As we have noted, the same charities tended to be seen as the antithesis of social progress by the left. Rather, their empathy with voluntary action lay with the institutions of working-class mutual aid and with movements promoting political change, increasing class consciousness and encouraging a supportive working-class culture.

In the 1980s and 1990s, a new political role was to emerge for voluntary and quasi-voluntary organizations. The state found voluntary action attractive as a mechanism for change, a powerful instrument capable of disempowering or undermining other players in the political game. This was to be of critical significance in the tense and sometimes fraught power struggles between a right-wing central state and often left-wing dominated local government. For the former, voluntary or quasi-voluntary housing associations and schools in particular were to offer a politically and electorally acceptable way of being seen to fund collective services, while at the same time weakening local government and — superficially at least — "rolling back the state". For the so-called "urban left" local authorities of the early 1980s, by contrast, the provision of financial and other support for "constituences of the disadvantaged" — including groups for ethnic minorities and women, and groups promoting the rights of state welfare recipients — was regarded as a useful means of politicization, mobilizing new constituencies of support (Gyford, 1985; see Chapter 5).

1.2 Voluntarism and the impetus from government

As interest has grown in the UK, four forms of government encouragement for the voluntary sector have become increasingly important over the past 20 years. The state has sought to enhance the sector's visibility, provide funding, offer regulatory support and expand tax concessions.

Enhancing visibility

Ministerial speeches and departmental policy documents have often alluded to the assumed positive attributes of the voluntary sector that we have outlined, enhancing its visibility and stature, and made much of the notion of "partnership" between government and voluntary organizations. Within the state bureaucracy, since its formation in 1973, the Home Office's Voluntary Service Unit (VSU) has been active in promoting both the voluntary sector and volunteering through the collection and dissemination of information, and via a small number of funding schemes. In England, the VSU works closely with many of the sector's infrastructural, promotional and support bodies (such as the National Council for Voluntary Organisations and the Volunteer Centre UK). These bodies attempt to perform resourcing and co-ordinating roles for the sector, and the VSU provides core funds for many of them.[2] The symbolic importance of the VSU has been welcomed by many commentators, and it has been applauded as an enclave of voluntary sector understanding within central government, although its resource base has also been dismissed as tokenistic (Brenton, 1985; and see Hazell and Whybrew, 1993; note that the VSU allocated grants worth £12 million in 1991/92). In addition, while it claims to coordinate government policy, the VSU's influence within government has been very limited, since other departments have been reluctant to accept "interference" in what they perceive to be their own internal responsibilities. The voluntary sector's profile has been raised in the 1990s through the spotlight cast by a 1990 "Efficiency Scrutiny" of government funding of the sector, and through annual meetings of the sector's four national generalist intermediaries with a newly-convened "Ministerial Group on the Voluntary Sector" for a general exchange of views. To date, the former has had a mixed reaction from the sector's support bodies, following diverse experience of implementation (e.g. Mabbott, 1992a; Garfield, 1994).

Funding

A second way in which government has encouraged the voluntary sector is through *direct financial support* (some but not all of which was the subject of the recent scrutiny). The national lottery is a recent new addition to the existing battery of funding opportunities provided by government. As we describe in more detail in Chapter 4, total UK statutory funding of the sector, broadly defined (from all tiers of government, including local, central, foreign and supranational — such as the European Community) stood at some £11.6 billion in 1990. This represented just under 6 percent of total UK government current expenditure in that year.[3]

Historically, and employing a broad definition of the sector, over the past 50 or so years, funding for the universities and maintained voluntary (mainly church) schools has dominated central and local government support, respectively. Education remains the largest single area of state expenditure on this broader voluntary sector. In recent years, the most significant new injections of public funds have tended to come in the form of contractual or quasi-contractual funding for particular programmes or purposes, under which providers in the voluntary sector have been mobilized to deliver specific services in pursuit of departmental policy objectives. Housing provision and training schemes for the unemployed have been the leading examples. While central government funding of the sector under most if not all potential definitions has undoubtedly increased as a whole over the past 20 or so years, whether or not it did so between the mid-1980s and mid-1990s depends upon the definition of the sector which is employed (see Chapter 4).

At the same time, *local* government support, dominated by funding from social services and education committees, has increased markedly in real terms since the mid-1980s, despite the financial squeeze from central government. Nevertheless, local government funding of the voluntary sector remains low when compared to the overall amounts spent, at between 2 and 8 percent of current expenditure (depending on whether a narrow or broad definition of recipient organizations is employed; see below).

Regulatory support

The third form of government "encouragement" — through regulation — has grown in importance in recent years, sometimes
building upon a variety of provisions in particular fields from
earlier periods. Some measures are currently still in the process
of establishment or consolidation, including legislative measures
introduced by the Charities Acts of 1992 and 1993 . These seek to
modernize the regulatory environment and ensure adequate accountability and supervision, the first major legislation in this area
since 1960. In addition to this generic legislation, the state also
interacts with voluntary bodies through regulations in specific
fields. For example, in the case of central government, the Housing
Corporation regulates (as well as funds) housing associations
while, at the level of local authorities, inspection units deal with
voluntary sector social care facilities.

Of course, regulations seen as inappropriate can be inhibiting
rather than supportive. A "Deregulation Task Force", set up in
1994, gave the sector, via umbrella and intermediary bodies, the
opportunity to air their grievances concerning governmental
regulations and requirements across a range of areas, including
the new generic charities legislation.

Tax concessions

Tax concessions, which make up the other main form of increasing
government encouragement, were significantly expanded during
the 1980s, driven partly by the generally favourable climate of
encouragement for voluntarism, and partly in response to the
sector's lobbyists. By the turn of the decade, these concessions
were worth just under £1 billion a year.[4] These lobbyists had
pointed to the combined adverse and unintended effects on the
sector's resource base of two tax changes: reductions in income
tax rates (making "tax-efficient" donations more costly to
individual donors) and the associated switch to indirect taxation,
particularly VAT.

The most significant tax extensions have been geared towards
individual and corporate donors, including liberalization of the
complex tax-exemption arrangements for planned "covenanted"
giving, and the introduction of tax exemptions for particular

forms of one-off giving. The latter includes the "Gift Aid" scheme established in 1990, which is expanding rapidly — and possibly at the expense of traditional covenanted giving — and the much smaller payroll giving project instigated in 1986. In addition, some advantages have also been made available to charities themselves, including a limited number of concessions in the VAT area, and the extension of mandatory relief on business rates.

Of course, these encouragements have come with many and varied strings attached, raising issues which we explore in the pages that follow.

1.3 Developing theoretical perspectives

Academic interest in the roles and activities of the voluntary sector has a long pedigree in Britain. For example, major social and political thinkers of the late 19th and early 20th century, ranging from Herbert Spencer to Beatrice and Sidney Webb, were preoccupied with the refinement of theory pertaining to the appropriate division of labour between the state, charity and self-help in meeting social need (Lewis, 1995a). Furthermore, the outstanding work on the history of voluntary action, David Owen's *English Philanthropy 1660-1960*, was written as long ago as the early 1960s (Owen, 1964). Yet in an interesting parallel with the view from government and the general public, many of the modern disciplinary social sciences — including economics, sociology and political science — until quite recently have tended to work predominantly with a two-sector, public versus private model as the basis for analytical distinctions.[5] Similarly, in social policy analysis, the dominance of the Fabian socialist tradition, with its rush to condemn the profit-oriented market while equating an expanding state teleologically with social progress, tended to obscure, or at least underplay, the continued contribution of voluntary organizations in British society.

More recently, however, an international academic research community with an interest in the non-profit sector has emerged. Perhaps with the highest profile during the 1980s because of the elegance and parsimony of their theoretical arguments, were the economic theories of American academics Burton Weisbrod,

Estelle James, Henry Hansmann and Avner Ben-Ner.[6] Weisbrod (1975, 1977) developed a body of theory conceptualizing the voluntary sector as a response to demand for public or quasi-public goods and services supplied by neither the market nor the state. In orthodox economics, the private market is usually seen as an efficient mechanism for ensuring provision in line with citizens' tastes and preferences. However, this optimality breaks down in the case of jointly consumed, non-excludable and non-rival goods — in part because of the so-called free-rider problem, wherein the benefits of consumption can be reaped without paying. This instance of "market failure" is then taken as providing an efficiency rationale for government provision (with consumer preferences expressed through the democratic process). Yet Weisbrod points out that the state itself is likely to be willing and able to meet only some of the demands that arise in this fashion, and the combination of both market and government "failures" leaves a residual demand — failures to which voluntary organization is then seen as an efficient response.

James (1987) takes this demand-side argument a stage further by positing that "excess and differentiated demand" for this type of good may be a necessary but not a sufficient condition, for the existence of voluntary organizations: the supply side also needs to be theorized. She argues that the relative strength of the voluntary sector will also be predicated on the availability of appropriate entrepreneurship, while posing the question as to why this is likely to arise under non-profit, rather than for-profit, auspices. Supported by a wide range of cross-national comparative evidence in the education field in particular, she isolates religion, the pursuit of status, prestige and political power, and the goal of disguised profit distribution as critical motivating factors for those who decide to adopt the non-profit form.

Hansmann's (1980) "contract failure" theory, like Weisbrod's, takes the free market as the benchmark for thinking about the voluntary sector's role, but focuses on a different set of difficulties in its operation. The theory places particular emphasis on what is often taken as a defining characteristic of voluntary organizations — the non-distribution constraint under which they operate. From this perspective, legal and constitutional constraints on organizations' abilities to distribute net earnings act as a powerful signal to consumers about the motives, intentions and behaviour of those who control them. In situations of consumer vulnerability, where the characteristics of output are difficult or impossible to measure or monitor (particularly through separation of the funder and direct consumer), non-profit organizations, according to Hansmann, are likely to be regarded as more "trustworthy" than for-profit organizations. This is because the latter's organizational goals mean that they have a more obvious incentive to cut corners on quality, or otherwise opportunistically "take advantage" of the situation. The existence of non-profits which act in accordance with consumer expectations is then efficient from a societal viewpoint because this implies that the costs of monitoring or exploitation which would be incurred in a purely for-profit world are avoided.

Finally "stakeholder theory" in many ways represents an attempt to synthesize and provide micro-economic foundations for the bodies of theory described thus far, with a sharp focus on the economic aspects of the process and conditions of non-profit formation (Ben-Ner and Van Hoomissen, 1993). Non-profit organizations are portrayed as coalitions of stakeholders providing "trust goods" and "collective goods", both for their own benefit (as simultaneously demanders and suppliers), and for the benefit of "non-controlling stakeholders" who do not have a direct input into organizational governance. The latter frequent this type of organization because they identify with the core coalition of demanders-suppliers, and recognize that because the supplying coalition are themselves demanders, it would be self-defeating for them to cut corners on the quality of provision.

The body of sociological and political theory that has emerged to advance understanding of the voluntary sector is unsurprisingly rather more complex, and is difficult to summarize briefly. Instead, it may be helpful to identify four major themes which have arisen in the international literature: two relating to these organizations' relationships with the state; and two to their relationships with the structure of society as a whole.

The first important theoretical theme has been developed directly in response to the economic theories described above, as well as to "conservative" political theory (Salamon, 1987, 1995; Kuhnle and Selle, 1992). These, it is argued, are inherently misleading because they create the expectation of conflict and competition rather than cooperation between the state and the voluntary sector. The assumption of competition is seen as erroneous because of the ample, if fragmented, evidence that was beginning to emerge during the 1980s that, in many countries (including the US), the two sectors tend to operate in concert or "partnership", rather than discretely and separately. The voluntary sector, it is argued, historically and currently has tended not to act as a "gap-filling" response to the failures of the other sectors, or in competition with them: rather, the sectors have tended to develop a relationship of mutual dependence and cooperation. Most importantly, the state has clearly become a major funder and regulator of non-profit activity in many countries, and it is suggested that the dominant economic formulations are unable to make sense of this empirical reality. Salamon's (1987) "voluntary failure" theory then developed a new perspective on state-voluntary sector relationships. While government and the marketplace may have certain weaknesses, it is argued that the voluntary sector itself also tends to exhibit its own failings. These include particularism, amateurism, paternalism and insufficiency, which in turn may prompt various forms of state intervention.

A second theme also focuses attention on the relationship between the voluntary sector and the state. One particular theoretical tradition sees "the third [voluntary] sector offer[ing] a buffer zone between state and society, and mitigating social tensions and conflicts. Third sector organizations take on functions which the state, for various reasons, cannot fulfil or delegate to for-profit firms" (Seibel and Anheier, 1990, p.14). One variant of this is Seibel's (1990) characterization of the sector as a "shunting yard for [unsolvable] social political problems". Under this argument, the sector emerges as a major player funded by government not because of any superiority in terms of efficiency. (Many reasons why voluntary organizations are likely to be highly inefficient are identified.) Rather, it is well positioned to allow the government to create the *impression*, as political imperatives dictate, that "something is being done" about issues that are inherently intractable.

A third theme is "structural" and relates to the sector's ability to grow in different national settings, in part taking us back to the issue of non-profit entrepreneurship. Salamon and Anheier (1994) have argued that the existence of an educated urban middle class — reflecting an advanced state of economic development — is one of three factors conducive to the existence of a strong voluntary sector. Other features argued to be of import are the existence of a common law (as opposed to a civil law) legal system, and a lack of political centralization. A common law system, with its presumption in favour of the right of association, together with a decentralized political framework, it is argued, create a greater "social space" or more "open field" in which non-profits can flourish.

The final theme relates to distributional concerns. It has been suggested by some scholars that the operations of non-profit organizations may mirror the interests of elites, or the capitalist system. Some commentators, arguing from a Marxist or near-Marxist perspective, have conceptualized philanthropy as an expression of social control by dominant status groups, effectively blocking social progress. Such theorizing is consistent with the political left's antipathy towards charity to which we have already referred (see Williams, 1989; Wolch, 1990; and Beckford, 1991 for interesting recent formulations sympathetic with this tradition).

1.4 The comparative non-profit sector

The expectations generated by the increased attention from the public and the media, government and academia have not, however, been informed by a clear understanding of what the voluntary sector is, how it is financed, or how it links with the state and private business. This is as true in the UK as it is in most other countries. It was in this context that the Comparative Nonprofit Sector Project was launched in 1990, directed by Lester Salamon and Helmut Anheier of the Johns Hopkins University, Baltimore, USA. The UK was one of the first countries to sign up for the project, with financial support from the Joseph Rowntree Foundation, Charities Aid Foundation and Home Office. The international project's aims were to close gaps in knowledge about the

---

Box 1.1   Aims of the Comparative Nonprofit Sector Project

- To provide a systematic basis for comparing the experience of voluntary organizations in different parts of the world.

- To describe the scope, scale and legal position of the voluntary sector in each participating country, and to develop an understanding of its evolving role.

- To examine the voluntary sector's relations with other institutions, especially government and business.

- To improve awareness of the sector on the part of public and private leaders and the general public.

- To provide a sounder basis for evaluating policies which concern the voluntary sector.

---

sector in a comparative context using common definitions, equivalent research frameworks and consistent instrumentation in pursuit of an agreed set of common objectives (see Box 1.1).

Other participating countries were Brazil, Egypt, France, Germany, Ghana, Hungary, India, Italy, Japan, Sweden, Thailand and the United States. Alongside the UK, full statistical data were collected in seven of these countries — France, Germany, Hungary, Italy, Japan, the United States and Sweden (although Sweden joined the project later, and so was not included in the first stream of published comparative results). Each country had a team of "Local Associates" to carry out the country-specific research tasks, while the Baltimore team provided central support and direction.

1.5 The question of definition

One of the first activities of the Comparative Project was to address the definition of the sector. What is this phenomenon to which renewed public and political interest has been directed, which government appears so keen to support? The task of definition is far from trivial. Indeed, researchers who have attempted a definition or classification often remark that the array of organizational forms, activities, motivations and ideologies that exists between the state and the market is so confusing as to render the task inherently impossible. Moreover, there is no single "correct" definition to be used in all circumstances, and the preferred approach will depend upon the purposes for which it is required (Johnson, 1981; 6, 1991).

To define the sector for the purposes of comparative cross-national research, the international research team built up what has been labelled a "structural operational definition". This approach identifies characteristics which organizations should possess in order to be meaningfully described as "non-profit" or "voluntary". On the evaluative criteria of economy, significance and explanatory power, the structural operational definition performs better than the obvious alternatives, including legal, economic/financial and functional approaches (Salamon and Anheier, 1992a, 1996b). A similar "first principles" approach has been adopted before by policy analysts who have addressed this issue explicitly in the UK (for example, Johnson, 1981; Brenton, 1985; Knapp et al., 1987). The characteristics required for organizations to be included are listed in Box 1.2, while Figure 1.1 illustrates how this definition's coverage squares with some of the major types of organization in the UK. The area enclosed by the bold line represents the set of registered charities and is contrasted with the shaded area, showing organizational coverage when the structural operational definition is applied to the UK. With the exception of voluntary controlled schools, purely religious trusts and bodies linked to specific statutory agencies, all bodies that are charitable in law were covered by our interpretation of this definition, whether registered, exempted or excepted, or for some other reason unregistered. Other non-charitable bodies which appeared to meet all our criteria to a meaningful degree were also included, and some economically significant examples are given at the foot of the figure. Other non-charitable bodies included in our definition were entities considered "too political" to be regarded as charitable in law; "exclusive" self-help or mutual aid groups which have been denied charitable status; and any voluntary bodies which have either made a conscious decision not to be officially sanctioned as charitable bodies because the advantages are thought to be outweighed by the concomitant constraints, responsibilities and costs, or because they are unaware of their eligibility for charitable status. (Technically, some of the

Box 1.2   The structural operational definition

Organizations appearing to meet all of the following criteria were regarded as voluntary bodies for the purposes of cross-national comparison.

Formal. Only structured entities with constitutions or formal sets of rules, perhaps (but not necessarily) registered with a public authority or voluntary intermediary body, were included. This ruled out the large set of informal household and neighbourhood support activities, which are particularly important in the community development and social welfare fields.

Independent of government and self-governing. Groups were required to be constitutionally or institutionally independent of government, and self-governing — that is, with their own internal decision-making structures, and not directly controlled by a private (for-profit) entity or by the state. This criterion does *not* exclude from the sector constitutionally independent organizations heavily dependent on the private market or the government for their resources.

Not-profit-distributing and primarily non-business. Organizations were ruled out if they were empowered to distribute net earnings to controlling persons (even if on solidaristic principles) or had a commercial orientation which made them indistinguishable from for-profit firms. Cooperatives, financial and other mutuals (including building societies, most friendly societies and motoring organizations) were among the exclusions.

Voluntary. A meaningful degree of voluntarism in terms of money or time through philanthropy or voluntary citizen involvement was required to qualify an agency as belonging to the sector.

Two further criteria were adopted for the purposes of statistical mapping only. *Party political* organizations were excluded. And *sacramental activities*, taken to include places of worship and the central infrastructure and support bodies of the churches, were omitted — although they are recognized in the classification scheme.

organizations in the last category may legally be charitable without realizing it.)

There is one criterion sometimes employed in identifying voluntary organizations which is conspicuous by its absence from the listing shown in Box 1.2. This is the requirement that

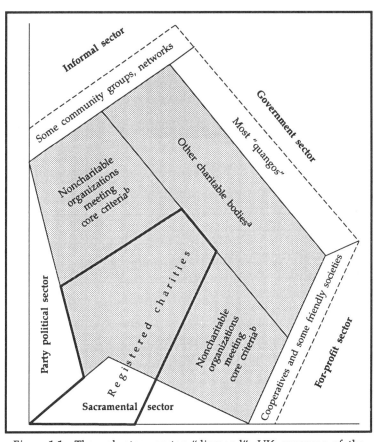

Figure 1.1 The voluntary sector "diamond": UK coverage of the structural/operational definition

a Includes exempted and excepted charities (other than sacramental bodies in this category), some of which are often referred to as "quangos", or thought of as public sector bodies, including the national museums and voluntary aided schools.

b Includes most housing associations, self-help groups, non-partisan "political" groups; trade unions, and professional, trade and business-support agencies; most recreational organizations (including sports and social clubs); and many community businesses.

Note: In addition to sacramental bodies, voluntary controlled schools, and trust funds and fundraising bodies linked to specific statutory bodies have been excluded from the structural/ operational definition as applied here, although charitable.

organizations should be "other-regarding", "altruistic" or operate for "the public benefit" to be included as part of the voluntary sector — one interpretation of which is an important element in the legal definition of "charity". This criterion was *not* employed for the purposes of cross-national comparison since it was not possible to agree on how it might be applied in practice internationally.

Even within the UK, there is no universal agreement as to what "public benefit" actually means, and the way in which it has been interpreted in charity law has been contested by numerous commentators in a highly charged ideological debate. For its supporters, the current system (described in Chapter 3) is flexible, adaptive and a pragmatic solution to an inherently complicated problem. They suggest that the concept of charity as now legally interpreted is instinctively and universally understood by the British public, and that the creative use of analogy through case law for gradual and sensitive modernization helpfully avoids the need for complicating (and potentially complicated) primary legislation.

To its critics, however, charity law is seen as having developed in such a way as to become removed from its original unifying purpose of helping the poor and deprived, and of therefore being anti-working class and perpetuating privilege. Under this view, the Charity Commission and the judiciary's interpretation of the core "public benefit" criterion is regarded as inequitable, inconsistent and restrictive (Chesterman, 1979; Gladstone, 1982; Brenton, 1985; Wolch, 1990; Beckford, 1991). Because charitable status gives tax advantages and acts as a *de facto* seal of approval, its denial to mutual aid bodies and pressure groups has been seen as unjust and stifling of social change, while its possession by many fee-paying and socially exclusive institutions — particularly many "public" (charitable) schools funded by private fees — has been regarded as reactionary and divisive. It is noteworthy that this aspect of the legal framework was not dealt with in the early 1990s' spate of charity legislation which was primarily concerned with regulatory issues. According to Stephen Lee, director of the Institute of Fund Raising Managers, to have addressed the topic of definition "would have led into a parliamentary minefield which would have blown up any prospect of a non-partisan approach to the Charities Bill" (quoted in Windsor, 1994, p.2).

Having settled on a definition, the next step was to agree a classification of organizations by field of activity. A number of alternatives have previously been used by researchers and umbrella bodies. This study had to select just one. An "International Classification of Nonprofit Organizations" (ICNPO) was specially developed by the Johns Hopkins University team in collaboration with the researchers in each of the participating countries, categorizing organizations by "industry" (Salamon and Anheier, 1992a, 1996b). The ICNPO is summarized in Box 1.3. Like the definition, the classification aims to be sensitive to what appear to be the relevant features of voluntary organization activities across the globe. Inevitably, it therefore represents a compromise between different national realities and contexts. However, our experience of its application shows that it works relatively well in the UK. Perhaps the major conceptual problem to arise is that the classification scheme tends to focus attention on the sector's service provision functions at the expense of its mutual aid, campaigning and advocacy. One way out of this *impasse* is to recognize that, for many purposes, organizations will need to be classified by both industry *and* societal function, generating a two-dimensional matrix (Kendall and 6, 1994). Indeed a third dimension, to recognize variation between types of beneficiary, may also be useful (Hems and Passey, 1996). Difficulties and ambiguities in the practical application of the ICNPO in the UK are briefly described in Chapter 4.

Finally, armed with this classification scheme, we need to revisit the question of definition, since some of the organizations which have all the characteristics listed in Box 1.2 — and are thus part of the sector for international comparative purposes — would probably not feature in most people's understanding of "the voluntary sector" in the UK. This problem arises both as a corollary to our exclusion of a "public benefit" or "altruistic" criterion in the definition, and because the criteria that have been used tend not to be met or unmet in an absolute sense, but are relevant to varying degrees: in other words, the boundary around the sector is blurred. We coped with this difficulty in the UK by developing a "narrow voluntary sector" definition to run alongside the broader, structural operational definition. Our objective was to get closer to what is probably the taken-for-granted understanding of what is meant by "the voluntary

Box 1.3   The International Classification of Nonprofit Organizations

Group 1: Culture and Recreation

1 100 Culture
Media and communications
Visual arts, architecture, ceramic art
Performing arts
Historical, literary and humanistic societies
Museums
Zoos and aquariums

1 200 Recreation[b]
Sports clubs
Recreation and social clubs

1 300 Service Clubs

Group 2: Education and Research

2 100 Primary and Secondary Education[b]
Elementary, primary and secondary education

2 200 Higher Education[b]
Higher education (university level)

2 300 Other Education
Vocational/technical schools
Adult/continuing education

2 400 Research
Medical research (in-house only)
Science and technology
Social sciences, policy studies

Group 3: Health

3 100 Hospitals and Rehabilitation
Hospitals
Rehabilitation

3 200 Nursing Homes
Nursing homes

3 300 Mental Health and Crisis Intervention
Psychiatric hospitals
Mental health treatment
Crisis intervention

3 400 Other Health Services
Public health and wellness education
Health treatment, primary outpatient
Rehabilitative medical services
Emergency medical services

Group 4: Social Services

4 100 Social Services
Child welfare, child services, day care
Youth services and youth welfare
Family services
Services for the handicapped
Services for the elderly
Self-help and other personal social services

4 200 Emergency and Relief
Disaster/emergency prevention and control
Temporary shelters
Refugee assistance

4 300 Income Support and Maintenance
Income support and maintenance
Material assistance

Group 5: Environment

5 100 Environment
Pollution abatement and control
Natural resources conservation and protection
Environmental beautification and open spaces

5 200 Animals
Animal protection and welfare
Wildlife preservation and protection
Veterinary services

Group 6: Development and Housing

6 100 Economic, Social & Community Development
Community and neighbourhood organizations
Economic development
Social development

6 200 Housing
Housing associations
Housing assistance

6 300 Employment and Training
Job Training programmes
Vocational counselling and guidance
Vocational rehabilitation and sheltered workshops

Group 7: Law, Advocacy, and Politics

7 100 Civic and Advocacy Organization
Advocacy organizations
Civil rights associations
Ethnic associations
Civic associations

7 200 Law and Legal Services
Legal Services
Crime prevention and public safety
Rehabilitation of offenders
Victim support
Consumer protection associations

7 300 Political Organizations[a]
Political parties and organizations

Group 8: Philanthropic Intermediaries and Voluntarism Promotion

8 100 Philanthropic Intermediaries and Voluntarism Promotion
Grant-making foundations
Voluntarism promotion and support
Fundraising organizations

Group 9: International Activities

9 100 International Activities
Exchange/friendship/cultural programmes
Development assistance associations
International disaster and relief organizations
International human rights & peace organizations

Group 10: Religion[a]

10 100 Religious Congregations and Associations
Congregations
Associations of congregations

Group 11: Business, Professions and Unions[b]

11 100 Business, Professional Associations and Unions
Business associations
Professional associations
Labour unions

Group 12: (Not Elsewhere Classified)[a]

12 100 NEC

---

a   Not included for statistical mapping purposes (BVS or NVS).
b   Not included for statistical mapping in NVS only.
    The ICNPO was developed by Salamon and Anheier (1992b, 1996b).

Box 1.4   ICNPO groups of organizations often not thought of as part of "the voluntary sector" in the UK

- *Recreational organizations (ICNPO subgroup 1 200).* These, which are mostly not charitable under existing law, may be thought of as lacking an "altruistic" core.

- *Primary and secondary education (ICNPO subgroup 2 100).* This group includes (a) charitable "independent" schools resourced largely by high private fees, and thus often thought of as "exclusive", or lacking in "altruism"; and (b) charitable maintained voluntary aided and special agreement schools whose current expenditure is fully funded by local government. Although the majority of their governors are appointed by their founding trusts (which are usually denominational in character), they are usually thought of as being part of "the state system", and therefore effectively not "independent" of the state.

- *Higher education (ICNPO subgroup 2 200).* Institutions in this group, including all the major universities, although exempted or excepted charities, are similarly thought of as being subject to so much state direction and control that they are not truly "independent" of the state.

- *Trade unions, professional and business associations (ICNPO group 11)* which, like recreation, are mostly not charitable, may also be excluded from the sector because they are thought to lack an "altruistic core".

---

sector" in this country. Those groups of organizations excluded from the narrow definition but included in the broad, structural operational definition are shown in Box 1.4. It should be stressed that this is a tentative attempt to identify *de facto* usage and should be treated as a working approximation. Moreover, what "the voluntary sector" means or should embrace is itself likely to change over time and is, in the jargon of political theory, essentially contestable, and contingent on the world view or ideology of the observer (Jeffries, 1993).

1.6 Plan of the book

Having addressed the question of definition, the primary aims of this book are to deal with the other components of the UK part of the international study (as set out in Box 1.1), although we shall see that the issue of definition is never far from the surface.

Chapter 2 charts the sector's history, based on a review of secondary sources. The third chapter analyses the sector's legal treatment, while Chapter 4 reports on the research component which was by far the most time-consuming and problematic: the quantative mapping of the sector. Central to the international comparative study was the collection of comprehensive statistics on the voluntary sector's activities, and its income, expenditure and employment. Although this research task drove us to distraction, it lay at the heart of the project strategy and it represents, we hope, one of its most important contributions.

Chapter 5 analyses developments in relationships between the state and the voluntary sector over the past 20 years or so. The next two chapters then focus on the particular histories and recent experiences of three key fields of activity — education (Chapter 6), and health and social services (Chapter 7). Policy-related insights for Chapters 5 to 7 were developed from an extensive literature review and detailed interviews with more than 40 key actors with a strong interest in the UK voluntary sector. Interviewees were chosen so as to gain the perspectives of people in the voluntary sector and key stakeholders outside it. Thus, representatives of central and local government, business, trade unions and the leading religious denominations were among those interviewed. Within the sector itself, representatives of key umbrella or intermediary bodies were interviewed, together with "specialist" interviewees in each of a number of key subsectors, including education, health and social services.

The final chapter briefly discusses the overall light which this new UK empirical evidence sheds on the main theoretical perspectives, although this is necessarily speculative as data were not collected in a form which was amenable to vigorous hypothesis testing. The main aim of the final chapter is to focus on some of the policy challenges that the voluntary sector faces towards the end of the millenium.

Finally, one point should be made about geographical coverage in the pages that follow. The statistical data we report are generally UK-wide. Although we deal briefly with Northern Ireland, Scotland and Wales in Chapters 2 and 5, we are well aware that the remainder of the book strongly reflects an orientation towards England. This is partly because of our institutional base; partly because we struggled hard enough to stick to the constraints of word length with a primary focus on England alone; and partly because much less is known about voluntary action outside England (a bias to which we concede we are ourselves in part contributing). As long as the United Kingdom remains precisely that, it should be an important objective of researchers to explore in more detail the implications of cultural diversity *within* the UK than we have been able to do here.

Notes

1 The figures in Table 1.1 should be treated as indicative only, and cannot be taken as an accurate record of the scale of sectoral activity. It seems likely that a rather large, but unknown, number of organizations on the register at any given time have been effectively defunct or moribund, or double-counted as subsidiaries of other listed organizations. We know, for example, that a large proportion of the 171,000 organizations on the register in 1990 were inactive (Posnett, 1993; Hems and Osborne, 1995). Fortunately, the Charity Commission's ongoing modernization and "cleaning" of the register means that we now have a much better idea of the number of bodies that are active (see Chapter 3). The figures for the early 1990s show that significant numbers of bodies are now being removed from the register, partly for this reason.

2 Arrangements in other parts of the UK vary, with the Scottish system of support for infrastructural bodies probably somewhat less well developed from the sector's perspective, while the experience in Wales and Northern Ireland has been more satisfactory (see Chapter 5).

3 While the scale of this funding is extremely significant for the sector itself, as we describe below it is important to keep it in perspective from the point of view of government. With the exception of a few programmes — central government funding of voluntary sector housing, employment and training measures, some urban policy measures, and funding for overseas develop-

ment — expenditure on the voluntary sector still tends to represent only a very small proportion of individual departments' or quangos' overall spending. One consequence of the proportionately low level of funding for the voluntary sector is that it is unlikely that the matter will even be on the agenda in the annual Public Expenditure Survey negotiations between the Treasury and individual spending departments. Although there is a civil servant within the Treasury's public expenditure department responsible for the coordination of voluntary sector spending and taxation policy, this is only one small part of that person's overall responsibilities.

4 This figure is an estimate of the value of concessions from both central and local government. It includes an estimate of just under £200 million from output VAT relief on fees paid to independent charitable schools, hidden support from the state which is often overlooked (Robson and Walford, 1989; and see Chapter 6). It does not include the value of exemptions from capital gains tax for charities in general, which are thought to be large, particularly for many older charities and would likely push the value of concessions in 1990 over the £1 billion mark.

5 This is a general tendency only; there are, of course, specific exceptions. Perhaps the most obvious arises in the political science literature through the various traditions of analysis dealing with the impact of pressure group activities on the political process (see Dunleavy and O'Leary, 1987; and Dearlove and Saunders, 1991, for reviews). These approaches do not, however, attend to the service provision role of voluntary organisations.

6 Only a brief sketch of some of the most important perspectives is possible here. For useful overviews of economic theory, see James and Rose-Ackerman (1986), Hansmann (1987) and Gassler (1990). A forthcoming issue of *Voluntas* reflects the state of the art in the mid-1990s. It reports some theoretical refinements and a build up of empirical evidence, but no major theoretical innovations beyond the four bodies of theory referred to in the text. For reviews of sociological and political theory, see in particular DiMaggio and Anheier (1990), and the various contributions in Anheier and Seibel (1990).

Chapter 2

HISTORY OF THE VOLUNTARY SECTOR*

2.1 Introduction

This chapter charts the historical development of the UK voluntary sector, offering a description of its evolution over time. It takes a broad perspective, exploring developments which have relevance across most of the sector, but with a bias towards social welfare, which reflects the availability of evidence. Six periods are distinguished, and for each we sketch the elements of political context and social structure which have had the most obvious impact on the pattern of voluntary sector development.

Of course, to attempt a comprehensive overview of the development of such a diverse part of British society as the voluntary sector in so few pages is to court disaster. While in the past specialized studies of the history of the voluntary sector have been few, threads of that history can be found throughout the historical canon. The recent formation of a Voluntary Sector History Society demonstrates a growing and welcome interest in this field. This new interest promises to draw on a widening range of methodologies and to build a richer body of material than has previously been available. In the meantime, our intention in this chapter is modest: we use secondary sources to draw attention to some of the factors which have been important in the evolution of the sector, and to provide a backdrop against which to view the recent and current developments which dominate the rest of the book.

---

* This chapter was written by Marilyn Taylor and Jeremy Kendall.

2.2 Origins and early history: the medieval and Tudor periods

What the philanthropist of Tudor times tried to do forms the basis of the legal definition of charity. No other single period of English history is so important to the formation of the modern concept of charity (Chesterman, 1979, p.28).

The story of the British voluntary sector goes back way into the history of the British people with the development of traditions of mutuality and altruism in its society. Little is known about the development of formal voluntary action before the late Middle Ages, but friendly societies claim origins at least as far back as 55 AD (Gosden, 1973, p.3), and Rubin (1988) describes how some 500 voluntary hospitals were founded during the 12th and 13th centuries (cited in Davis Smith, 1995).

By the medieval era Roman Catholic Church institutions had come to occupy a central position in the delivery of formal philanthropy, under the auspices of both religious orders and secular clergy (Ware, 1989b). Almost all forms of medieval giving, whatever the ultimate purpose and direction, were administered in the first instance by the Church, with the chantry — the endowment of a priest to say prayers for the donor after death — a particularly popular mechanism. The dispensation of alms and care for the poor was a natural corollary to Catholic doctrine, and was given formal expression in the Church's own ecclesiastical Poor Law. Parish priests and, to a lesser extent, monks were legally bound to expend an appropriate proportion of their revenue (partly derived from tithes) on furnishing alms-houses, doles and elementary education for the poor (Chesterman, 1979).

Rosenthal (1972) argues that most medieval forms of philanthropy had the purchase of prayers as their ultimate goal — the benefactors of the time were "extremely conspicuous in the consumption of spiritual goods" (p.39) — while Jordan (1959) points out that little or no distinction was made between religious and social goals. But dissatisfaction with the Church, the monasteries and the functioning of the ecclesiastical courts had set in by the 15th century. Jordan notes that bequests to monasteries were in decline well before the end of that century, while wills dedicated for religious uses fell off sharply after 1510. (They represented 53 percent of bequests between 1480 and 1540, but only 7 percent between 1560 and 1600.) Those anxious for the fate of their souls were increasingly likely to endow chantries away from the monastery or the Church, a development which Rosenthal sees as preparing for the more individual expressions of religious sentiment and lay control of priests that characterized the 16th century.

More secular forms of philanthropy, though still based in a strong religious faith, arose from the feudal responsibility of the aristocracy towards those who lived in their manors, the agricultural estates which formed the mainstay of the primary producing medieval economy. Chesterman summarizes how

A lord was bound by personal obligations embedded in customary land law to ensure that at least the basic essentials of life were provided for any of his tenants who suffered exceptional hardship (1979, p.11).

Meanwhile, the guilds and livery companies of the 14th century marked the beginnings of an organized secular "independent sector" based on mutuality and the rise of trade, albeit for a relatively small proportion of the population. They were set up to protect trade and settle quality of workmanship, but also allowed men of lesser rank to invest in endowments, developed primitive forms of social insurance for their members, and took some responsibility for maintaining almshouses and doles for local paupers (Chesterman, 1979). They might maintain a school or a bridge, or put on miracle plays for the education and entertainment of the populace. There were also religious guilds: "lay associations of men and women that devoted themselves to a variety of religious and social undertakings". Like the more well-known craft guilds, they existed primarily to help their members but, unlike them, "drew their members from a variety of professions and made no attempts at industrial regulation" (McCree, 1993, p.196). A total of 473 were counted in the late 14th century.

The guilds had ceased to play a role in welfare provision well before the end of the 16th century (which also marked the end of the Tudor era), fading much earlier in the UK than in continental Europe (Black, 1984). The exceptions to this were the London livery companies, which gained a considerable reputation as trustees of charitable funds and were often preferred to the Church: in 1510, John Colet, who founded St Paul's School in London, left it not to the Church but to the Company of Mercers. The London livery companies remain major, if sometimes mysterious, philanthropic institutions to the present day.

The Crown had always been wary of the Church's accumulation of tax-free wealth, and Mortmain legislation was introduced from the 13th century onwards to limit the capacity of the Church to take property beyond the state's tax base. But these legal obstacles to growth were replaced by outright assault during the Reformation. Influences as diverse as the growing corruption of the domestic Church as an institution, the advent of printing (hence the increased capacity for independent expression), foreign policy considerations and the monarch's marital difficulties led, in the early 16th century, to the breach between the English state and the Church of Rome (Haigh, 1985). As supreme head of a newly independent Church of England, Henry VIII steered the state religion increasingly towards Protestantism. Henry and his successor, Edward VI, also dramatically weakened the Church's capacity to deliver welfare services in subsequent years through the dissolution and confiscation of the property of the major medieval church institutions: the monasteries and the chantries. Although the final piece of legislation justified this enormous transfer of wealth on theological grounds (Davies, 1985), the primary motive for the Crown's intervention was to raise funds to finance its foreign conflicts.

The selling of this land, alongside the growth of foreign trade and the enclosure of land formerly under common ownership, helped to create a much enlarged social and political elite by the early 17th century. Jordan describes this process as the rise of "a powerful and responsible gentry and ... of a principally Puritan urban aristocracy — the merchants — to the seats of economic power" (1959, pp.15-16). It was an elite that was already taking its responsibilities seriously. Briggs (1994) states that charitable giving may have declined overall in real terms after the Reformation, but, as the significance of religious gifts faded, the value of other more obviously socially useful gifts appears to have increased (Jordan, 1959). Williams goes so far as to describe the generosity of the gentry and the merchants as "a form of feudal tax evasion" (1989, p.7) to secure land to a stated purpose prior to death and thus avoid the levies usually payable on dying — a view endorsed by Whitaker (1974).

The objects of this benevolence were almshouses, hospitals, houses of correction, workhouses, work programmes, apprenticeship schemes, grammar schools, universities, loan schemes for young men starting up in business, municipal betterment and so on. Chesterman (1979) reports that the number of almshouses increased from 40 to 350 between 1540 and 1660. The scope of state activity also expanded. Public authorities took on more responsibilities, in compensation for the disappearance of religious foundations (Briggs, 1994), and legislation followed in the later 16th century to allow justices of the peace and town councils to give poor relief, although some had already embarked on this course.

This generosity was needed. The rapid growth of a landless underclass matched the expansion of society's upper echelons. The existence of a manageable population of the poor had traditionally been accepted as an inevitable feature of the social order, while effectively providing an opportunity for the elite to perform good works (Golding and Middleton, 1982). But detached from the customary support systems of Tudor feudal society — and with the monastic network no longer in place to provide support — the landless poor now appeared to the elite to be posing a major threat to social order and stability (Williams, 1989). This expanded population of beggars in towns and vagrants in rural areas included peasants thrown off the land through the move toward enclosures, those affected by war and epidemics, and former monks and nuns (Ware, 1989b; Chesterman, 1979).

Most historians would agree that the 16th and early 17th centuries were therefore characterized by unprecedented concerns about the apparent extent of social instability. The Tudor state reacted to these trends by elaborating a variety of legislative measures. The central plank of this strategy was the incremental development of an increasingly sophisticated Poor Law, in conjunction with a parallel growth of legislation aiming to encourage secular charity and protect against fraud. The two legislative streams were interdependent. Taxation or "poor rates" to fund local government's anti-poverty measures were made compulsory in 1572. But private philanthropy was still seen as essential if the burden of taxation was to be kept in check, and was regarded as the prime conduit for meeting social needs.

The two growing bodies of legislation were consolidated in the famous *1601 Statute on Charitable Uses*, which placed charitable law firmly in the context of the relief of poverty, and attempted to define the respective responsibilities of local government and private philanthropy in tackling it. Underlining a division that had been recognized in existing Poor Law as far back as the 14th century, the poor were divided into the employable and the unemployable. The former (who were seen as "undeserving") would, in theory, be under the control of parishes (the local, not the central, state) which would provide outdoor relief or, as time went on, the deterrent of the workhouse in order to "encourage" them back into the labour force. Private philanthropic resources could then supposedly concentrate on the provision of support for the unemployable ("the deserving") in the secure knowledge that "because vagrancy and idleness were proscribed by Law, those who gave now knew they aided in relieving the really worthy poor" (Jordan, 1959, p.98). The codification of charitable law which the Statute provided meant that the Court of Chancery finally ousted the ecclesiastical courts as a means of enforcing charitable use; privileges to charitable institutions were confirmed and enhanced; and temporary "roving" commissioners could be appointed to investigate the administration of charities (Davis Smith, 1995).

2.3 The pre-industrial era (1660 to 1780)

Religious and political upheaval dogged the 17th century: 1642-60 were the years of civil war and the brief reign of Nonconformist republicanism in Britain, with an equally brief reign of religious toleration from 1647 until the monarchy was restored in 1660. With the Restoration, religious intolerance returned, favouring first the Protestant and then the Catholic Church. The bloodless Glorious Revolution of 1688 finally re-established the privileges of Protestantism and restricted the powers of subsequent monarchs by bringing in the precursor of modern parliamentary democracy, but with an electorate heavily based on property rights and with political power effectively concentrated in the hands of the land-owning elite and its commercial and mercantile allies.

The Tudor system of charity administration had fallen into decline under the pressures of the civil war (Ware, 1989a). The trust form's preeminence ceased, and court indulgence towards charitable giving gave way to concern to preserve land for the heir-at-law, agricultural production and commerce, enshrined in the 1736 Mortmain Act (Chesterman, 1979; Williams, 1989). Thus, the governing elite was confident enough in the stability of the early 18th century social order not to feel reticent about blatantly generating laws in their own interests. Chesterman (1979) argues that the ruling class became effectively dominated by the interests of mercantile and agricultural capital, and as such began to move away from paternalism to repression of the poor. *Inter alia*, the 1662 Act of Settlement confined the poor to their parish of origin if they were to receive relief, and there were increasingly harsh penalties for crimes against property.

However, a somewhat more tolerant climate was to develop during the course of the 18th century, and Rodgers (1949, pp.8-9) goes so far as to describe this era as the "golden age of philanthropy". The value of endowments grew significantly with the increase in the value of land during this period. In the towns, merchants continued to be influential in the philanthropic world, searching perhaps for a new kind of immortality in what Owen describes as "richesse oblige" (1964, p.15). In rural areas, the disadvantaged still tended to rely on the gentry and the aristocracy, and in some areas charity sermons provided a new source of funds. The latter part of the century witnessed a large number of humanitarian reforms to the national system of Poor Law administration, partly repealing the laws of settlement, softening the workhouse test, introducing outdoor relief and topping up low wages to reflect the rising cost of bread (Dean, 1991).

One of the most significant aspects of the 18th century was the growth of an entirely new form of giving — associative philanthropy — parallel, Owen suggests, to the growth of joint stock companies in business (1964, p.3; see also Prochaska, 1990). The charity school movement was an early example, with the Society for the Promotion of Christian Knowledge demonstrating what could be achieved through a national body with local committees (see Chapter 6). As the century progressed and it became increasingly "out of the question for the philanthropist, however well disposed, to seek out for himself the causes of greatest need and to become familiar with them" (Owen, 1964, p.92), a range of other societies and associations were formed to act as intermediaries between donors and beneficiaries. These societies were based on subscription, with subscribers often having the power to exercise patronage by recommending beneficiaries: a sure route to the social prestige which has been one motivating factor of philanthropy.

Mutual aid was also on the increase. That the term "friendly society" was in common currency by the 18th century is suggested by the existence of a chapter about friendly societies in one of Daniel Defoe's published essays in 1696, while in the early 18th century a pamphlet quoted by Gosden (1973) urges the formation of friendly societies as a way of diminishing the burden of the poor on the rates.

2.4 The industrial revolution (1780 to 1840)

The period of the industrial revolution witnessed a number of significant changes in society, which are summarized in Box 2.1. As UK society left what was called by some historians the "age of enlightenment", so the "cheer, joviality and ... brutality of the early eighteenth century" (Rodgers, 1949, pp.15-16), along with its humanitarian ethos and "slightly careless" benevolence, gave way to a more calculating approach, often of a puritan character. For example, middle-class philanthropists segregated the sexes and introduced hard labour to prisons, and even barred country dancing and ballad sellers.

However, the most spectacular manifestation of the new harshness of moral tone came with the eventual tightening up of the Poor Law in 1834, which put deterrence at the top of the agenda (see Box 2.2). While some of the aristocracy and landed gentry may have resented the loss of control that the centralization in this law implied, the view that came to dominate in the ruling class was that a "more disciplined" workforce was required to enable growth and stability at a time when the

---

Box 2.1   Changes in the structure of UK society in the late 18th and early 19th centuries

Rose (1981) has identified four revolutions as taking place over the late 18th to 19th centuries:

- *Industrial* — with major technological change and concentration of the labour force in urban centres;
- *Political* — with ideas for political reform triggered by the French Revolution;
- *Religious* — with the Evangelical Revival and the rise of Methodism; and
- *Artistic* — with the advance of Romanticism.

He suggests that the period witnessed the "end of the protective role exercised by the higher orders in the old hierarchical society" (p.257), with society bound together by the "strings of patronage" and the "ropes of dependence". Rather, society was increasingly structured by the "horizontal lines" of class interest and class consciousness in which each layer's interests differed, in contrast with the congruence of interests throughout the ranks of pyramidically organized and patriarchal pre-industrial "old society" (see also Perkin, 1969).

The horizontal solidarities and vertical antagonisms of class may have been thrown into sharper relief, especially by the early 19th century, but relics of "old society" interest and connection persisted nevertheless. This resilience had implications for voluntary action. Most obviously, class consciousness overlaid, rather than superceded, feelings of religious identity. In the political arena, an important feature of British society was the ongoing struggles of Nonconformist dissenters to achieve political rights and liberties.

French Revolution had stirred up very real fears of insurrection. A growing number of influential philanthropists frowned on alms-giving which was apparently not carefully targeted (Owen, 1964, p.98). Malthus went so far as to argue that large charities with their lack of discrimination were pernicious and should be abandoned. Small voluntary charities, on the other hand, were argued to be acceptable because the recipients could not help but feel grateful and those who were refused charity could not complain of injustice or a denial of their rights (Knott, 1986).

Moralization was part of the philosophy which underlay the

Box 2.2   Attitudes towards poverty and Poor Law reform

Fears of social disorder generated by the French Revolution joined with concerns about "over-population" to create a mood of intolerance in the late 18th century. The more relaxed attitudes earlier in the century had tempered the harsh language of the 1601 Act and were seen to have blurred the distinctions between deserving and undeserving poor as well as blunting the deterrent effect of the workhouse and the incentive to work. Parish-based relief was increasingly seen as unsuitable to an industrial world which now demanded mobility of labour (Beveridge, 1948). But between 1784 and 1813 the cost of poor relief trebled. Hardship spread rapidly in response to the combined pressures of Industrial Revolution, famine, war and population increase. In 1802, one in ten of the population was on relief (Golding and Middleton, 1982).

The reform of the Poor Law in 1834 sought to replace parish-based relief with a more centralized system, which would reduce local autonomy and reinstate the deterrent of the workhouse by abolishing outdoor relief. For the able-bodied poor, the principle of "less eligibility" captured the idea that the system should provide incentives to seek work, become self-sufficient and avoid the danger of "dependency" on the state. Under this principle, poor relief should be less attractive than the situation of the poorest labourer. Since the prime aim of the Poor Law was to ensure commitment to the work ethic, comparatively little attention was given to measures to provide relief for people unable to work (Hill, 1970). That was left largely to the voluntary sector in a doctrine of "mutually exclusive spheres" formalized in the 1869 Goschen minute and championed by the influential Charity Organisation Society formed in that year (see section 2.5 and Box 2.4).

Poor Law, and this was paralleled by a surge of other moral welfare activities over the century, often associated with the growth of the Evangelical movement at the turn of the century. The Society for the Suppression of Vice clocked up 623 successful prosecutions for breaking the Sabbath laws in 1801-2 alone (Thompson, 1980). Another product of the Evangelical movement was the Proclamation Society which prosecuted an obscure bookseller for publishing Paine's *Age of Reason* (Owen, 1964). Fear of crime and the lack of an efficient police force also led individuals to join together in associations to look after themselves and their possessions (Rodgers, 1949), with societies like those for the Reformation of Manners and for the Protection of Persons and Property, which acted as a kind of private prosecution service and brought many "miscreants" before the courts.

In contrast to the reactionary stance of these organizations, there were still forces for tolerance in the voluntary sector, many within the same Evangelical tradition. The "supreme accomplishment of the Evangelical reform forces", wrote Owen (1964, p.129), was the Anti-Slavery Movement, whose influence stretched across the globe. Another reformist group was the Society for Bettering the Condition and Increasing the Comforts of the Poor, which fought to continue and extend the late 18th century modifications in the old Poor Law (Dean, 1991). It was one of the few organizations of this time to see a role for the state in welfare, and was also active in factory reform, coordination, the dissemination of philanthropic ideas and initiatives, and sponsorship of education for the female poor.

Other developments of the late 18th century included soup kitchens, fever hospitals, medical dispensaries, institutional training for disabled people, and the ecumenical industrial and Sunday schools movements. There was also a concern to cross the widening class divide (Rose, 1981). Town missions were set up at the beginning of the 19th century, partly inspired by the work of Thomas Chalmers, who attempted to introduce the paternalism of the country village into the slums of Glasgow. The missions urged the middle classes to go out to the poor to give them support, to educate them in the basics of health care and child care and, not least, to spread to them the Christian gospel. They were seen by the churches as a means of "cop[ing] with the sheer size and paganism of the towns" (Perkin, 1969, p.122). A Society for Promoting District Visiting was formed in 1828, concerned with the prevention of distress and the promotion of family life and social harmony (Prochaska, 1988, p.43). As the century progressed, their efforts were to be supplemented by the introduction of voluntary district nursing and health visiting schemes, concerned to educate women in the rudiments of self-help in health.

This educational approach may have offered more than the punitive alternative of the Poor Law and the workhouse. However, such visiting schemes were often seen as selfish interference in their lives and culture by those on the receiving end.

There is strong evidence that the Victorian poor were not content with their lot. Contemporary reports suggest irritation with the moralising cant of the relief workers, and resentment at providing a hobby for the Evangelical middle class whose women were precluded by custom from gainful employment (Williams, 1989, p.44).

Simey goes even further, describing the popularity of philanthropy during the Victorian era as "nothing less than ill-informed and ill-inspired meddling with the working classes" (1951, cited by Williams, 1989, p.47).

Visitors were mainly women: over the coming years, charity was to prove one of the few occupations permissible for middle-class women and one of the few ways in which they could acquire status in the community. Indeed, Prochaska has pointed to an "explosion of societies run by women ... in the nineteenth century, institutional expressions of a vital female culture with financial resources" and claims that many of the voluntary traditions of modern social welfare are deeply rooted in female culture which "found a compelling, and relatively unrestricted, avenue for expression in charitable work" (1988, pp.23-4).

Urban concentration accelerated the development of working-class organizations, particularly in the forms of friendly societies and trade clubs, which combined the insurance and social functions of friendly societies with controls over apprenticeship and defence of wages. Beveridge finds evidence of the first building society in 1781 and there were a growing number of burial clubs (the worst possible disgrace was a pauper's funeral). The 1793 Friendly Societies Act gave them recognition by providing them with a legal structure and put them on a more secure basis, although many failed to register, and secretiveness, especially under fear of upper-class scrutiny, remained a significant feature.

By the end of the century the trade clubs were joining together to become trade unions and becoming both more powerful and more threatening to the ruling classes. Equally threatening was the growth of more radical middle- and working-class organizations pushing for electoral reform. Corresponding Societies took up the cause of reform, with the London Corresponding Society arguably being the "first distinctively working-class political body in English history" (Cole, 1948, p.29, quoted in Hill, 1970; but see Perkin, 1969, ch. 6).

Fears of unrest fanned by the flames of the French Revolution led to a brief period of suppression of the freedom of association, with the passage of three laws in quick succession: the Seditious Meetings Act 1797; the Corresponding Societies Act of 1799, which rendered all such societies with branches illegal; and Combination Acts of 1799 and 1800, brought in to discourage the increasing strength of the trade clubs and emerging trade unions. Friendly societies were almost caught in the backlash, and in 1835 the government of the day was still contemplating legislative measures that would have had the effect of suppressing the great majority of them as well as the trade unions. But the restrictive Acts of the turn of the century did not have a long life. Trade unions were released from the Combination Acts in 1824. By then both they and the friendly societies were increasingly being seen by the better off as a way of developing providence among the poor and as a demonstration that the "respectable" poor could help themselves.

2.5 The mid-19th century to 1905

For every cure of every sorrow by which our land or our race can be visited there are patrons, vice presidents and secretaries. For the diffusion of every blessing of which mankind can partake in common there is a committee (Stephen, 1849, p.581, quoted in Prochaska, 1988, pp.39-40).

The 19th century, especially its second half, is seen by many commentators as the heyday of British philanthropy (Davis Smith, 1995). By 1890, Prochaska (1990) reports, the average middle-class household was spending more on charity than any other item in its budget except food, while Owen (1964) notes that the income of London charities at this time exceeded that of a number of nation states. The huge number of charities operating at that time provided donors with ample opportunity to exercise choice, and to some this proliferation of charity appeared to be creating problems of duplication. The same or similar tasks were often undertaken by many different denominations or sects: in parts of London, four or five visiting societies besieged poor households each week (Prochaska, 1988). But Thane (1982) suggests that giving across the country was highly localized: even in the same part of the country, one town or district might do much better than a neighbouring area.

The period witnessed a growing demand for reform and coordination in the charitable world. After some procrastination, the legal profession's calls for modernization of the legal framework were heeded in a number of legislative measures — outlined in Box 2.3 — but these were restricted to endowments, and did not apply to "collecting" charities.

Much philanthropy depended on individual alms-giving, appeals and other forms of fundraising, and there were growing concerns in the emergent urban elite about the effects of "indiscriminate" generosity. In the mid-19th century, charitable giving far exceeded the gross government expenditure on poor relief (Chesterman, 1979; Prochaska, 1988).

This apparently unfocused giving often appeared to be at odds with the tenets of the new Poor Law. How could pauperism be defeated when it was rewarded by uncoordinated and "sentimental" donations? Some argued for the control of these "improvident" outpourings in the belief that the problem of poverty could be resolved through a form of social Darwinism that allowed the unfit to "quietly go out of existence" (Stedman Jones, 1971, p.311). In response to these calls, in 1869 the Charity Organisation Society (COS) was set up to tackle the problem of coordination and was a formidable actor on the late Victorian stage. It was ultimately to fail in persuading society of the validity and practicability of its moral vision (Box 2.4), but in its heyday it was a major player in the political arena. *Inter alia*, it launched a powerful critique of "voting charities" in health care, was at the forefront of campaigns to reform charity law, and brought much abuse to court as well as distributing a cautionary list of abusers to donors. Furthermore, its contributions to the introduction of casework techniques in welfare and the establishment of social work as a profession were considerable.

The COS also sought new methods to reform the poor. One was to move the poor away from their environment to areas where there were jobs or where the discipline of work could be instilled. The labour colony movement sought to remove the feckless hard core of paupers from their urban environment into more uplifting surroundings (Stedman Jones, 1971). In the

---

Box 2.3   19th century reform of charity law

In 1880, *The Times* defined charity as "an institution that labours under a perpetual tendency to fall out of repair" (Owen, 1964, p.276). There had been no major reform of the law since 1601. Charity law reform grew out of long dissatisfaction with the machinery of litigation, the growing number of obsolete trusts and the difficulty of reforming them, the chaotic state of the law, and considerable evidence of abuse. But it took a long time to achieve any progress. No less than 13 Bills were defeated before the 1853 Charitable Trusts Act: there were a lot of vested interests at stake (Williams, 1989), and further legislation was needed in 1860 to make up for its timidity. Both Williams and Owen argue that charitable law had developed into something that was as much about protecting property from "philanthropic excess" as about protecting charity. And over the years, the legal process increasingly separated the definition of charity from its historical context within the Poor Law.

The 1853 Act set up a central, permanent Charity Commission, and ensuing legislation in 1855 and 1860 gave it some teeth. Legislation over this period extricated charity from the labyrinthine process of Chancery, the object of Dickens' contempt in Bleak House, by giving the Commissioners "scheme-making" powers (i.e. the powers to redefine obsolete charities). But scheme-making applied only to small charities — a relatively small proportion of the country's charitable resources — and was restricted to illegal or impossible objectives. And while the powers of the Charities Commission were increased, there were no new staff. Progress was slow. Chesterman claims that the effect of the legislation on the overall use of charitable resources was slight. The Commission gradually introduced a representative element into the body of charitable trustees and local charity administration was improved — a task greatly aided by the reconstruction of local government in the latter half of the century (Owen, 1964). Parliament also took steps to reform educational endowments and the endowments of the City of London (see Chapter 6). But the movement for more far-reaching reform ran into the ground as the worst anomalies were taken care of and as the state itself began to take more responsibility for welfare.

1870s, a labour exchange was set up in central London by the COS which "migrated around 300 surplus women and children up to the textile districts" of the north (ibid., p.277).

Box 2.4   The failures of the Charity Organisation Society

Building on the principles of the 1834 Poor Law (see Box 2.2), the Charity Organisation Society set its face against "indiscriminate" alms-giving and sought to coordinate charitable activity. It introduced the idea of "scientific charity", advocating the full investigation of need before administering aid to avoid the allocation of resources to anyone deemed "undeserving". Significantly, many of its members were also members of the local statutory sector "Boards of Guardians", with others drawn from the Church, the law, medicine, the armed forces and the civil service: a "new urban gentry visiting its status on the poor" (Stedman Jones, 1971, p.268). However, unlike the traditional rural aristocracy and landed gentry, this group had little economic contact with those who depended upon them. COS's own leading thinkers saw its attempts at moralization as progressive and conducive to participatory citizenship (Lewis, 1995a). But COS was subject to growing criticism from contemporaries as the century wore on. It appeared to many that the "mutually exclusive spheres" doctrine — with its strict casting of the state in a residual role — was an inadequate response to chronic poverty, and it was in any case proving extremely difficult to operationalize (Prochaska, 1988). Moreover, critics of its moral stance suggested that it "was more interested in preventing unsound charity practices than preventing distress" (Owen, 1964, p.37), or that its concern was to "inculcate appropriate moral sentiments among the recipients and to influence their conduct in a way which suited the givers" (Chesterman, 1979, p.79). Finally, its influence probably failed to reach far north of the Midlands (Stedman Jones, 1971), and even in its southern power base it made little real progress towards the coordination of charitable effort, despite its best intentions (Chesterman, 1979).

As the century drew to its close, the nature of voluntary action was changing. Charitable funds were still pouring in: the first street collection or "flag day" was held for the Royal National Lifeboat Institution in 1891, and any crisis or riot would still unleash an influx of funds. But changes in the structure of industry were putting pressure on traditional sources of philanthropic funds. Cahill and Jowett have suggested that "the formation of limited companies and the emergence of absentee directors" (1980, p.362) separated the philanthropists from their beneficiaries. At the same time, the "suburbanization" of towns with the growth of transport reduced "geographical and social contact between local business and professional elites and the poor of their towns" (Thane, 1982, p.63). Moreover, Cahill and Jowett suggest that the new commercial elite had little interest in philanthropy: their "upbringing and interests predisposed them to see their works not as their life but simply as a way to generate income as quickly as possible to satisfy other interests" (1980, p.362). Meanwhile in the areas which they left behind, standards of local administration deteriorated; rateable burdens increased; and the remaining population became more demoralized.

Some philanthropists deliberately sought to bridge this gap by moving back into the poorer areas. Those involved in the settlement movement wished to counteract the break-up of cities into preserves of the rich and leisured and warrens of the poor and labouring (Beveridge, 1948). The first settlement at Toynbee Hall was founded in 1884 and there were 30 by the end of the century. Beveridge saw them as "indispensable centres of criticism and unveiling of social evils" (p.132) and an attempt to bring civic skills into areas which lacked them. They formed a part of the "new conceptions of public duty, new developments of social enterprise, new estimates of the natural obligations of the members of the community one to another" which Joseph Chamberlain claimed on the eve of the great Liberal split of 1886 (Briggs and Macartney, 1984, p.2). The leaders of the settlement movement pushed for a "new liberalism", arguing for the recognition of working-class grievances if revolution was to be avoided (Means, 1976), reinterpreting freedom in a positive sense — "freedom to" — which was contrasted with the freedom "from" at the core of classical liberal thinking. Many of these people eventually became civil servants or went into government where they were in a powerful position to promote their own interpretation of social problems, and how they might be solved by a professional meritocracy (Perkin, 1969, 1989). Sir William Beveridge — for many, the "architect" of the welfare state in the next century — was himself a graduate of Toynbee Hall.

Other organizations sought to improve conditions in the city. With the public health movement of the 1840s and massive population growth, progressive philanthropists had become increasingly aware that the conditions in which the poor lived were unlikely to encourage self-improvement. This gave rise to a number of housing projects over the following years, mainly financed by investment, thus combining benevolence with the prospect of some profit, albeit at a low return.

This new activity developed against a background of changing industrial conditions: increased leisure, the growth of the suburb, the reduction in child labour. In response, the voluntary sector entered new territory in the fields of leisure, adult and civic education, and environmental improvement. The growth of children's holiday organizations gave children and families a chance to escape from the urban environment. The Boys Brigade, Boy Scouts and Girl Guides, Sea Cadets and a number of other organizations devoted to training young people were formed at this time, partly reflecting concern with national efficiency and a new emphasis on investment in human capital that was also leading the state to finance voluntary schools for the first time (see Chapter 6).

For the employed classes, growing leisure time led to an explosion of recreational activities. The tradition of mutuality was also extending — at least among the better-off working classes — with the growth of building societies, working men's clubs and cooperatives, temperance halls and massed choirs. The Women's Cooperative Society sought to extend the benefits of cooperation into the poorer classes and, in so doing, introduced many women to local government and public life. Indeed, the turn of the century saw the growth of many women's organizations — most notably the suffragette movement — to establish the independent woman's voice in a range of institutions, from the Church to the professions, and to campaign on a variety of issues.

Among the already enfranchised, a number of more or less explicitly political groups developed especially around socialist principles: the Fabian Society in 1884, the more radical Social Democratic Federation and eventually the Independent Labour Party, formed in 1893. Trade unions were given legal protection in legislation in the 1870s: the labour movement was moving into the mainstream.

At the same time some of the traditional working-class organizations were faltering. The friendly societies, though still growing in number — membership was universal among the more secure, "respectable" working class by the end of the century — were in serious difficulties. As their members lived on into old age, the societies found themselves paying out levels of sick benefit for which they had not made provision (Gosden, 1973). If a society failed, its members' savings were lost and it was extremely difficult for anyone over 40 to find another society that would take them on. They were also facing increasing competition for savings, from trade unions who discovered that benefit provision kept members with them between periods of militancy and from commercial concerns, as well as the Post Office Savings Bank. Many friendly societies began to move away from their roots in mutuality (Beveridge, 1948).

While the mid-19th century had witnessed the economic prosperity that was the fruit of the Industrial Revolution, by 1870 the end of Britain's industrial hegemony was becoming apparent (Payne, 1985). With a slowdown in the growth of industrial production and increasing competition from abroad, it appeared to many leading thinkers that charity and self-help alone were not equal to the task of meeting the needs of the disadvantaged and the casualties of structural change. Recession and hard winters struck, and the innovative social surveys of Charles Booth and Seebohm Rowntree towards the end of the century dramatically raised awareness of the extent of poverty. Although the validity and interpretation of these findings were vehemently contested by the COS (Stedman Jones, 1971, ch. 5), the apparent levels of distress associated with the unreformed *status quo* led increasing numbers of people to conclude that charity and self-help in isolation could not deal with the problems created by industrialization.

In this context, the state was beginning to take on work that had previously been confined to the voluntary sector. It had begun to take responsibility for public health, it made provision for Poor Law infirmaries independent of the workhouse and, as we have noted, it had begun to put money into schools, although it did not take on a major role in direct provision until the 1870s.

2.6 The entry of the state (1905 to 1945)

Since 1914, the most important single factor affecting the activities of private philanthropy in England has been the massive growth in state welfare (Chesterman, 1979, p.81)

At the turn of the century, the relief of poverty and the promotion of welfare were still largely in the hands of the voluntary sector. Voluntary institutions in the 1900s were, with the major exception of education, "very remote from contact with organizations of the state: they expected no public financial support and were subject to little or no state regulation" (Harris, 1990, pp.113-4). But the realignment of politics with the growth of the Labour Party, the impact of the Boer and First World Wars, and the post-war cycle of depression tipped the balance of provision over the first half of the 20th century decisively towards the state, and Chesterman (1979) also reports an increase in the welfare provision made by employers.

Increasing economic competition from abroad, coupled with the discovery of the poor medical condition of recruits to the armed forces drove home to the nation the "economic and military importance of building, from birth, a strong and stable race" (Thane, 1982, pp.42). To rely solely on the voluntary sector appeared increasingly unwise, since the money it could generate seemed to fall far short of the nation's requirements for a healthy and well-educated population. While the voluntary sector was still typically regarded as the first line of defence in many areas, the view that this front line needed reinforcements came to be more widely held by politicians and opinion formers. The field of income maintenance saw the development at the turn of the century of a temporary agency relationship between the state and working-class mutual aid (Box 2.5). The voluntary sector continued to play a major role in health and education. However, two major government committees met between the wars to tackle the issues raised by voluntary failure in the hospital and university sectors. Both recommended enhanced state financial aid, though in the hope that it would be a temporary measure (Owen, 1964).

The needs exposed by the war therefore led to state investment in the upcoming generation, especially in the provision of

---

Box 2.5 Early 20th century income maintenance and state involvement

State unemployment assistance in 1905 was followed by pensions in the 1908 and 1911 Acts, covering respectively compulsory old age pensions and social insurance. The entry of the state into social insurance had long been resisted by the friendly societies and the trade unions, who were suspicious of public intervention, despite their financial difficulties (Gosden, 1973). They did not relish the prospect of further competition for the working man's savings, nor the close supervision of their affairs that would be entailed. But their resistance faded with the severity of their financial situation. Government rewarded their eventual support by recognizing their existing contributions in its own scheme and by using them as agents, placing national insurance under their supervision. But Beveridge reports that the societies became "more official and less personal; more of insurance agencies and less of social agencies" (1948, pp.78-9). There was pressure to concentrate in larger units, leading to the disappearance of a large proportion of smaller agencies.

---

medical inspection, school meals and infant welfare. In addition, local authorities funded voluntary agencies to provide accommodation and support for elderly people and people with disabilities. Charity, argues Thane, "increasingly operated in close cooperation with, and often subsidized and directed by, statutory authorities" (1982, p.171). Indeed Beveridge in 1948 was highly critical of the extent to which, between the wars, voluntary organizations became "agencies" of the state.

While the state had increased its range of responsibilities by giving powers to local authorities to invest in welfare, public expenditure cuts after the war meant that in many cases, and especially in medical care and social welfare, the advance of the state was slow. The voluntary sector remained a major actor. Even where the state was now playing the major role, there were new demands to be met and gaps to be filled, and fresh attempts were made to build up coherent mechanisms for voluntary sector infrastructural support through the development of "intermediary bodies", as charted in Box 2.6.

Furthermore, ex-servicemen and women often looked to the

Box 2.6 The emergence of intermediary bodies in the early 20th century

The capacity of the voluntary sector to respond to new needs was reinforced by the growth of its infrastructure. Early in the century, a series of initiatives attempted to do what the Charity Organisation Society was failing to do. Between 1904 and 1911, no less than 60 local Guilds of Help were formed, aiming to pull together all possible resources to tackle the persistent problems of poverty. On the face of it they had similar aims to the COS, aiming to coordinate philanthropic effort and through social casework, not only to validate claims but also to give a personal touch to alms-giving. But the crucial difference lay in their attempts first, to build bridges between state-sponsored social welfare and the philanthropic community, and second, to enrol the help of the working class, although with limited success in the latter case. As such, they "marked the end of the old order which rested on the implicit assumption that social services was good done by a favoured class to those less fortunate" (Cahill and Jowett, 1980, p.360). One major motivation for their efforts was the need that they saw to provide an alternative to the Independent Labour Party which was gaining strength at local level.

There was some conflict between the Guilds of Help and local branches of the COS as well as another set of coordinating bodies that were making their appearance — local Councils for Social Welfare (Knight, 1993). But after the First World War a more co-operative spirit was abroad and, along with representatives from charities to help servicemen and their families, support grew for a national coordinating body, which led to the formation of the National Council for Social Service in 1919.

With the continued growth of local voluntary service councils (who had overtaken and absorbed local Guilds of Help), the dream of local coordination began to take some shape. The National Council was a particularly useful channel for government funds aimed at promoting voluntary endeavour, and it administered government funding for voluntary initiatives on unemployment in the mid-1930s.

It was later renamed the National Council for Voluntary Organisation, funded by government to undertake a range of support functions for the sector, including training, advice and information.

voluntary sector and mutual aid for help, and a number of disability and relief organizations were formed to meet their needs. Youth, nursery and play provision was largely in the hands of the voluntary sector. Leisure organizations continued to grow. Voluntary organizations continued to provide the majority of approved schools for young offenders in the inter-war period, with state funding. As the Depression began to bite at the end of the 1920s, unemployment absorbed a great deal of charitable energy, and unemployment clubs grew all over the land.

Charity committees of middle-class women concerned with child welfare were formed to focus particularly on war refugees and families of dead and wounded servicemen (Thane, 1982). In education, alongside its provision of primary, secondary and higher education, the voluntary sector was developing a new role in relation to adults, through community centres, unemployment clubs, the Workers' Educational Association and women's organizations. In health, while the state of medical advance may have been sounding the death-knell for the beleaguered voluntary hospital (Titmuss, 1958), the voluntary sector was assuming a central position in the field of medical research, particularly in relation to heart, cancer, stroke and chest conditions. Although local authorities were taking increasing responsibility for social housing, having been authorized to build public housing at the end of the previous century, the voluntary sector continued to play its part and the National Federation of Housing Associations was formed in 1935.

Another bout of environmental activity came towards the end of the 1920s, and the sector also retained an important role in campaigning for groups neglected by public policy. There was, for example "a small but remarkable rise in the volume of protest against the long-established codes of morality" (Pym, 1974, p.21). Organizations like the National Council for Civil Liberties, the Progressive League, the Abortion Law Reform Association, the National Council for the Abolition of the Death Penalty — all small, middle-class organizations — developed innovative ways of operating in a new, enfranchised, political environment. The National Council for One-Parent Families (then referred to as Unmarried Mothers and their Children) was formed in 1918. Women's organizations continued to campaign for action over infant mortality. Others were led by the war to form associations to promote international understanding and peace, while charities were also formed to support the Republican side in the Spanish Civil War.

The Second World War provoked a surge of concern about social problems and the respective roles of state and voluntary organizations. Once again, new voluntary organizations were formed to assist in dealing with the emergencies of war, with considerable support from the state, as in the case of the Women's Voluntary Service (a body whose role was the stimulation of volunteering to meet emergency needs, but which was fully funded by government). Citizens' advice bureaux were set up under the auspices of the National Council for Social Service (NCSS) to deal with the social dislocation of war, and other bodies established in war-time included the National Old People's Welfare Committee with its network of local committees (also under the auspices of the NCSS) and Oxfam.

2.7 The post-war period: from 1945 to the mid-1970s

Between 1944 and 1948 major legislation was enacted, preserving the sector's role in education and social services, but superseding it in health care and income maintenance through the introduction of direct central government provision (Box 2.7). The net effect of these reforms is usually interpreted as effectively relegating the sector to becoming a "junior partner in the welfare firm" (Owen, 1964, p.527). Some, particularly on the left, expected and hoped that those voluntary services that remained would "wither away" along with their aura of middle-class patronage, as an effective strategy for reducing class divisions would render them irrelevant. Attlee and Crossman were notable exponents of this view. There had already been considerable hostility and mutual distrust between some Labour local administrations and the sector between the wars (Harrison, 1987). However, in the post-war years, many Labour politicians were much less judgemental. Many parts of the sector were perceived to have progressed from encouraging "hierarchical values and pieties" in the 1930s to embracing a more

---

Box 2.7 The "welfare state" legislation of the 1940s

- *The Education Act 1944* established free secondary education as a universal right. This was to be funded by local and central government. Provision was both through schools run directly by local authorities and through voluntary schools.

- *The National Health Service Act 1946* established free health care as a universal right. This was both funded and directly run by central government (primarily out of general taxation), and involved the nationalization of most existing voluntary hospitals.

- *The National Insurance Act 1946* established a single, unified administrative structure for social insurance, funded through flat-rate contributions from employees and employers. This was now administered directly by central government, ending the agency relationship with the friendly societies.

- *The National Assistance Act 1948* repealed existing Poor Law legislation, creating a single, national means-tested allowance available to all those not in employment whose financial resources fell below a standard set by Parliament. The Act also made local authorities responsible for providing residential care for the elderly, either directly or through the voluntary sector.

"egalitarian" and "less snobbish and socially divisive" ethos after the war, and such "progressive" agencies were to be encouraged (Prochaska, 1992).

At the same time as registering enthusiasm for an expanded role for the state, many on the left were keen to suggest that the sector, newly enthused with democratic principles, should cooperate with the state in certain areas, and could thrive by adapting and pioneering. Herbert Morrison, as Lord President acting as coordinator of the government's social policy, was a leading exponent of this view (see Deakin, 1995). Nonetheless, the expansion and high profile of state provision was bound to have implications for the voluntary sector. At the practical level, many voluntary bodies found it difficult to recruit high-quality staff, and it is common to see the post-war period as one where the voluntary sector marked time (see, for example, Wolfenden, 1978).

Friendly societies were major victims of change alongside the hospitals (see Chapter 7). Beveridge (1948) had wished to see friendly societies running the state-funded social security scheme, but his study found that many were moribund, had lost their base in face-to-face association, and by this stage most were national affiliates with relatively little local control (Davis Smith, 1995). Unions were alive and well, but Beveridge felt they had become embroiled in party politics and could no longer be seen as voluntary associations, nor provide the basis for the delivery of state welfare through mutual aid. For the time being, the sector also appeared to have lost its role in combating unemployment because of the pledge, initially successful, to full employment levels (Deakin, 1995).

The radical nature of the shift in the balance of power towards the state prompted Beveridge to recommend a review of the legal environment for the sector, a process which eventually culminated in new legislation in 1960 (see Box 2.8). The Nathan Committee (1952) gave an official seal to the importance of

---

Box 2.8   The Nathan Report and the 1960 Charities Act

The profound implications of the legislative changes of the 1940s led Beveridge to recommend a Royal Commission to survey charitable trusts. This recommendation eventually bore fruit through the appointment of a special committee to consider and report on changes in law and practice relating to charities (except as regards taxation), chaired by Lord Nathan. This Committee cleared the ground for the Charities Act 1960, which for the first time:

- gave the Charity Commission jurisdiction over "collecting" charities (that is, fundraising rather than endowed charities);

- set up a central register of charities;

- allowed the Commission to pool the assets of small charities for joint investment; and

- introduced a more relaxed *cy-près* regime (see Chapter 3).

The Act cleared a lot of dead wood by consolidating previous legislation, but did not deal with the definitional issues raised by the Committee, and proceeded fairly cautiously on the other recommendations (see also Chapter 3).

---

philanthropy in a period of considerable uncertainty for the sector. And, despite many fears, the voluntary sector was to exhibit its usual resilience and adaptability in the face of change (Younghusband, 1978; Finlayson, 1990).

There was in fact considerable space for the voluntary sector in post-war reconstruction, even if its organizations still had to step carefully through the ideological suspicions of some Labour administrations at local and national level. First, where services had been taken over by the state, charitable funds could be turned to new fields of endeavour within the same territory. Thus, with the nationalization of the voluntary hospitals network:

Philanthropists especially concerned with medical care are no longer obliged to see their gifts swallowed up in the running expenses of hard-pressed hospitals, but are free to support more interesting ventures in research, training, or administrative experiment (Owen, 1964, p.547).

Second, there was some continuity with the past in the sense that substantial amounts of public money continued to support existing voluntary provision in some fields. For example, in primary and secondary education, this was in support of voluntary schools, which continued to be funded alongside those run directly by local government. In higher education, provision continued to be provided independently of direct state control in the universities. In these fields, unlike hospitals, nationalization did not even reach the mainstream political agenda, but existing voluntary provision continued to receive grants from local and central government.

Third, many personal social services and related activities, particularly outside the residential care sector, stayed beyond the reach of the state, either in terms of governance or of financial support. These services were not a priority for state intervention or funding, thus leaving a major area of social provision initially beyond the purview of the state. Nonetheless, some organizations were able to secure significant amounts of funding from central and local government as state finance followed increasing recognition of the pervasiveness of continued need in the personal social services field (see Chapter 7).

Fourth, the expanded role of the state in many fields itself appeared to create a new need for advice and information services. And finally, some areas remained almost uniquely the domain of voluntary bodies with no discernible impact from state expansion: the Royal National Lifeboat Institute's continued provision of the nation's sea rescue service is one example, while many conservation organizations like the National Trust and the Royal Society for the Protection of Birds would continue with little change.

Despite these opportunities, there was still cause for concern. The increasing taxation required to fund new statutory services put pressure on voluntary fundraising. Would people pay twice? Chesterman (1979) reports on a survey in 1948 which found that 99 percent of people interviewed believed philanthropy had been made superfluous by the welfare state, and the Wolfenden report (1978) suggested that individual giving had not kept pace with inflation. But Prochaska (1992) reports continued giving to hospitals despite their takeover by the state.

In certain specialist areas — provision for people with visual and hearing impairments, for example — voluntary organizations retained their virtual monopoly (Brenton, 1985). Furthermore, Wolfenden identified the trends in the voluntary sector between the war and the 1970s as favouring: self-help; specialist conditions; lobbying; and secularization. Social welfare organizations, counselling organizations, cultural and leisure activities, a variety of self-help groups and medical research groups (physical and mental health) grew considerably during the years between the war and 1960.

It became clear by the 1960s that poverty and other social problems had not been eradicated by the consolidation of the welfare state. The social movements of the 1960s across the world influenced British communities: feminism, civil rights, the consumer movement, the re-emerging environmental movement and the peace movement. Increased government involvement in a wide variety of aspects of social and economic life triggered reaction: communities and consumers knew where to direct their dissatisfaction and had been led to expect that they had a right to do so.

The roots of new campaigns often lay in the previous decade: the Anti-Apartheid Movement, the Consumers Association and the Campaign for Nuclear Disarmament, for example, were already up and running by the 1950s. They were joined in the 1960s by such organizations as Friends of the Earth, Shelter (homelessness), the Child Poverty Action Group and Chiswick Women's Aid. Unfettered by past assumptions, they gave a "kick start" to a new image of the voluntary sector (Young-husband, 1978, p.263) and one which was more acceptable to the Labour movement than the "philanthropy" of previous eras. The 1960s also saw the growth of volunteer bureaux and consumer aid centres, followed by more militant law and welfare rights centres. By 1973 there were 566 citizens' advice bureaux (ibid.).

The new campaigners appeared to come mainly from the educated middle class and they were joined by an army of crusading volunteers mobilized at home and abroad by organizations like Voluntary Service Overseas, Community Service Volunteers, the Young Volunteer Force Foundation and the London-based Task Force. Along with the rising profession of community development workers, they provided echoes of the settlement movement of the late 19th century.

While government continued to expand its own services, it was also looking for new ways of working with the voluntary sector. In 1964 the Housing Corporation had been established to channel funds to housing associations. Major government initiatives on social work — the Social Work (Scotland) Act of 1968, the Seebohm report of the same year, and the Local Authority Social Services Act 1970 which it prompted — led to the creation of large-scale social services departments in local authorities, but underlined the contribution of voluntary and community activity in this field. The major reorganization of local government in 1972 led indirectly to increased support for the local voluntary sector infrastructure as local councils for voluntary service, needing to cover larger areas, successfully turned to local authorities for funding support (Younghusband, 1978). Local and central government funding of the sector as a whole grew during the 1960s and 1970s, although not all local authorities were involved: some traditional metropolitan, Scottish and Welsh Labour local authorities still distrusted the sector, while traditional Conservative authorities often expected it to pay for itself (Taylor and Lansley, 1992).

The large-scale housing and road developments of the post-war years were beginning to provoke protests from displaced communities, and this contributed to government initiatives to promote participation in planning (Skeffington, 1969). Faced with unrest in the urban areas and the "rediscovery" of poverty, government also began to put money into community organiz-ations, influenced by the anti-poverty strategies of the United States (Taylor, 1995). Thus the late 1960s were marked by the introduction of the Urban Programme (see Chapter 5), the Educa-tional Priority Areas and the national Community Development Project. Local authorities began to invest in community develop-ment: by 1975 there were an estimated 276 full-time community workers in social services departments alone (Thomas, 1983). In Scotland, community activity was given a further boost in the 1970s by the Alexander report on adult education (1975). These funding initiatives from central and local government supported a new wave of community and service user organizations. At local level, tenants' organizations and claimants' unions, advice and law centres, play groups and toy libraries, black and minority ethnic organizations and women's organizations responded to the perceived failings of public services, both by putting pressure on government and by developing their own activities and services. A national Self-Help Support Centre was set up in 1977.

The late 1960s and early 1970s were still a period of economic expansion, and thus there were rewards for the community activist and campaigner. But the bubble was to burst in the mid-1970s and unemployment began to rise, particularly among the young. This was an era of fiscal austerity, with important implications for the state and voluntary sectors alike. Chapter 5 takes up the story of how relations between these two sectors were to evolve between the 1970s and the mid-1990s.

2.8 Conclusion

It is always dangerous to generalize, especially in the discipline of history where apparently obvious progressions and periodiz-ations are all too often undermined by a closer look at the rich texture of economic and social life. Changes linked to one par-ticular date or event are seen, on closer inspection, to have been evolving in some corners of society for a number of years and almost as soon as they bed down in legislation and practice, a new contradictory strand begins to take shape in another corner. Similarly, major movements, like the Evangelical movement of the Victorian era or the social movements of the 1960s, prove to have within them the seeds of very different developments and to set off hares that run in apparently quite different directions. While sweeping statements about organizational development and external stimuli in society's structure and ideology are hazardous at the best of times, caution may be particularly apposite in the domain of voluntary organizations. While their spontaneity and responsiveness to changes in society are often remarked upon, they also often appear to be the embodiment of ossification, introversion and continuity with the past. It has been impossible to capture adequately this contradictory character of the sector in any single short account.

However, one of the abiding characteristics of the voluntary sector during this history has been its breathtaking diversity and its capacity to provide an institutional outlet for people — often as moral or social entrepreneurs (Obelkewich, 1990) — when neither business nor the state appears to offer a legitimate, feasible or appropriate context for the pursuit of their aspirations. Not surprisingly, this appears to make the historical development of the sector a function of a large number of interdependent variables at any one time. These include the changing structure of society in terms of status and class groups, and the relationship between them; the character of the state, its relationship with religion and how it relates to both the demands of elites, and to popular aspirations in terms of policy goals and legal structure; tensions, and sometimes conflicts between different ideologies or belief systems and the institutions through which they are expressed; the prevailing economic climate, and both the needs of the economy and its capacity to foster development; scientific advance; changing currents of both popular and minority concern; and changing socio-demographic and environmental factors as well as unforeseeable "acts of God".

These factors would probably be relevant in any country at any one time, but there are perhaps three characteristics about the UK which appear to have had consistent relevance over time. First, the particular history of the sector in the UK has certainly been a function of the lengthy *stability* of this country. Northern Ireland excepted, there has been no civil war within these shores since the 17th century. As a result, the sector as it currently exists contains a remarkably rich variety of institutions established over successive centuries, with new types and forms of organizations adding to, and not supplanting, existing organizations in each era. The legal system has been an important force for continuity, with the protection of charitable assets allowing large numbers of ancient foundations to continue operating over hundreds of years.

Second, the *tolerance* generally shown towards free association outside the state, as an integral part of the liberal ideology that has dominated belief systems, has also been conducive to a strong tradition of voluntary action. (Of course, as we have described, punitive legislation brought in at the end of the 18th century disallowed the formation and activities of reformist "political" organizations and trade unions, and attempts were also made to ban non-Anglican education in the early 18th century. But both instances were exceptional and short-lived.) The exclusion from the institutions of the state of significant sections of the population, either formally — as occurred prior to the 19th century — or informally, as with "outgroups" still marginalized, albeit more subtly, by virtue of race, gender, disability or poverty in the 20th century — has helped to guarantee a need for organization under voluntary auspices.

Finally, and also of overarching relevance, has been British society's chronic preoccupation with *gradations of status*, while at the same time allowing for considerable movement or fluidity between status groups. If conspicuous philanthropy is, at least in part, a means of signalling "arrival" at a higher tier of society, or of reinforcing existing social status, then this function may carry particular weight in the UK.

It is evident that the philanthropic mode of voluntary action has been used by powerful elites as a means of legitimizing and reinforcing the *status quo*: as a kind of social cement or glue. As such, it has been a reactionary force, serving to underpin and enhance the status of individuals and groups within the social order. It has been a route for the aspiring classes to gain acceptance in that social order and, as Stedman Jones and others would argue, by the judicious use of funds to encourage the respectable working classes into acquiescence. But it has also played a major role in change by both the powerful and the powerless. For the drivers of economic change, it has acted as a sticking plaster on the casualties of that change, underpinning and paving the way for new power structures: a role shared in the 20th century with the state. But at the same time it has been a channel for dissent, both in religion and in politics. It has been a way for groups excluded from political and economic power to gain a stake in society, develop networks, discuss and formulate strategies and gain an organizational base. In this respect, no amount of centralized planning or even more subtle forms of hegemony can dictate the pattern of voluntary action, unless it is entirely outlawed. This seems to have been the lesson of the past and an important lesson to take forward into an uncertain future.

Chapter 3

LEGAL POSITION OF THE VOLUNTARY SECTOR*

3.1 Introduction

The historical analysis in the previous chapter demonstrates, among other things, the increasingly sophisticated and wide-ranging arrangements developed by the state to encourage and control voluntary organizations. This includes the construction and refinement of an elaborate legal framework. Beyond the regular courts, specialized arrangements for the monitoring and control of the endowed charity sector came first with the "roving" Charity Commissioners introduced at the time of the 1601 Statute, investigating breaches of trust on a county-wide basis (Davis Smith, 1995). In reaction to widespread evidence of abuse and inefficiency, a permanent national Charity Commission was eventually established for England and Wales in the 19th century (Box 2.3, p.42), while the 1960 Act brought fundraising and commercial charities within the Commission's purview, and introduced a register (Box 2.8, p.53). Legislation introduced for the sector in the 1990s, although still primarily concerned with registered charities, represents a further broadening of legal control. The fundraising and collecting activities of all "charitable institutions", embracing "charities and voluntary organisations established for charitable, benevolent and philanthropic purposes", increases the

---

* This chapter was written by Geraint Thomas and Jeremy Kendall.

ambit of statutory regulation more widely than ever before (Driscoll and Phelps, 1992, section 13).

The range of legal structures now available to voluntary organizations represents a historical legacy, with each developed originally as a response to the needs of the dominant mode of voluntary action in a particular era. This is most obvious in the case of two of the most important structures currently available. The "charitable trust", with origins in the medieval period, came to prominence in Tudor times originally as an adaptation of general trust law to the requirements of the individualistic philanthropy of gifts and bequests that characterized the period. And the most common mechanism for incorporated philanthropy, the "company limited by guarantee", was a "conscious and significant step" by the legislature to encourage the associative philanthropy of the 19th century (Chesterman, 1979, p.200). Whether these and the other legal structures currently available are appropriate for the needs of the 21st century is one of a number of legal controversies to which we return at the end of this chapter.[1]

The significance of the current pattern of *fiscal* privilege is a relatively modern phenomenon, reflecting the fact that the all-pervasiveness of taxation has been uniquely associated with the late 19th and 20th centuries. While piecemeal tax advantages were available in education from as early as the 15th century, the exemption from income tax for any "corporation, fraternity or society of persons established for charitable purposes" initially emerged as that tax was first introduced at the onset of the 19th century. The automatic link that currently exists between legal and fiscal status was in fact not a conscious decision of Parliament. Rather, it was concretized in case law as a result of a majority decision of four to two in the High Court in the famous *Pemsel* case of 1891, which, as we see in section 3.2 below, has also had wider implications for the legal interpretation of the meaning of "charity". The subsequent extension of exemptions and reliefs from other modes of taxation since this decision has been the outcome of deliberate decisions by the legislature in response to the lobbying efforts of those representing interests within the sector (see especially Chesterman, 1979, pp.58-62; and see Chapter 1).

In this chapter we consider in detail how the law concerning these organizations currently operates. While, like Chapter 2, constraints of space force us to concentrate on developments in England and Wales, it is important to observe that the legal environment experienced by voluntary organizations in the UK is complicated by the existence of three different legal traditions. This reflects different patterns of historical development in each of the UK's constituent nations. Although in one of the areas of law with the most important policy implications for the sector — the tax treatment of "charities" — the concept of "charitable status" is now used uniformly across the UK, in other respects there are differences. English law, which covers England and Wales, is based on common law, the ancient law of the land deduced from custom and interpreted by judges, which has been exported in part to the USA, Ireland, Canada and Australia, among others. Scotland falls under the auspices of separately developed Scots law, based on Roman law and a close relative of civil law, in common with the legal systems of mainland Europe. Northern Ireland represents something of a "halfway house" (Woodfield et al., 1987). In practice, the same legal meaning of "charity" is shared by the laws of England, Wales and Northern Ireland, whereas Scots law, though broadly similar, embraces some marked differences. Each nation also has its own particular arrangements for the administration of charities.

The day-to-day administration of any voluntary organization (be it charitable or not) obviously rests with those directly charged with that task. Their administrative and managerial powers are derived from the governing or founding instrument or from general law and the relevant statutes. The latter include the Charities Act 1993 (consolidating the Charities Act 1960, Part I of the Charities Act 1992 and the Charitable Trustees Incorporation Act 1872), the Trustee Act 1925, the Trustee Investment Act 1961, the Charities Act 1985, and the Charities Act 1992.

Thus, the trustees of a charitable trust will generally have available the powers conferred on trustees by the Trustee Act 1925 and the Trustee Investment Act 1961, as well as those contained in their trust instrument. Similarly, the directors of a charitable company will be subject to the Companies Acts and to their own Articles and Memorandum, while members of an unincorporated association will generally be bound by the terms of their contract *inter se*. However, charitable organizations, as well as some non-charitable ones, are also subject to regulation and control by certain statutory authorities, with arrangements for the former in particular recently modernized through the Charities Act 1993. We provide details of these complex arrangements in the sections that follow.

It is important to make two fundamental points at this stage. First, although there are large areas of overlap, the set of organizations with charitable status is not the same as either the "broad voluntary sector" (the structural operational definition) or the "narrow voluntary sector" that we introduced in Chapter 1. The expression "voluntary organization" is *not* synonymous with the term "charity". We should note here that the implications of the three different approaches are significant in terms of coverage. The broad voluntary sector embraces the entire set of organizations that are charitable in law (with the exception of places of worship and purely religious trusts, voluntary controlled schools, and trust funds and appeals linked to specific statutory bodies) as well as large numbers of voluntary bodies without charitable status. Organizations that are excluded in moving from our broad to a narrower definition include some which are charitable in law (including aided voluntary and independent schools and universities), and some which are not (for example, sports clubs and trade unions).

The expression "voluntary organization", while the most often used descriptor in common parlance and in government policy documents, in fact has no precise legal meaning. Unlike the civil law systems that operate in continental Europe, the term "organization" has no distinct or useful general definition in English law (other than in occasional statutes, such as industrial relations legislation). Instead, the system identifies entities as "persons", which may be either individual or corporate (having a distinct personality from that of individual members). It is these legal "persons" which are legally empowered to act in terms of holding or selling property in their own right, suing or being sued in their own name, entering into contracts, and being liable in tort, for example. This legal identity or personality of a voluntary organization is therefore constituted by the aggregate of individuals that control it or by the corporation established for this purpose (if it is incorporated). Some organizations, such as registered friendly societies, are effectively "quasi-corporations", and occupy an intermediate position.

The word "voluntary", in its technical sense, refers to transactions rather than organizations. First, it connotes absence of compulsion so that, for example, an act carried out in pursuance of a statutory duty, or simply to comply with the law, would not be a voluntary act.[2] Second, it is also used to describe an absence of "consideration" (i.e. that an act is done without a *quid pro quo*, such as a payment of money, or a return promise, or marriage). Thus, the act must be performed out of free will or choice, such as the making of a gift, and not under compulsion or as part of a "bargain". Thus, the term "voluntary contributions" may mean that the contributions are not compulsory or, alternatively, that they are without consideration.[3]

The second crucial point to emphasize is the distinctiveness of the legal status of "charity" from any particular legal form or structure. Again, this is a point of contrast with European civil law countries, in which the acquisition of the nearest equivalent status to that of a UK "charity" tends to be linked to the adoption of a specific legal form, or to the process of incorporation. In the UK, agencies enjoy charitable status because their organizational *substance*, as reflected in their objectives, has been recognized as charitable in law, irrespective of the form or nature of their legal personality. No generalized legal structure has been tailor-made for the universe of charitable or indeed non-charitable voluntary bodies. As we have already pointed out, these may have been incidentally adapted to the needs of voluntary organizations from what has historically been more generally available. Alternatively, they adopt structures designed in discrete specialist pieces of legislation, such as the "housing association" and "friendly society". Each option has its advantages and disadvantages, and the appropriate structure is likely to be connected with the scale of activity proposed, and with the amount and value of property which the body proposes to have.

In the next section we outline the legal meaning of the expression "charity", while section 3.3 looks at the structures which voluntary organizations can adopt. Section 3.4 considers the legal arrangements for the sector's administration and control. Section 3.5 addresses the issue of the sector's tax treatment, and the final section looks at some of the current legal issues and debates concerning the voluntary sector.

3.2 The legal meaning of charity

Although we have noted that the ambit of this book's analysis goes deliberately beyond the legal concept of "charity", its controversial interpretation is central to an understanding of the legal and fiscal position of the sector in the UK. There is in fact no statutory definition of the words "charity" or "charitable" in English law. (On charity law generally, see Tudor, 1995, pp.1-8; Keeton and Sheridan, 1992, ch. 1; Picarda, 1995.) Section 96(1) of the Charities Act 1993 defines "charity" as "any institution, corporate or not, which is established for charitable purposes and is subject to the control of the High Court in the exercise of the court's jurisdiction with respect to charities".[4] "Charitable purposes" are purposes which are exclusively charitable according to the law of England and Wales. The word "institution" includes any trust or undertaking.[5] Statute law (including tax law) does not, therefore, define what is charitable or identify which organizations qualify for charitable status. For the definition of the basic terms it is necessary to look to the substantial body of case law that has grown up over centuries.[6]

If a purpose is to be charitable according to English law, it must fall "within the spirit and intendment" of the preamble to the Charitable Uses Act 1601.[7] The preamble provided a catalogue of charitable purposes:

[the] relief of aged, impotent and poor people, [the] maintenance of sick and maimed soldiers and mariners, schools of learning, free schools, and scholars in universities, [the] repair of bridges, ports, havens, causeways, churches, sea-banks and highways, [the] education and preferment of orphans, [the] relief, stock or maintenance for houses of correction, [the] marriages of poor maids, ... [the] aid or ease of any poor inhabitants concerning payments of fifteens, setting out of soldiers and other taxes.

The preamble was not intended to define charitable purposes but it did contain a non-exhaustive list or index[8] of purposes which, in 1601, were regarded as charitable. An object or purpose could be held charitable if some analogy could be found between it and an object mentioned in the preamble. In time, the courts went further and granted charitable status to an object if they could find an analogy between it and an object already held to be charitable.[9] Consequently, although it is still said that an object or purpose cannot be charitable unless it is

within the spirit and intendment [of the preamble,] it is now accepted that what must be regarded is not the wording of the preamble itself, but the effect of decisions given by the courts as to its scope, decisions which have endeavoured to keep the law as to charities moving according as new social needs arise or old ones become obsolete or satisfied.[10]

In 1891, the mass of case law was classified by Lord Macnaghten in *Pemsel's Case:*[11]

"Charity" in its legal sense comprises four principal divisions: trusts for the relief of poverty; trusts for the advancement of education; trusts for the advancement of religion; and trusts for other purposes beneficial to the community, not falling under any of the preceding heads.

This classification has constantly been referred to in later cases; and it is now undoubtedly the starting point when the question of charitable status has to be determined, although the courts recognize that there may well be purposes which do not fit readily into any one of these categories, and that the law of charities may have evolved since 1891.[12]

There are two additional requirements. First, a purpose must be *exclusively* charitable. The inclusion of non-charitable objects along with charitable ones will invalidate the entirety.[13] Second, in order to be recognized in law as charitable, a purpose must not only be beneficial (in the sense that it falls within one of the four categories) but it must also be for the benefit of the *public*, i.e. it must benefit the whole community or an appreciable section of the community. This requirement of public benefit varies in its application to each of the four heads of charity, as we now discuss. We then consider how "public benefit" has been interpreted in each case.

Poverty and its relief have never been defined for the purposes of the law of charities. The usual starting point are the remarks of Lord Evershed M.R. in *Re Coulthurst's Will Trusts:*[14]

It is quite clearly established that poverty does not mean destitution.

It is a word of wide and somewhat indefinite import, and, perhaps, it is not unfairly paraphrased for present purposes as meaning persons who have to "go short" in the ordinary acceptation of that term, due regard being had to their status in life and so forth.

Thus, the law's concept of poverty is a relative and not an absolute one;[15] it takes into account the circumstances and expectations of the individuals in question. In accordance with these statements, the courts have upheld, as charitable, gifts for ladies in reduced circumstances,[16] for the aid of distressed gentlefolk,[17] for poor pious persons,[18] and many, many more (Tudor, 1995, pp.30-31).

Second, the concept of *education* in the law of charities has broadened considerably since the preamble to the 1601 Statute referred to "the maintenance of schools of learning, free schools and scholars in universities" and now extends to "the improvement of a useful branch of human knowledge and its public dissemination".[19] It includes purposes as general as "the advancement and propagation of education and learning in every part of the world"[20] and as specific as establishing a single library or museum, a single teaching post or a scholarship. Educational institutions may be charitable even though they are essentially fee-funded or otherwise exclusive (such as independent schools) provided that any profits they make are applied solely towards their educational objects (including payment of staff) and are not distributed to the institution's owners or shareholders.[21]

Third, although the only *religious* purpose referred to in the preamble to the 1601 Statute is the repair of churches, this category now includes virtually anything[22] which is for "the promotion of spiritual teaching in a wide sense, and the maintenance of the doctrines on which it rests, and the observances which serve to promote and manifest it". There is no definition of "religion" for these purposes, but it is considered that it must possess two essential attributes, namely "faith in a god and worship of that god". As between different religions, the law stands neutral, but it assumes that any religion is at least likely to be better than none.[23] However, social movements founded on Christian ethics and organizations based on ethical or moral principles are not charitable under this head (although they may be for the advancement of education).[24]

Finally, *other purposes beneficial to the community* comprises the residual head of charity and the one under which most new registrations by the Charity Commissioners are made (Charity Commissioners, 1985, para. 8). However, there is no satisfactory test to determine whether a particular purpose falls within it, but the benefit to the public must be within "the spirit and intendment" of the preamble to the 1601 Statute, or at least within the cases previously decided.[25] The boundaries of this particular category are recognized to be vague, but they clearly encompass a wide and disparate range of purposes. Included are a wide variety of health and social care activities across diverse client groups; the promotion of racial harmony and relief for unemployed youth; environmental, animal welfare and cultural groups; fire brigade and lifeboat services; advice on and campaigning for road safety; promoting the efficiency of the armed services and the police; preserving law and order or the independence of the judiciary; and even a gift to the Inland Revenue (Chesterman, 1979, pp.166-7). The advancement of industry, commerce, agriculture, horticulture and craftsmanship may also be charitable (Charity Commissioners, 1973, paras 69-75).[26]

How is the requirement of benefit to the public, or an appreciable section of it, interpreted? The requirement differs in respect of each category.[27] In relation to the relief of poverty, the requirement of public benefit has been reduced almost to vanishing point, so that a gift in favour of "poor relations" or "poor employees" is capable of being charitable.[28] In relation to the advancement of education, the requirement has been more stringently applied,[29] but not as stringently as in relation to the fourth category (other purposes beneficial to the community).[30] Most purposes accepted within this category must generally be for the benefit of "the public". This is interpreted to mean that gifts for the benefit of groups of persons bound together by some personal or contractual nexus are not charitable.[31] On the other hand, the inhabitants of a geographical area, such as a county or town or borough, *are* regarded as a section of the public.[32]

It is sometimes stated that a purpose may fall within one of the four *Pemsel* categories and have an element of public benefit, but may still be held non-charitable because it is infected by some disqualifying factor. Chesterman (1979, pp.174-88) identifies the three main disqualifications as "self-help", "profit distribution" and "politics". Whether these are in fact distinct or additional disqualifications is open to doubt: they may simply be factors which have the effect that a particular purpose is not exclusively charitable within one of the four recognized categories, or, more likely, that the public benefit test is not regarded as having been satisfied.

Finally, a further condition to note, which appears to go beyond the second requirement of non-profit-distribution, is that of "disinterested management": organizations which provide material remuneration for those that control them (their boards, management committees or trustees) cannot generally have charitable status (although there are a very small number of exceptions to this general rule). To become a charity an organization must generally accept the restriction that its board or management committee are trustees and, as a result, cannot be "salaried" or paid in any way linked to performance, although "legitimate expenses" may be reimbursed. These restrictions apply whatever structure the organization adopts.[33]

3.3 Legal structures adopted by voluntary organizations

In section 3.1, we drew attention to the historical origins of the "trust" and "company limited by guarantee".[34] These remain two of the most important legal structures to this day. The *trust* form does not, in fact, correspond to a distinct legal person. It has been defined[35] as

an equitable obligation, binding a person (who is called a trustee) to deal with property over which he has control (which is called the trust property), for the benefit of persons (who are called the beneficiaries or cestuis que trust), of whom he may himself be one, and any one of whom may enforce the obligation (see Underhill and Hayton, 1995, p.3).

"Trust" and "foundation" are often used interchangeably and non-specifically in everyday language to describe parts of the voluntary sector. But in a legal sense, the terms are not synonymous. Technically, foundations are a different subset of organizations, being eleemosynary corporations founded by the Crown or by an individual. The law distinguishes two species of foundation, namely the *fundatio incipiens*, which may be created directly by Royal Charter or Act of Parliament, or by private individuals acting under Royal licence; and the *fundatio percipiens*, or endowment, in which the first gift of revenues is the foundation (and the person who gives them is the founder).

The most common form of incorporation in the sector, with the concomitant advantages of a distinct legal personality and limited liability for its members, is under the 1980s Companies Acts as a *company limited by guarantee*. Less common forms of charitable corporation result from the incorporation of the trustees of a trust or association (see below) under the Charitable Trustees Incorporation Act 1872, as consolidated in the Charities Act 1993; and incorporation by Royal Charter, ecclesiastical decree or Act of Parliament.

The third main generic structure adopted by voluntary bodies is the "unincorporated association", sometimes regarded as the voluntary equivalent of "partnerships" in the for-profit sector, from which it differs by having members and "non-commercial" purposes. Although there are statutes dealing with the particular cases of registered friendly societies and industrial and provident societies whose structures are described below, associations in general are not governed by statute, and most of the law relating to them is judge-made. An "unincorporated association" has been judicially defined as

two or more persons bound together for one or more common purposes, not being business purposes, by mutual undertaking, each having mutual duties and obligations, in an organization which has rules which identify in whom control of it and its funds rests and upon what terms and which can be joined or left at will. The bond of union between the members of an unincorporated association has to be contractual.[36]

Two of the remaining three legal structures adopted by voluntary bodies can be regarded as rendering them "quasi-corporate" unincorporated associations. First, *friendly societies* are unincorporated mutual insurance associations in which members subscribe for provident benefits for themselves and their families, and these have recently been subjected to modernizing legislation following campaigning by the Friendly Society Liaison Committee, partly to meet the requirements of recent EC Directives. They have formed part of a group of benefit thrift and provident societies, others being building societies, cooperative societies and trade unions. Most of these are excluded from our broad definition of the sector because of their quasi-commercial character.

Although registered friendly societies are governed by the Friendly Societies Acts of 1974 and 1992, they are but one of six classes of societies which can be registered under that Act, the others being cattle insurance societies, benevolent societies, working men's clubs, old people's home societies, and specially authorized societies. The permitted purposes of a *registered* friendly society are defined by the 1974 Act.[37] There is no legal definition of *unregistered* friendly societies, which are therefore in the position of ordinary unincorporated associations.

Second, *industrial and provident societies* were originally societies whose purposes were to make profits by the personal exertions of their members and to distribute the profits by way of provident provision for their members' future. They are now governed by the Industrial and Provident Societies Acts 1965, 1967, 1968, 1975 and 1978. They may be registered under the 1965 Act for the purpose of carrying on any industry, business or trade, whether wholesale or retail, if either (1) the society is a bona fide cooperative society, or (2) in view of the fact that the business of the society is being, or intended to be, conducted for the benefit of the community, there are special reasons why the society should be registered under the 1965 Act, rather than as a company under the Companies Act.[38] ("Cooperative society" does not include a society which carries on, or is intended to carry on, business with the object of making profits mainly for the payment of interest, dividends or bonuses on money invested or deposited with, or lent to, the society or any other person.[39])

Third, a *housing association* is a society, body of trustees or company (a) which is established for the purpose of, or among whose objects or powers are included those of, constructing, improving or managing or facilitating or encouraging the construction or improvement of accommodation, and (b) which does not trade for profit or whose constitution or rules prohibit the issue of any capital with interest or dividend exceeding such rate as may be prescribed by the Treasury (whether with or without differential as between share and loan capital).[40] Provisions affecting housing associations, or tenants or tenancies of such associations, will be found not only in the Housing Associations Act 1985 but also in a mass of other legislation (including the Housing Act 1985, the Landlord and Tenant Act 1985, and the Housing Act 1988).[41] These bodies may take the form of a corporation, a trust or an association.

3.4 The regulation and control of voluntary organizations

We begin this section with a description of the arrangements that apply to charitable bodies in England and Wales, before considering the UK-wide treatment of non-charitable voluntary bodies. Arrangements for supervision differ in Northern Ireland and Scotland. In neither case is there a body equivalent to the Charity Commission (see below), and arrangements for supervision are subsequently less developed. Section 10 of the Charities Act 1993 (concerning disclosure of information to and by the Charity Commissioners), however, does apply to the whole of the UK. In Northern Ireland, the Department of Finance and Personnel has certain powers as a result of the Charities Act (Northern Ireland) 1964, although sections 15(2) and 100 of the Charities Act 1993, concerning charities governed by royal charter, also now apply there. In Scotland, while sections 70, 71, part of section 86 and section 100 of the 1993 Act, concerning charity trustees' powers of investment, do apply, the main statute is the Law Reform (Miscellaneous Provisions) (Scotland) Act 1990. This has established an index of "recognized bodies" at the Scottish Inland Revenue open for public inspection, and the granting of supervisory and investigatory powers to the Lord Advocate, similar to those of the English Charity Commission, which are described below.[42]

The regulation and control of charities in England and Wales

All charities, other than exempt charities and excepted charities, must be registered with the *Charity Commissioners*.[43] An excepted charity (but not an exempt charity) may be entered on the register, and removed therefrom at its own request. An *exempt* charity, i.e. one which is exempt from the jurisdiction of the Charity Commissioners, cannot be registered. The Second Schedule to the Charities Act 1993 lists those institutions which are exempt. The list includes Winchester and Eton schools, various universities and museums, Trustee Boards, the Church Commissioners and societies registered under the Industrial and Provident Societies Acts. An *excepted* charity (other than an exempt charity) is any charity which is exempted by order or regulations, including most maintained voluntary schools, boy scouts' and girl guides' organizations, non-exempt universities, and a large number of charities connected with the advancement of religion,[44] and any charity having neither a permanent endowment nor the use or occupation of any land, and whose income from all sources does not in aggregate amount to more than £1,000 a year.[45] An excepted charity (like an exempt one) is not, therefore, required to register, but (unlike an exempt charity) it is not necessarily excepted from the other requirements of the 1993 Act.

It is the duty of the trustees of any charity which is not exempt or excepted from registration to apply for it to be registered. It is also their duty to notify the Commissioners if a registered institution ceases to exist, or if there is any change in its trusts, or in the particulars of it entered on the register, and to supply particulars of any such change and copies of any new trusts or alterations to the trusts. The register, and copies or particulars of the trusts of any registered charity, are open to public inspection at all reasonable times.[46] Any institution which no longer appears to the Charity Commissioners to be a charity shall be removed from the register, as also shall any charity which ceases to exist or does not operate.[47]

The Chief Charity Commissioner and two other Commissioners (and, since 1988, also two part-time Commissioners) are appointed by the Home Secretary, at least two of whom must be barristers or solicitors.[48] They are charged by the 1993 Act with

the general function of promoting the effective use of charitable resources by encouraging the development of better methods of administration, by giving charity trustees information or advice on any matter affecting the charity and by investigating and checking abuses [and their object is] so to act in the case of any charity...as best to promote and make effective the work of the charity in meeting the needs designated by its trusts.

The Commissioners do not themselves have power, however, to act in the adminstration of the charity.[49] They have the same powers as are exercisable by the High Court in charity proceedings for establishing schemes for the administration of a charity, for appointing, discharging or removing charity trustees, or removing an officer or employee, and for vesting or transferring property.[50] However, they are not to exercise their jurisdiction in any case which is of a contentious character, or which involves any special question of law or of fact, or which they consider more fit, for other reasons, to be adjudicated by the court.[51] There are also provisions for appeals to the High Court against any order of the Commissioners, by the Attorney General, by the charity or its trustees, or by any person removed from office.[52]

The Commissioners may institute inquiries with regard to charities or a particular charity. For this purpose, they have a range of ancillary powers, such as power to call for documents, to compel attendance of witnesses, to inspect documents, to furnish accounts and statements in writing, to publish the report, and so forth.[53] Where they are satisfied that there has been any misconduct or mismanagement in the administration of the charity, they may exercise a wide range of powers. *Inter alia*, these include the power to suspend any trustee or other person connected with the charity from the exercise of his or her office or employment, to appoint additional trustees, and to restrict the transactions which may be entered into in the administration of the charity without their approval. They may also remove any charity trustee or other officer or employee of the charity or, by order, establish a scheme for the administration of the charity.[54] They also have wide powers to appoint charity trustees.[55]

Charity trustees (other than where the charity is a company) must ensure that accounting records are kept which are sufficient to show and explain all the charity's transactions. Trustees are required to prepare in respect of each financial year of the charity (unless it is a company) a statement of accounts complying with the form and contents of accounts prescribed by regulations. If the charity's gross income in any financial year does not exceed £25,000, the charity trustees may elect to prepare a receipts and payments account and a statement of assets and liabilities instead. The records must be preserved for at least six years.[56] Charitable companies are also obliged to keep accounting records but under a completely separate legislative regime (namely under section 221 of the Companies Act 1985). Charities whose gross income or total expenditure exceeds £100,000 must have their accounts audited by a qualified auditor. Those whose income or gross expenditure is below that sum may instead elect to have their accounts examined by an independent examiner. Charity trustees must prepare in respect of each financial year a report on the activities of the charity during that year and such other information relating to the charity or to its trustees or officers as may be prescribed by regulations made by the Home Secretary. This report is open to public inspection and also has to be supplied (for a small fee) to any person who makes written request for a copy.[57]

While the Charity Commission is the principal regulatory body for charities, other institutions are also involved, including the Official Custodian for Charities, the Attorney General, local authorities and, in some cases, Visitors. First, the *Official Custodian for Charities* was constituted by section 3 of the Charities Act 1960 to act as trustee for some charities as specified in that Act. The office is continued by section 2(1) of the Charities Act 1993, but the Custodian's functions were drastically reduced by section 29 of the Charities Act 1992 (which remains in force) which requires her to divest herself of most of the investments which she currently holds.

Second, since the Crown — as *parens patriae* ("parent of the country") — is the ultimate guardian of charity, it is the duty of the Attorney-General (who represents the Crown for all forensic purposes) to intervene to protect charities and to give advice and assistance to the court in the administration of charitable trusts.[58] Third, *local authorities* have a number of supervisory functions. The Charities Act 1993[59] authorizes the council of a county or of a district or a London borough to initiate, and carry out in cooperation with the charity trustees, a review of the working of any group of local charities with the same or similar purposes in the council's area, and to report to the Commissioners on its findings after consultation with the trustees. Local councils are also authorized to make arrangements for coordinating their activities with those of charities offering similar or complementary provision in the interests of persons who may benefit from those services.

Finally, *Visitation* is a form of supervision of the domestic affairs of some charitable institutions (see Tudor, 1995, pp.369-88; Picarda, 1995, ch. 41). It usually applies to corporations, although the trust deed of any unincorporated charity can also appoint a Visitor of the charity. The Visitatorial jurisdiction has expanded in recent years because of the foundation of new universities.[60] The powers vested in a Visitor usually include power to appoint and remove members and officers of the corporation (e.g. the election of the master or fellows of a college, the pensioners of a hospital), to regulate the management of the corporation's property, to determine questions of construction arising under the statutes of the foundation, and to hear and adjudicate upon claims and complaints concerning the internal affairs of the corporation made by members (e.g. expulsion of students from colleges or universities, or the conduct of examinations).

The identity of Visitors depends upon the type of corporation. Corporations may be ecclesiastical or lay corporations. In the case of ecclesiastical corporations (for the furtherance of religion and for perpetuating the rites of the church), the Visitor is generally "the ordinary" under canon law (i.e. a bishop or his official, exercising judicial power), although, in some cases, it is the patron. Lay corporations are subdivided further into eleemosynary and civil corporations. Civil corporations have the Sovereign as their Visitor, and include the Sovereign herself, municipal and commercial corporations, the Universities of Oxford and Cambridge, and some learned societies (such as the Royal Society and the Royal College of Surgeons). Eleemosynary corporations are those lay corporations constituted for the perpetual distribution of the free alms or bounty to those persons directed by the founder. Typical examples are many hospitals, colleges and corporate schools. The founder of an eleemosynary corporation has full power to make regulations, including making express appointment of the Visitor.

The regulation and control of non-charitable organizations

In general, non-charitable organizations are not subject to overall regulation and control. However, registered industrial and provident societies, registered friendly societies and registered housing associations are subject to the requirements of the enactment directly applicable to them. Registered *industrial and provident societies* are subject to the provisions of the Industrial and Provident Societies Acts 1965 to 1978. Once registered, societies must register or deposit with the appropriate registrar all applications to register, amendments of rules, annual returns, applications for approval of a change of name, notices of changes of registered offices, special resolutions for amalgamations, transfers of engagements or conversions, notices of appointments of receivers and receivers' returns, instruments of dissolution, winding-up resolutions and other documents required to be registered under the winding-up provisions of the Insolvency Act 1986.

Registered *friendly societies* now come under the jurisdiction and control of the Friendly Societies Commission. The general functions of the Commission shall be to promote the protection by each friendly society of its funds; to promote the financial stability of friendly societies generally; to secure that the purposes of each friendly society are in conformity with the Friendly Societies Act 1992; to administer the system of regulation of the activities of friendly societies; and to advise and make recommendations to the Treasury and other government departments on any matter relating to friendly societies. The Commission has power to do anything which is calculated to facilitate the discharge of its functions, or is incidental or conducive to their discharge.[61]

Housing associations are eligible for registration with the Housing Corporation in England, Scottish Homes in Scotland, and Housing for Wales in Wales, if they are (a) a registered charity or (b) a society registered under the Industrial and Provident Society Act 1965 which fulfils certain conditions. These quangos each maintain a register of housing associations, which is open to public inspection.[62] Once a housing association is registered with the Corporation, it becomes subject to a wide range of controls and restrictions imposed by the Housing Associations Act 1985. For example, the consent of the Corporation is required for any disposition or loan by a registered housing association (and also for any disposition of grant-aided land by an unregistered association).[63] No gift may be made, and no sum may be paid by way of bonus or dividend, to a person who is or has been a member of the association (or a member of such person's family, or a company of which he or she is a director); and no payment or grant may be made to committee members.[64] No amendment of the rules of a registered housing association which is also registered under the 1965 Act, and whose registration has been recorded by the Registrar (except a change in its name or its registered office) is valid without the Corporation's consent.[65] Associations must comply with the regulations issued under the 1985 Act and the Registered Housing Associations (Accounting Requirements) Order 1988 as to the production of annual accounts. The Corporation has power to remove or appoint committee members of the association,[66] to direct an inquiry or an audit and, if misconduct or mismanagement is found in the administration of the association, to direct the transfer of the association's land to another housing association or the Corporation,[67] and so forth.

3.5 The tax treatment of voluntary organizations

The distinction between voluntary organizations which enjoy charitable status and those which are non-charitable has considerable significance for tax purposes (see Whiteman, 1988, ch. 26; Vincent, 1991). In the case of charities, the tax advantages conferred by numerous provisions in the fiscal legislation take two general forms: first, there are exemptions, reliefs, concessions and privileges conferred on, or enjoyed by, charities themselves by virtue of their charitable status; second, there are several reliefs available to taxpayers who make gifts to charities.

The tax treatment of charities

Income tax and corporation tax
There is no general exemption from income tax for charities, but particular exemptions have been granted, by section 505 of the

Income and Corporation Taxes Act 1988, in respect of tax under different Schedules. These exemptions have been increased by extra-statutory concessions, and additional concessions may be allowed in practice. These income tax exemptions and reliefs are extended to corporation tax by section 9(4) of the 1988 Act. The various types of income which are exempt are detailed in section 505, although other minor exemptions are scattered elsewhere in this legislation.

If a charity carries on a trade, such profits will be exempt from income tax, but only if (1) the profits are applied solely for the purposes of the charity and (2) either (a) the trade is exercised in the course of the actual carrying out of a primary purpose of the charity or (b) the work in connection with the trade is mainly carried out by beneficiaries of the charity.[68]

If a charity incurs a loss on its charitable non-trading activities, it cannot offset the loss against its profits from a trade.[69] It is doubtful (but not clear) whether a charity can offset losses on an exempt trade against profits made on a non-exempt trade.

Capital gains tax
Charities are generally exempt from capital gains tax under section 256 of the Taxation of Chargeable Gains Act 1992, provided that the gains are applied for charitable purposes. However, in order to prevent avoidance of the tax by means of a temporary charitable trust, section 256(2) imposes a liability when assets cease to be held on charitable trusts. On such an occasion, the trustees are regarded as having made a deemed disposal of the assets, and the disposal is chargeable to tax, without the benefit of any exemption.

Business rates and council tax
The system of local taxation now comprises two distinct taxes, namely the uniform business rate (which, as the name implies, is a tax on businesses) and the council tax, a local tax on individuals assessed by reference to dwellings. Voluntary organizations benefit from concessions on the latter, in as much as some of the categories of person with which they deal, including, *inter alia*, those with health problems, hostel residents and care workers, are disregarded (or "invisible") for the purposes of the personal element which partly decides the overall liability. As far as the

former tax is concerned, charities are entitled to mandatory 80 percent relief, provided the hereditament is wholly or mainly used for charitable purposes;[70] and local authorities have a discretion to increase the relief to 100 percent in respect of charities within their own jurisdictions, provided the same condition is satisfied.[71]

Value added tax

Charities are *not* exempt from valued added tax (VAT). While there are a few exemptions, reliefs or privileges for VAT purposes, charities are generally liable to VAT on all goods and services purchased by them.[72] They are also under a liability to register and account for VAT in respect of the supply of goods and/or services in the course of the furtherance of a business. "Business" includes every trade, profession or vocation (and is thus a wider concept than "trading"). "Supply" includes all forms of supply except anything done otherwise than for a consideration. To the extent that charities provide services and goods which are entirely free (which is often the case), their "supplies" necessarily fall outside the scope of VAT.

The manner in which the VAT legislation applies to the activities of charities is extremely complicated (see Vincent, 1991, ch. 21). Some of these activities are regarded as non-business activities and are outside the scope of VAT, e.g. fees paid to independent schools, and fees and donations in respect of the conduct of religious rites or services (e.g. weddings); voluntary services given entirely free of charge in pursuit of the charity's objects; giving flags or emblems as an acknowledgement of a donation (unless offered for a minimum sum); the receipt of sums from advertisers in charity programmes or brochures (subject to certain restrictions); and the supply of welfare services consistently below cost.[73]

Where the activities of charities are regarded as "business" for VAT purposes, the relevant supplies will be (a) standard-rated (i.e. a charge to VAT at 17.5 percent added to the supply), or (b) zero-rated (i.e. VAT at 0 percent added to the supply), or (c) exempt. The requirement to register is dictated by the volume of taxable supplies, which include those subject to VAT at either the standard rate or the zero rate (but not those which are exempt).

Other taxes

Chapter III of the *Inheritance Tax Act 1984* contains elaborate provisions for the taxation of trusts in which no interest in possession subsists (generally referred to as "discretionary trusts").[74] Charities are *not* exempt from national insurance contributions and must account for Pay As You Earn (income tax) on employees' salaries in the normal way. However, expenses paid by a charity to a director, or higher-paid employee, whose total emoluments are less than £8,500 a year are not subject to the legislation which normally charges "benefits in kind" provided for directors and higher-paid employees.[75] Charities are not liable for stamp duty on conveyances, transfers on sale or leases,[76] and are also exempt from pool betting duty in respect of lotteries, provided they are small lotteries incidental to exempt entertainments or private lotteries or societies' lotteries.[77]

Tax incentives to donors to charities

There is no general relief from tax for a taxpayer who makes gifts to charity, but there are several specific reliefs which have become more numerous and generous over the years.

Deeds of covenant

Under a deed of covenant, the taxpayer enters into a binding legal obligation to make regularly recurring payments (of fixed or variable amounts) for a fixed period of time, and can receive tax relief if the fixed period exceeds three years (hence the emergence of the "four-year covenant"). The donor pays a sum which is actually *net of income tax* to the charity, but they can set the gross amount of the covenanted payment against their income and claim relief against higher rate income tax (if this is relevant). The receiving charity itself can then reclaim from the Inland Revenue the basic rate income tax deducted by the donor.[78] Similar covenants can be entered into by companies, with similar results. For corporation tax purposes, the covenant is a charge on income, and it is a common practice for trading subsidiaries of charities to use such covenants to convert their profits into exempt income in the hands of the receiving charity.[79] The charge is not, however, incurred exclusively for the purposes of the company's trade, so a loss created by the amount payable under the covenant cannot be carried back or forward against past or future profits.

Single donations ("Gift Aid")

Relief from income tax has been available, as from 1 October 1990, to individuals who make a single donation to charity, provided certain conditions are satisfied. These conditions currently include the requirement that the amount of the donation must not be less than £250 net of basic rate income tax.[80] The individual will obtain tax relief at his or her highest rate of income tax. Gift Aid is also available to companies, subject to similar conditions.

Capital gains tax

The disposal of an asset (such as by way of gift) may give rise to a charge to capital gains tax if the value of the asset at the date of disposal is higher than its value at the date of its acquisition. However, where the chargeable asset is disposed of to a charity, the value at which the asset is deemed to pass is such that neither a gain nor a loss arises on the disposal, and thus no capital gains tax is chargeable.[81] This relief applies only to the chargeable asset and not to the proceeds of sale of the asset. Therefore, if the disposal of a chargeable asset would give rise to a chargeable gain, the donor should make a gift of it to the charity which can then dispose of it free of capital gains tax.[82] If the disposal would give rise to a loss, the donor should sell the asset and give the proceeds to the charity.

Other specific reliefs

Three other reliefs can be noted. First, under a *payroll deduction scheme* (introduced in 1986), an employee may authorize his (or her) employer to deduct sums from gross pay before deduction of income tax (but not before deduction of national insurance contributions) and to pay these over to charity. Maximum gifts must not exceed £900 a year per employee.[83] Second, there are *reliefs where employees are seconded to charities*. The employees' salaries, national insurance contributions, pension contributions, and so forth, continue to be paid by their employers. Such expenditure may be deducted by the employers for tax purposes, provided that the secondment is temporary.[84] Finally, gifts (or "transfers of value") to charity, whether made during the donor's lifetime or on death, are exempt from *inheritance tax*, provided the gift is absolute.[85]

The tax treatment of non-charitable organizations

Non-charitable organizations do not generally enjoy exemptions or privileges under existing fiscal legislation. For the purposes of the Income and Corporation Taxes Act 1988 and the Taxation of Chargeable Gains Act 1992, a "company" includes any corporate body or any unincorporated association, and both are subject to corporation tax on their income and chargeable capital gains.[86] Despite the fact that an unincorporated association does not possess a separate legal identity, it is the association which is liable to tax and not its individual members.[87] Liability is assessed according to normal income tax principles (see generally Warburton, 1986, ch. 6). Thus, associations are not liable to tax on their subscription income because it does not fall within one of the income tax schedules.[88] Similarly, an association is not liable for any surplus made on the provision of services solely to members, e.g. profit on the sale of alcohol, because of the principle of mutual trading.[89] (This principle ceases to apply, however, if the association takes money from non-members, e.g. a golf club charging green fees, for it will then be trading in the normal way.[90])

For VAT purposes, an association will be a taxable person if it makes supplies in the course of its business and is otherwise not excepted. If it makes no supplies, for example because it is wholly involved in research funded by grants, or because it gives items to members and does not sell them, it will not be liable to VAT. However, the principle of mutual trading does not apply to VAT and the provision of goods and services to members will therefore be a supply, even if there is no sale.[91] A member of an association will not generally be able to deduct their subscription when computing their taxable income unless the association is recognized by statute or is one approved by the Inland Revenue (usually as one connected with the individual's profession).[92]

Non-charitable organizations are not entitled to mandatory relief from the local authority charge to *uniform business rate*. However, local authorities may grant discretionary relief to certain non-charitable bodies in specific cases.[93] It will also be recalled that many groups are exempted from the council tax. It may be that some of these exemptions are relevant to a non-charitable organization.

It should also be noted that there are certain miscellaneous privileges for all of the types of organization we identified in section 3.3 if they are non-charitable, provided they satisfy certain limited (and often unusual) conditions. For example, an approved housing association can claim exemption from corporation tax only if the rules of the association restrict membership to actual or potential tenants, alongside a number of other conditions.[94] And in the case of registered friendly societies, stamp duty is not chargeable on certain transactions, while they are also entitled to exemption from income and corporation taxes under a number of specific conditions.[95]

3.6 Legal trends and debates

In this concluding section, we begin by describing a small number of areas which have consistently generated high degrees of controversy, not only in recent years but also in the much longer term: the questions of definition; tax privilege; and political activity. It is important to bear in mind in what follows that none of these topics is remotely new as an issue for debate among members of the legal profession, or in the wider political context in which they should be located. Our third topic, the political activities of charities, was the most recent to emerge — in the early 20th century — while the other two comfortably predate recent times. A detailed analysis of the question of the appropriateness of the existing law's approach to defining "public benefit", "need" and "disadvantage" can be found in Francis Moore's 1607 "Reading" on the Elizabethan Statute of Charitable Uses. The second topic, the fiscal regime's treatment of the sector, was the subject of a House of Commons speech by the aspiring Prime Minister William Gladstone in 1863, in which he launched into a strong critique of the "undiscriminating" link between organizational status and fiscal privilege, the inequity of exempting schools for the rich, and the weakness of existing supervisory arrangements for the charity sector in particular (Randon and 6, 1994).

The question of definition

As noted in Chapter 1, the recent legislation on charities, following on the recommendations of the 1989 White Paper, left the case law-based *status quo* completely unchanged in this area. In the longer term, especially as awareness of the scale of tax expenditures on the sector grows, and as long as legal status continues to be the primary means for establishing fiscal privilege (see below), this issue is likely to remain an important topic of legal, and indeed wider, public debate

A number of official inquiries over the past 40 or so years have in fact recommended varying degrees of reform, although their suggestions have tended to be quietly shelved in the face of hostility from the legal establishment. As far back as 1952, the Nathan Committee recommended that a new statutory definition should be enacted (Cmnd 8710, 1952, paras 120-40). Since then, there has been considerable judicial reluctance to endorse this recommendation, most judges sharing the view expressed by Sachs L.J. that "any statutory definition might well merely produce fresh litigation and provide a set of undesirable artificial distinctions".[96] The House of Commons Expenditure Committee took a similar view when it investigated the matter in 1975. It recommended that legislation be introduced whereby all charities should be required to satisfy the test of purposes beneficial to the community; and that those charities which had formerly been admitted to one of the first three of Lord Macnagten's categories (poverty, education and religion) should continue to qualify only if they also satisfy this main criterion. It was asserted, however, that such a change would probably not affect the great majority of charities, and no real attempt was made to formulate a precise or workable definition of what kind of purpose was, or should be, beneficial to the community (House of Commons, 1975, vol. I, paras 31-2, 34, vol. II, pp.48 *et seq*).

Unlike Nathan and the House of Commons Committee, the Goodman Committee, which looked at the question in 1976, came to the conclusion that the formulation of a statutory definition was neither feasible nor desirable. It considered, on the one hand, evidence suggesting that the scope of charities should be restricted to the relief of the poor and of people suffering from deprivation of one sort or another and, on the other hand, evidence that the benefits accorded to charities should be extended to other (presently non-charitable) voluntary bodies (Goodman, 1976). The latter suggestion involved extending the privileges of charity to all non-profit-distributing organizations. Under this formulation, recreational associations, professional bodies, political parties, self-help groups and pressure groups of all kinds would have qualified as charities. The Committee rejected such an extension of the categories of charities. It also rejected the idea that it was possible to formulate a definition of charity. Instead, the Committee recommended that an updated version of the preamble to the 1601 Statute be produced, a reformulation of the categories of charities in simpler and more modern terms, which would preserve the flexibility of the law and the mass of case law decided over past centuries. Like the previous Committees' recommendations, even this much less radical proposal was not taken forward by government.

The reform of tax privileges

The current treatment of charities and other voluntary organizations under tax legislation is under criticism from two directions. The first, and lesser, criticism is that the relevant tax exemptions and privileges could be extended and improved, a position taken (unsurprisingly) by many within the sector itself. For example, charitable bodies could be exempted from the scope of VAT, the income tax treatment of their trading activities could be relaxed considerably, and relevant statutory provisions could be simplified or consolidated. The second, and far more important, criticism is that the conferring of charitable status in itself brings with it an almost automatic enjoyment of tax exemptions and privileges. This of course means that charitable bodies as a group are subsidized by the public simply for meeting the legal requirements we have identified in previous sections. In as much as the legal interpretation of "charity" — which currently in practice usually determines the scope of automatic fiscal benefits — diverges from the popular view of the types of organization that "deserve" tax concessions or have "public benefit" or appropriately "needed" objectives, then difficulties are presented in defending the *status quo*. What is more, in the sense that meeting these requirements is concerned with structures and inputs rather than outputs or outcomes, recipients of this hidden state support are not required to be socially efficient. Both arguments would tend to suggest that these concessions could be "indiscriminate", inefficient and/or unjust.

Most legal debate on this topic has concentrated on the first issue: which objectives and means should be regarded as charitable and, hence, under the current system, gain almost automatic tax relief. The type of institution whose privileges under the present regime are most often contested are the fee-paying "independent" schools with charitable status which benefit from the general reliefs available to charities, while parents also benefit from the specific VAT exemption on fees not accessed by charities in general. Although the founding charters of many of these schools rate the education of the poor as one of their primary objects, it is clearly the case that, in practice, it is predominantly the very wealthy who directly benefit from their provision. This is not a new phenomenon but has been the case in some schools since at least the 16th century. The education provided is largely paid for by charging high fees, and the proportion of pupils who would qualify as "poor" or "disadvantaged" appears to be small, in spite of government support through an "assisted places scheme".[97] As a result, it is often alleged that such schools are not sufficiently "altruistic" to qualify as charities, and those people who place a premium on egalitarian goals are especially likely to baulk at the privileges conferred on these establishments.

A counter-argument is typically made that these schools are in fact operating "for the public benefit" since they generally advance education in the same way as (or better than) any other school. More particularly, the schools promotional body — the Independent Schools Information Service — has sought to legitimate their privilege by referring to their supposed usefulness to their local communities (Davison, 1992). An argument to justify the position is also made that they relieve a part of the burden on the state, that parents have already paid, through their taxes, for their share of the cost of state education (upon which they are then not making any demands); and even that their position can be defended on the grounds of internationally recognized rights to freedom of choice (Lester and Pannick, 1991). What is more, it can be argued that there are immense practical difficulties to reform: how, technically, could the general principles of the law of charities be reformulated so as to exclude these schools from benefit? If profit-*making* (as opposed to profit-distributing) agencies were to be prohibited, many other charitable organizations would also lose their status.

In theory, the issue of fiscal privilege can be treated separately from that of charitable status. As long ago as 1955, the Royal Commission on the Taxation of Profits and Income (the Radcliffe Commission) (Cmnd 9474, ch. 7)[98] discussed the possibility of distinguishing between charitable bodies which should enjoy tax privileges and those which should not, considering that the automatic link that currently exists between fiscal and legal status could be broken. This point was taken by Lord Cross in delivering the judgment of the House of Lords in *Dingle v. Turner*.[99]

It is, of course, unfortunate that the recognition of any trust as a valid charitable trust should automatically attract fiscal privileges, for the question whether a trust to further some purpose is so little likely to benefit the public that it ought to be declared invalid and the question whether it is likely to confer such great benefits on the public that it should enjoy fiscal immunity are really two quite different questions. The logical solution would be to separate them and to say — as the Radcliffe Commission proposed — that only some charities should enjoy fiscal privileges. But, as things are, validity and fiscal immunity march hand in hand.

It can of course also be argued that there are many *non-charitable* voluntary bodies whose purposes and activities are sufficiently beneficial to the public that they too should have the same automatic tax privileges as those currently enjoyed by charities. However, each of these issues — the significance of tax privileges in determining whether charitable status ought to be granted, the denial of tax privileges to certain charities or their extension to certain non-charitable organizations — really raises the same fundamental question of what kind of purpose, or wider aspects of organizational substance or behaviour, should merit special status in law? Whether this is considered to be a question of what should really be considered charitable or, alternatively, a question of what merits preferential tax treatment, it is ultimately a political question to be resolved by the legislature, and not one for the courts or lawyers to determine.

Political activity

Organizations whose purposes are "political" cannot be charitable. Even if they would otherwise fall within the preamble to the 1601 Statute, bodies for which a direct and principal purpose is (a) to further the interests of a particular political party, or (b) to procure changes in the laws of the UK or of a foreign country, or (c) to procure a reversal of government policy or of particular decisions of governmental authorities in the United Kingdom or in a foreign country, cannot be regarded as being for the benefit of the public in the manner which the law regards as charitable.[100] This prohibition has emerged gradually since the end of the 19th century, which explains why some older, essentially "political" voluntary organizations, such as the Howard League for Penal Reform and the Lord's Day Observance Society, are registered charities. This principle poses considerable difficulty for organizations whose purposes are essentially "propagandist" or who see their purposes as best served by campaigning for political changes or by means of political action, such as those concerned with the enforcement of human rights, or changes in the law. It is the case that, if the main objects of the organization are exclusively charitable, the mere fact that it may have incidental powers to employ political means for their furtherance will not deprive them of their charitable status. However, the dividing line between what is objectionable and what is not in practice has often appeared blurred.

Despite the Commission's clarificatory guidelines developed during the 1980s, it has often appeared difficult for some charities to steer a course between what is permissible and what is not. Frequent complaints are received by the Attorney-General about the use of students' unions' funds for purposes which go beyond those permitted for such funds (which is to represent and foster the interests of the students at an educational establishment in such a way as to further the educational purposes of the establishment itself). Students frequently assume that, by majority or even unanimous vote, a union's constitution may be amended so as to authorize the application of union funds towards political objectives (such as political campaigns or causes, or industrial disputes).[101] In 1978, the activities of three charities involved with international relief (War on Want, Oxfam and Christian Aid) were considered worthy of investigation by the Commissioners; and so, too, were the activities of three domestic charities in 1979 (Abortion, the RSPCA and the Howard League for Penal

Reform) (see Charity Commissioners, 1978, paras 21-29; 1979, paras 18-22).

As with the issue of tax treatment, while some observers feel that current arrangements are too generous, others take the view that they are not generous enough, and add that the system produces "inconsistent and arbitrary results" (see Randon and 6, 1994, p.23, and references therein). Most recently, the tenor of the 1991 report into Oxfam's activities, which was critical of the charity, and publicly threatened trustees with sanctions in the event of recurrence of "political abuse", raised further concerns about the restrictiveness of the Charity Commission (Burnell, 1992). Those who believe that poverty, particularly in the Third World, can be eradicated only by tackling its social and economic roots rather than by traditional reactive methods, have portrayed the existing constraints as an unnecessary brake on social progress.

New guidelines published by the Commission in 1994 have been interpreted as offering some improvement on some of the ambiguities and uncertainties following from the Oxfam enquiry. For example, they have been welcomed by the National Council for Voluntary Organisations as "much clearer and more consistent...with a much more positive tone" (Morrison, 1994). Yet in an international context, the regime still appears rather illiberal. A recent 24-country comparison between charities in charity law countries and "non-profit organizations" in countries with civil law and mixed legal systems found that only the former were characterized by the existence of any constraints whatsoever on their campaigning role, and this could not be explained by "clear, comprehensive jurisprudential rationales" (Randon and 6, 1994, pp.51). Moreover, even within the charity law countries, arrangements in England and Wales compare unfavourably with North America in the sense of allowing far more discretion to the monitoring agency. (In the US and Canada, straightforward limits on expenditure, enforced by the tax authorities, apply.) We should add that voluntary bodies, of course, always have the option of not applying for charitable status, and hence avoiding any constraints whatsoever, or of establishing a separate, non-charitable campaigning structure. Such dual structures characterize the non-charitable Liberty and its charitable subsidiary Cobden Trust, and Amnesty International and its Prisoners of Conscience Fund, for example. However, there are practical disadvantages, including the need to keep separate accounts, payrolls and other records.

Future issues

The issues we have identified have been controversial for many years (and even centuries in the case of the question of definition). We conclude by simply identifying two areas whose salience has become obvious much more recently, and as a result have been subjected to little legal analysis to date. Neither issue was addressed in the recent package of legislation. First, the potential tensions between European law, including competition law and provisions for a new European statute for associations, and charity law, have only just begun to be debated by lawyers, although the area has already been analysed by one eclectic researcher not afraid to grapple with legal problems (6, 1993). Second, an issue likely to receive increased attention in the near future is that of the adequacy or otherwise of the existing range of legal structures available to voluntary organizations. As we noted at the start of this chapter, the structures currently available for charities and other voluntary bodies have emerged for historical reasons. It has been argued that there is so much complexity and ambiguity in existing law in this area that the time has come for a new "charitable corporation" structure to be made available (Warburton, 1990). Although the possibility of a new structure was mooted in the 1989 White Paper, the government implicitly dropped this option by not pursuing it in the 1992 or 1993 Acts. There is a pressing need for legal studies to attend to these and a number of other areas in the coming years (Warburton, 1993).[102]

Notes

Note on citations

Most references in the following notes are to law reports and statutes. "Official" law reports are published by the Incorporated Council of Law Reporting. These include reports of decisions in the House of Lords and Privy Council, and in the three Divisions of the High Court, namely the Queen's Bench Division (or the King's Bench Division), the Chancery Division and the Family Division, and also appeals from each Division to the Court of Appeal. These reports are referred to respectively as "A.C." (House of Lords and Privy Council), "Q.B." (or "K.B.") (Queen's Bench or King's Bench Division, as the case may be, and appeals therefrom to the Court of Appeal); "Ch." (Chancery Division and similar appeals) and "Fam." (Family Division and similar appeals). In addition, there are two series of law reports, published weekly, one by the I.C.L.R., namely the Weekly Law Reports ("W.L.R.") and the other privately, namely the All England Law Reports ("All E.R.").

Until 1890, each volume in the various series had its own individual number (which ran consecutively from year to year). In these cases, it is the volume number rather than the date (which is placed in round brackets), which is important in locating the correct report. Since 1891, individual numbering of volumes has been discontinued, except when more than one volume is published in any particular year. In these cases, the date (which is placed in square brackets) is an essential guide to location. Thus, in note 2, A.-G. *[Attorney-General] v. Ellis* are the names of the parties involved in the case; [1895] is the year in which the case was reported; 2 Q.B. refers to the second volume of reports of cases in the Queen's Bench Division reported in that year; and 466 is the page number at which the report commences.

Earlier law reports (i.e. mostly pre-1865) are reported in different series bearing the name(s) of the compiler(s) of the reports (and are referred to accordingly as "Nominate Reports"). Thus, in note 7, the reference to "(1804) 9 Ves. 399" refers to the ninth volume in a series of reports of cases (between 1789 and 1817) in the then Court of Chancery compiled by Vesey Junior; and in note 18, the reference to "5 Beav." is to the fifth volume in a series of reports of decisions in the then Rolls Court Reports between 1838 and 1866 compiled by Beavan.

Law reports (sometimes condensed) are and have been published elsewhere, e.g. Tax Cases ("T.C."); Times Law Reports ("T.L.R."); Scots Law Times ("S.L.T."); and Value Added Tax Tribunal Reports ("V.A.T.T.R.").

Official copies of statutes (the Public General Acts) are published by HM Stationery Office (although the I.C.L.R. and some private law publishers also publish them). They are commonly referred to by their short title and the year of publication, e.g. the Charities Act 1993. A statute may also be cited by reference to the year in which it was passed and the individual number (the chapter number) given to it. Before 1963, a statute was referred to by the year of the monarch's reign and its own chapter number, e.g. in note 7, "43 Eliz. I, c. 4" refers to the fourth Act passed in the 43rd year of Elizabeth I's reign. The provisions of a particular statute will be set out in section, sub-sections, paragraphs and schedules, e.g. note 37 refers to section 7, sub-section (1), paragraph (a) of, and Schedule 1 to, the Friendly Societies Act 1992. Delegated legislation, in the form of regulations, rules, orders, by-laws, etc. are made by means of Statutory Instruments ("S.I.").

1 See generally (1994) 144 New L.J. (Christmas Appeals Supplement) 22 (J. Hill).

2 *A.-G. v. Ellis* [1895] 2 Q.B. 466.

3 *Savoy v. Art Union* [1896] A.C. 296, at p.305.

4 The requirement as to the control of the High Court is satisfied if the institution is subject to that jurisdiction in any significant respect. It is sufficient, for example, if the court can restrain the institution from applying its property in breach of trust or ultra vires: see *Construction Industry Training Board v. A.-G.* [1971] 3 All E.R. 449; affd. [1973] Ch. 173. See also sections 13(4), 15(1)-(3), 33(8).

5 Section 97(1).

6 The Recreational Charities Act 1958 is an exception, being the only statute to supplement the case law and to create a new (and limited) category of charitable purposes.

7 43 Eliz. I, c. 4. See *Morice v. Bishop of Durham* (1804) 9 Ves. 399, affd. (1805) 10 Ves. 522; *Scottish Burial Reform and Cremation Society Ltd v. Glasgow City Corporation* [1968] A.C. 138; *Ashfield Municipal Council v. Joyce* [1978] A.C. 122. The 1601 Act was repealed by the Mortmain and Charitable Uses Act 1888, although the preamble was partly preserved by section 13(2). The 1888 Act itself was repealed by the Charities Act 1960, section 38(4) of which provided, somewhat tortuously, that "any reference in any enactment or document to a charity within the meaning, purview and interpretation of the Charitable Uses Act 1601, or of the preamble to it, shall be construed as a reference to a charity within the meaning which the word bears as a legal term according to the law of England and Wales".

8 See, for example, *Commissioners for Special Purposes of Income Tax v. Pemsel* [1891] A.C. 531, at p.581, *per* Lord Macnaghten.

9 *Scottish Burial Reform and Cremation Society Ltd v. Glasgow City Corporation* [1968] A.C. 138, at p.147, *per* Lord Reid.

10 *Scottish Burial Reform and Cremation Society Ltd v. Glasgow City Corporation* [1968] A.C. 138, at p.154, *per* Lord Wilberforce; also at p.221, *per* Lord Upjohn.

11 *Commissioners for Special Purposes of Income Tax v. Pemsel* [1891] A.C. 531, at p.583. This classification was based, in fact, on Sir Samuel Romilly's argument in *Morice v. Bishop of Durham* (1805) 10 Ves. 522, at p.523.

12 *Scottish Burial Reform and Cremation Society Ltd v. Glasgow City Corporation* [1968] A.C. 138, at p.154, *per* Lord Wilberforce.

13 *Morice v. Bishop of Durham* (1805) 10 Ves. Jr. 522; *I.R.C. v. Baddeley* [1955] A.C. 572; *Ellis v. I.R.C.* (1949) 31 T.C. 178. Severance of the good from the bad is possible in rare and restricted circumstances, i.e. where the peculiar construction of the particular gift permits it (e.g. in *Salisbury v. Denton* (1857) 3 K. & J. 529), or under the Charitable Trusts (Validation) Act 1954 (which applies only to trust instruments coming into operation before 16 December 1952).

14 [1951] Ch. 661, at p.666. In *I.R.C. v. Baddeley*, Lord Simonds declared: "There may be a good charity for the relief of persons who are not in grinding need or utter destitution...[but] relief connotes need of some sort, either need for a home, or for the means to provide for some necessity or quasi-necessity, and not merely an amusement, however healthy."

15 *Re De Carteret* [1933] Ch. 103 is unusual in that an absolute concept of poverty may have been adopted.

16 *Shaw v. Halifax Corporation* [1915] 2 K.B. 170.

17 *Re Young* [1951] Ch. 344.

18 *Nash v. Morley* (1842) 5 Beav. 177.

19 *Incorporated Council of Law Reporting for England and Wales v. A.-G.* [1972] Ch. 73, at p.102, *per* Buckley L.J. In *Re Lopes* [1931] 2 Ch. 130, at p.136, Farwell J. suggested that "a ride on an elephant may be educational".

20 *Whicker v. Hume* (1858) 7 H.L.C. 124.

21 *Re Girls' Public Day School Trust* [1951] Ch. 400; *Abbey Malvern Wells Ltd v. Ministry of Local Government and Planning* [1951] Ch. 728.

22 For example, see *Re Delmar* [1897] 2 Ch. 163, and *Re Charlesworth* (1910) 26 T.L.R. 214.

23 *Neville Estates Ltd v. Madden* [1962] Ch. 832, at p.853, *per* Cross J.

24 *Re Thackrah* [1939] 2 All E.R. 4; *Oxford Group v. I.R.C* [1949] 2 All E.R. 537; *Re Macaulay's Estate* [1943] Ch. 435n; *Re South Place Ethical Society* [1980] 1 W.L.R. 1565; *R. v. Registrar General, ex p.*

Segerdal [1970] 2 Q.B. 697; *Re Porter* [1925] Ch. 746.

25 *Williams' Trustees v. I.R.C.* [1947] A.C. 47; *Re Macduff* (1896) 2 Ch. 451, at p.466; *A.G. v. National Provincial Bank* [1924] A.C. 262, at p.265; *Scottish Burial Reform and Cremation Society v. Glasgow Corporation* [1968] A.C. 138.

26 *Crystal Palace Trustees v. Ministry of Town and Country Planning* [1951] Ch. 132; *Yorkshire Agricultural Society v. I.R.C.* [1928] 1 K.B. 611; *Brisbane City Council v. A.G. for Queensland* [1978] 3 All E.R. 30; *Re Pleasants* (1923) 39 T.L.R. 675.

27 *Gilmour v. Coats* [1949] A.C. 426, at p.429, *per* Lord Simonds; *I.R.C. v. Baddeley* [1965] A.C. 572, at p.615, *per* Lord Somervell.

28 *Re Scarisbrick* [1951] Ch. 622; *Re Cohen* [1973] 1 W.L.R. 415; *Dingle v. Turner* [1972] A.C. 601.

29 *Re Compton* [1945] Ch. 123; *Oppenheim v. Tobacco Securities Trust Ltd* [1951] A.C. 297; *I.R.C. v. Educational Grants Association Ltd* [1967] Ch. 123; cf. *Re Koettgen's Will Trusts* [1954] Ch. 252. The status of this test is in doubt in view of the *obiter dicta* in *Dingle v. Turner* [1972] A.C. 601. *Re Clark* (1875) 1 Ch. D. 497; *General Medical Council v. I.R.C.* (1928) 97 L.J.K.B. 578; *Geologists' Association v. I.R.C.* [1928] 14 T.C. 271; *R. v. Special Commissions of Income Tax Ex Parte Headmasters' Conference* (1925) 41 T.L.R. 651; *Dingle v. Turner* [1972] A.C. 601 at p.625, *per* Lord Cross.

30 *Williams v. I.R.C.* [1947] A.C. 447; *I.R.C. v. Baddeley* [1955] A.C. 572.

31 *Re Drummond* [1914] 2 Ch. 90; *Re Hobourn* [1946] Ch. 86; *Re Mead's Trust Deed* [1961] 1 W.L.R. 1244.

32 *German v. Chapman* (1877) 7 Ch. D. 271; *Hall & Derby Sanitary Authority* (1855) 16 Q.B.D. 163; *Re Mellody* [1918] 1 Ch. 228.

33 See generally Charity Commissioners' *Decisions*, vol. 2, 1994, pp.14-23.

34 See generally (1994) 144 New L.J. (Christmas Appeals Supplement) 22 (J. Hill).

35 Approved by Romer L.J. in *Green v. Russell* [1959] 2 Q.B. 226, at p.241.

36 *Conservative and Unionist Central Office v. Burrell* [1982] 1 W.L.R. 522, at p.525, *per* Lawton, L.J.

37 Section 7(1)(a) and Schedule 1, and section 116 of the Friendly Societies Act 1992.

38 Section 1(1), (2).

39 Section 1(3).

40 Section 1(1) of the Housing Associations Act 1985. A development corporation is deemed to be a housing association, as is the Commission for the New Towns and the Church of England

Pensions Board. This definition applies generally, subject to modification in particular cases.

41 Section 1(3) of the Housing Associations Act 1985. Section 2 of the Housing Associations Act 1985.

42 See Barker et al. (1994). The impact of the new regulatory framework on Scottish charities, S.L.T. (News) 331. See also s. 80 of the Charities Act 1993.

43 Section 3(1) and (2) of the Charities Act 1993.

44 S.I. 1960 No. 2366 (Voluntary Schools); S.I. No. 2074; S.I. 1964 No. 1825 (Religious Charities); S.I. 1961 No. 1044 (Boy Scouts and Girl Guides); S.I. 1965 No. 1056 (Armed Forces); S.I. 1966 No. 965 (Non-exempt universities).

45 Section 3(5) of the 1993 Act. See also section 96(4).

46 Section 3(6) (7), (8) and (9) of the 1993 Act.

47 Section 3(4) of the 1993 Act.

48 Para. 1 of the Schedule 1 to the 1993 Act.

49 Section 1(3), (4).

50 Section 16(1).

51 Section 16(10).

52 Sections 4(3), 16(11), (12).

53 Section 8.

54 Section 18.

55 Section 18(5)

56 Sections 41 and 42.

57 Sections 45 and 47 of the 1993 Act. There are special provisions in section 46 in respect of the accounts and annual reports of exempt and other excepted charities.

58 *Wallis v. S.-G. for New Zealand* [1903] A.C. 173; *Re Royal Society's Charitable Trusts* [1956] Ch. 87; *National Anti-Vivisection Society v. I.R.C.* [1948] A.C. 31, at p.62; *Re Harpur's Will Trusts* [1962] Ch. 78, at p.94; *A.-G. v. Ross* [1986] 1 W.L.R. 252.

59 Sections 76-78.

60 *Patel v. Bradford University Senate* [1978] 1 W.L.R. 1488, at p.1500; *Herring v. Templeman* [1973] 3 All E.R. 569.

61 Section 1(4) and (5) of the 1992 Act.

62 Section 3 of the 1985 Act.

63 Section 9 of the 1985 Act.

64 Section 13-15 of the 1985 Act.

65 Section 19 of the 1985 Act.

66 Sections 16-18 of the 1985 Act.

67 Sections 28-30 of the 1985 Act.

68 I.C.T.A. 1988, s. 505(1)(e); Picarda (1995, pp.693-714). See also changes proposed in Clause 137 of the Finance Bill 1996.

69 *Religious Tract and Book Society of Scotland v. Forbes* (1896) 3 T.C. 415.

70 Local Government Finance Act 1988, s. 43 (5), (6).

71 Local Government Finance Act, 1988, s. 47.

72 Value Added Tax Act 1994, ss. 30, 31, Schedule 8, Group 15 (Charities), Schedule 9, Group 6 (Education), Group 7 (Health and Welfare), Group 8 (Burial and Cremation), Group 10 (Sport, etc.), Group 11 (Works of Art, etc.), Group 12 (Fund Raising Events by Charities, etc.); *Customs and Excise Commissioners v. Automobile Association* [1974] 1 W.L.R. 1447. See also Picarda (1995, pp.722-39); and (1995/96) *Charity Law and Practice Review*, vol. 3, issue 1 (Warburton).

73 Customs and Excise Leaflet No. 701/1.

74 Inheritance Tax Act, 1984, ss. 64, 65, 66.

75 I.C.T.A., 1988, s. 167(5)(b).

76 Finance Act, 1982, s. 129.

77 Lotteries and Amusements Act, 1976, ss. 3-5.

78 I.C.T.A., 1988, ss. 660(3); 683; F.A., 1989, ss. 56, 59. See also [1986] B.T.R. 101 (D. Stopforth); [1989] Conv. 321 (D. Morris); and I.R. Press Release and Statement of Practice, S.P. 4/90 (*Charitable Covenants*).

79 I.C.T.A., 1988, ss. 339, 505.

80 Finance Act 1990, s. 25; Finance Act 1993, s. 67(2).

81 Taxation of Chargeable Gains Act 1992, s. 257.

82 Under s. 256 of the 1992 Act.

83 I.C.T.A., 1988, s. 202; Finance Act 1993, s. 68; and S.I. 1986, No, 2211 (*Charitable Deductions [Approved Schemes] Regulations*). Clause 100 of the Finance Bill 1996 proposes to increase the limit to £1,200.

84 I.C.T.A., 1988, s. 86.

85 Inheritance Tax Act, 1984, s. 23.

86 The 1988 Act, s. 832(1); the 1992 Act, s. 288(1).

87 *Carlisle and Silloth Golf Club v. Smith* [1913] 3 K.B. 75; *Worthing Rugby Football Club Trustees v. I.R.C.* [1985] 1 W.L.R. 409.

88 *Carlisle and Silloth Golf Club v. Smith* [1913] 3 K.B. 75.

89 *I.R.C. v. Eccentric Club Ltd* [1924] 1 K.B. 390.

90 *Carlisle and Silloth Golf Club, supra; NALGO v. Watkins* (1934) 18 T.C. 499.

91 *Customs and Excise Commissioners v. Apple and Pear Development Council* [1985] S.T.C. 383; *British Olympic Association v. Customs and Excise Commissioners* [1979] V.A.T.T.R. 122; *Carlton Lodge Club v. Customs and Excise Commissioners* [1975] 1 W.L.R. 66.

92 Income and Corporation Taxes Act, 1988, s. 201.

93 Local Government Finance Act, 1988, s. 47(2).

94 Section 488, Income and Corporation Taxes Act, 1988.

95 Section 105(a) and (b) of the Friendly Societies Act, 1974, and sections 460-466 of the Income and Corporation Taxes Act, 1988.

96 *Incorporated Council of Law Reporting for England and Wales v. A.G.* [1972] Ch. 73, at pp.94-95.

97 See Chapter 6 below; only around one-fifth of all independent school pupils were funded under this scheme in 1990.

98 See also (1956) 72 L.Q.R. 187 (G. Cross) and (1977) 40 M.L.R. 397 (N. Gravells).

99 [1972] A.C. 601 at p.624.

100 *McGovern v. A.-G.* [1982] Ch. 321.

101 *Baldry v. Feintuck* [1972] 1 W.L.R. 552; *A.-G. v. Ross* [1986] 1 W.L.R. 252; the Charity Commissioners' *Annual Report* for 1983, Appendix A.

102 See also (1994) 144 New L.J. (Christmas Appeals Supplement) 22 (J. Hill). A joint project (between the NCVO, the Charity Law Association and the Charity Law Unit at the University of Liverpool) is currently engaged in comparative research on legal structures used by non-profit organizations in Australia, New Zealand, France and Germany, and on a new legal structure for UK charities.

Chapter 4

MAPPING THE VOLUNTARY SECTOR

4.1 Introduction

The statistical mapping of voluntary organizations lay at the heart of the research described in this book. It was essential to describe the basic contours of the sector — its financial and human resources in the various fields of activity — to provide the baseline for systematic analysis. As described in Chapter 1, the need to generate estimates capable of cross-national comparison led us to adopt a broader definition of the sector than is perhaps commonly (implicitly) used, but we also developed a narrower definition tailored to the UK context. The research challenge of embracing this full universe of organizations was considerable.

In section 4.2 we identify the mapping options available to us, and our chosen methodology. The rest of this chapter then focuses on the statistical findings of the study in terms of the overall scale of the sector and its components, employment and expenditures, sources of revenue and market shares. The data that underpin the various figures and charts are reported in Appendix 1. (The Appendices also report some of the more technical aspects of the methodology, including details of sampling frames, data sources and response rates.) Box 4.1 summarizes the definitions of the principal measures on which data were collected.

Box 4.1   Definitions used in the statistical mapping

The voluntary sector as a whole and its component parts were described along each of the following dimensions:

- *Full-time equivalent paid employment.* Paid employment in the voluntary sector includes many part-time, as well as full-time staff. Part-time jobs were weighted by the number of hours worked, assuming 37.5 hours per week to be equivalent to one full-time position.

- *Total operating expenditures.* The costs of an organization's general operations, including wages and other employment costs, purchases of goods (other than capital equipment), materials and services, and fees and charges paid. Some data on capital expenditures were collected but are not reported here. Note that operating expenditure is considerably broader than "final expenditure" as used for national accounts purposes to estimate value added by the sector's operations to the UK economy: the latter deducts fees and sales from total operating expenditure to avoid double-counting with consumers' and government commercial or contractual expenditures (Kendall and Knapp, 1990; Osborne and Waterston, 1994).

- *Total operating income.* Private earned income, income from government, and private donations (see text for further discussion). Not included here are sales of fixed assets and investments, or value of loans taken out (although these data were also collected).

4.2 The methodological approach

Two options for constructing our statistical map had *prima facie* appeal, but could not meet our needs. We begin this section by describing why they were inadequate, and then summarize the multi-faceted strategy that we did use.

The Charity Commission register

Previous attempts to generate global estimates of the size of the UK voluntary sector have concentrated on registered charities alone, or registered charities less some substantive omissions. One stream of relevant work was conducted by John Posnett for the Charities Aid Foundation (CAF) at five-yearly intervals since 1975 (Posnett, 1993). Another stream started at Cambridge University (primarily for 1970) and continued at Aston Business School (for 1990 and 1991) was conducted on behalf of the government's Central Statistical Office (CSO) for the purposes of national accounts (Moyle and Reid, 1975; Hems and Osborne, 1995). The Aston work has now fed into the Blue Book published annually by the Government Statistical Service, although the accounts for the sector are not separately shown but are subsumed under other aggregates. (See Kendall and Knapp, 1990, for a discussion of the application of national accounting conventions to the voluntary sector.) Posnett's surveys focused on the income and expenditure of registered charities in England and Wales, while the more recent Aston surveys also attempted to cover equivalent bodies in Scotland and Northern Ireland. In limiting their organizational scope to registered charities, both streams of work could use a single, well-defined sampling frame for England and Wales in the form of the register maintained by the Charity Commissioners since the Charities Act of 1960 (see Chapter 3). Although the state of repair of the register came in for criticism in the late 1980s (Woodfield et al., 1987), it has at least provided a single consolidated resource for researchers.

As we described in Chapter 1, however, registered charities comprise only a part of the broad voluntary sector. A comprehensive mapping needed to include not only charitable bodies not required to register (including exempted and excepted charities), but also agencies which meet the core criteria of the structural operational definition but which do not have charitable status.

Despite its partial coverage, we examined whether the register could be used as a "core" around which to build the wider estimate we required. However, without detailed data on the relative characteristics of the registered charity sector and the broad voluntary sector, it was impossible to exploit the register's uniqueness as a centralized resource. Today the relationship between charities and the broader sector is clearer as a result of *ex post* comparisons we can make between our comprehensive estimates and the narrower CAF and CSO surveys (Kendall, 1995).

An employment survey-led approach?

Despite its availability and familiarity, the register of charities was thus inappropriate because of its incomplete coverage. An alternative strategy — suggested by the international core research team in Baltimore, and inspired by the pioneering work of Independent Sector in the US (Hodgkinson et al., 1992; Hodgkinson and Weitzman, 1993) — was to use existing employment surveys as the basic building blocks for the wider estimates (Salamon and Anheier, 1996a). Most governments undertake regular censuses of workplace employment in different industries. If the collection of data distinguished between ownership sectors, it could provide the necessary basis for the mapping of the voluntary sector. The employment data could be combined with data on average wages in each industry to yield an estimate of the voluntary sector wage bill. The next stage would be to multiply these wage bill estimates by appropriate ratios to estimate total expenditure, and then to get an approximation of operating expenditures by deducting estimates of capital expenditure. Voluntary sector-specific figures for average wages, the ratios of wages to operating expenditures and capital expenditure would improve accuracy of the approach. The revenue side of the sector's account could be dealt with by small-scale surveys to establish the relationships between operating expenditure, total operating income and sources of income in each industry or field.

Variants of this strategy proved feasible in three of the seven countries on which full statistical data were collected in the international project. In France, the *Système de reportoire des enterprises et des établissements* (the SYRENE file) could be accessed to identify employees in the sector, and combined with wage data from the *déclarations annuelles de données sociales* (social security statistics). In Germany, the *Arbeitsstättenzählung* (Census of Workplaces) provided both paid employment and wages data. And in the US, the project's estimates leaned heavily on the model research already undertaken by Independent Sector (Hodgkinson et al., 1992).

In contrast, sector-specific data from employment and labour force surveys were not available in Hungary, Italy, Japan and the UK. The UK census only asks employers to identify their industry in terms of the Standard Industrial Classification (SIC), and does not ask for information on sector.[1] The only "sectoral" industry statistics published by the CSO compare the "private" and "public" sectors: they combine the triennial Census of Employment undertaken by the Employment Department (now consolidated within the Department of Education and Employment) with information provided to the Central Statistical Office directly by central government, nationalized industries and other public corporations, and separate survey data for local authorities (Fleming, 1988). An attempt had been made in the early 1980s to estimate voluntary sector employment using the Census, but it produced at best an indicative guestimate (Ashworth, 1984), because basic information on sectoral market shares in each industry were not available or fully utilized. We were able to make little use of the Census of Employment for our own mapping.[2]

The GUSTO approach

With the Charity Commission register and employment survey-based options ruled out, the only way to develop comprehensive estimates was to pursue a "modular approach". We could not rely on a single central survey in the absence of a sampling frame, even when supplemented by a small number of other gap-filling surveys. The modular approach instead involved the painstaking construction of separate estimates for ICNPO categories and sub-categories. The precise strategy varied according to the field of activity: for some it was possible to build an almost complete picture using existing data; in others, new surveys were needed. In many cases the most basic information was missing, so that a lot of researcher time was expended simply constructing the sampling frame.

With only the merest hint of irony, we termed our strategy the "GUSTO approach" to reflect the sequence employed in constructing our estimates. First, we obtained as much information as possible from **G**overnment statistics, and voluntary sector **U**mbrella body tabulations (including work commissioned or undertaken by CAF, NCVO and other intermediary agencies). **S**econdary analyses of these data were often needed to get them into the form required. **T**erritorial surveys were undertaken in a number of locales, either to cross-validate existing "top-down" sources, or to inform the assumptions necessary to move from the partial picture painted from extant data to the full canvass of statistics required. Our most comprehensive local survey was in Liverpool (Shore et al., 1994); others were undertaken in Kent, North London and Staffordshire (see Appendix 1, Table A.3, p.275). We were also fortunate to gain access to the local data gathered from across the UK during the CENTRIS study (Knight, 1993). The evidence from the territorial surveys suggests that, although our top-down strategy inevitably omitted some types of organization, these were probably small in terms of financial resources and paid employment.[3] Finally, in some ICNPO categories there was so little prior information that we had to conduct Original organizational surveys, sampling as necessary. Appendix 1 summarizes the key components of the "top-down" element of the strategy adopted in each ICNPO category. If available, locality data were also used to cross-validate the top-down statistical picture, and to fill gaps.[4]

A few difficulties encountered in using the ICNPO schema, however, had major implications for the relative size of different fields, and it is important to emphasize the conventions we developed to resolve these ambiguities. First, as mentioned in Chapter 1, advocacy and campaigning are key activities of many voluntary organizations. Many groups are also oriented towards the black community and other ethnic minority groups. Although advocacy and services for ethnic minority groups are identified separately within the ICNPO (subgroup 7 100), where possible we allocated organizations to other fields. For example, social services for particular ethnic groups are included in group 4, and campaigning or advocacy environmental bodies in group 5. Our statistics thus tend to understate the resources allocated to subgroup 7 100.

Second, to make our task manageable, and for similar reasons, we were also forced to treat community, economic and social development (ICNPO subgroup 6 100) in a "residual" fashion. Many voluntary organizations have a "developmental" orientation, but we reserved subgroup 6 100 for multi-purpose organizations which were operating across a number of ICNPO categories and could not be classified easily as any single one — without engaging in the almost impossible task of getting individual organizations to disaggregate their employment, expenditure and income by ICNPO subgroup.

Third, in group 8 (philanthropic intermediaries) we included all groups whose primary activity was the allocation of grants to other organizations, rather than the in-house delivery of services. Alongside endowed grant-making trusts, we therefore covered here federated fundraising organizations (such as Telethon and Children in Need) and — significantly in the UK — most medical research charities. There are a few important exceptions, but the latter typically raise money from the general public and make grants in support of research undertaken in both the broad voluntary and public sectors. These medical research charities could have been located in groups 2 or 3, but since most of their funds are channelled to organizations already in these categories (or to statutory bodies), we grouped them with other grant-making bodies so that potential double-counting of income could be identified. Group 8 also includes generalist (sector-wide) national and local intermediaries (local development agencies) as bodies involved in "voluntarism promotion": for example, NCVO and CAF, and Councils for Voluntary Service and Rural Community Councils were classified here (see Appendix 1); intermediaries for specific fields were located in their appropriate (other) ICNPO categories.[5]

The final convention to note is the exclusion of certain groups attached to specific public sector bodies, such as parent teacher associations, leagues of hospital friends and trust funds operating in support of NHS facilities (which were often actually established when these facilities were in the voluntary sector, prior to the establishment of the NHS). Although constitutionally independent and often with charitable status, these primarily fund particular public sector facilities or establishments, and were therefore regarded as part of that sector, rather than the voluntary sector.[6] (However, as noted above, we *did* include in our estimates for ICNPO group 8 general medical research charities and federated fundraising campaigns, some of whose funds may ultimately be applied in support of activities under public sector auspices.)

4.3 Overall scale

In principle, the overall size of the UK voluntary sector can be measured in terms of numbers of organizations or establishments, expenditure, income, paid employment, volunteers deployed, or through activity or output indicators. To date, no one has devised a sensible outcome measure for application across the sector as a whole, but a number of "market share" indicators are available in particular fields, as we illustrate later in this chapter, and in Chapters 6 and 7.

It was not possible to construct fully reliable estimates for the number of voluntary organizations corresponding to either our broad or narrow definitions of the sector using the GUSTO strategy. However, it is possible to suggest a "guestimate" by combining other statistics, as reported in Box 4.2. These figures are based on the Aston/CSO research on registered charities (Hems and Osborne, 1995) and information on non-charitable voluntary organizations from our own and the CENTRIS territorial surveys (Knight, 1993). Box 4.2 is broader in coverage than the figures reported in subsequent tables and charts, largely because it includes sacramental religious bodies and groups and funds linked to public sector bodies which we have noted were excluded in our GUSTO mapping. Although the figures in the box can only be tentative estimates, they are an improvement on Gerard's estimate of "350,000 or more organizations" (1983, p.17), and the figures reported by 6 and Fieldgrass (1992), which were themselves partly based on our own preliminary work.[7]

Figures for volunteering described in section 4.4 are far more reliable, being based on a large-scale purposive sampling of households in 1991 (Lynn and Davis Smith, 1991). We were unable to collect reliable information on volunteering from voluntary organizations themselves, a problem we also had with the in-kind contributions to the sector made by government, companies and others. With the exception of the data on volunteering and some data on individual monetary donations, the statistics reported in the remainder of this chapter are based entirely on our GUSTO mapping strategy, and confined purely to the activities of voluntary sector organizations.

Table 4.1 gives full-time equivalent employment (fte) and operating expenditures for the broad and narrow voluntary

Box 4.2 The estimated number of voluntary organizations in 1990

A. Number of active registered charities and
    equivalents excluding schools, universities etc.,
    housing associations, places of worship   97,478

B. Active voluntary aided etc. schools (some registered
    and some excepted charities)   5,174

C. Active registered charity independent schools   1,540

D. Active housing associations registered with housing
    quangos (some charitable, registered or
    exempted, others not charitable)   2,595

E. Exempted, excepted and unregistered charitable
    bodies other than those noted above (includes
    universities, places of worship)   90,000

F. Amateur sports clubs (generally not charitable)   150,000

G. Licensed non-profit social clubs not included above
    (generally not charitable)   17,902

H. Trade unions, professional, trade and business
    associations (generally not charitable)   3,633

I. All other non-charitable voluntary organizations,
    including tenants' and residents' associations,
    business support agencies, community businesses
    and miscellaneous other voluntary groups across
    all other ICNPO categories   10,000-50,000

Total implied for broad voluntary sector *plus* trust
    funds and groups linked to specific public bodies
    plus sacramental religious bodies   378,000-418,000

Total implied for narrow voluntary sector *plus* trust
    funds and groups linked to specific public bodies
    plus sacramental religious bodies   200,000-240,000

Sources: Active registered charity total less exclusions shown as A from Hems and Osborne (1995); B to H based on top-down data collected incidentally during GUSTO mapping, some of which were reported originally in 6 and Fieldgrass (1992), subsequently revised. The range shown for I is indicative, based on information from territorial surveys and CENTRIS analysis. This range may be a significant underestimate.

sectors, and summarizes operating income and its three major components. Comparisons between the columns reveal the impact of our exclusions on the overall size of the sector.

In thinking about its workforce and finance, it would be

Table 4.1

The UK voluntary sector, 1990

	Broad voluntary sector[a]	Narrow voluntary sector[b]
Fte paid employment — total	946,000	390,000
— as % of whole economy	4.0	1.7
Total operating expenditure (£ billion)	26.4	10.0
Total operating income (£ billion)	29.5	12.3
Sources of income:		
Government (£ billion)	11.6	4.3
Earned income (£ billion)	14.2	5.2
Private giving (£ billion)	3.6	2.9

a Broad voluntary sector: definition used for international comparative purposes.
b Narrow voluntary sector: broad voluntary sector less ICNPO groups 1 200, 2 100, 2 200 and 11 100.

tempting to equate the voluntary sector with the mobilization of unpaid volunteers and the receipt of private donations. Yet while it is indeed the case most voluntary organizations have no paid staff, the sector is still clearly a significant employer of paid labour overall. On the income side, the lion's shares of total revenue come from private earned income and from government. In both respects — paid employment and income sources — the UK voluntary sector is not greatly different from the equivalent sectors in other countries in the international project. The seven-country average for fte paid employment in the sector as a percentage of the whole economy is 3.4, compared to 4.0 for the UK. And like the UK, four countries — Hungary, Italy, Japan and the US — had commercial earnings as the largest single source of income. The sectors in Germany and France were dominated by public funding (Salamon and Anheier, 1996a).

Paid employment in the broad voluntary sector (BVS) represented nearly one-tenth of all jobs in the UK service sector — a useful comparator because this is where much voluntary sector activity is concentrated.[8] The narrow voluntary sector provided nearly 400,000 full-time equivalent jobs, 1.7 percent of the figure for the whole economy. On a headcount basis, the voluntary sector would probably account for a higher percentage of the workforce because there are so many part-time workers.

The sector's financial base is summarized by Figure 4.1. Under the broad definition, the operating income sources divide into roughly one-eighth donations, three-eighths government and four-eighths commercial earnings. The effect of narrowing the definition is almost to double the relative share of private giving because of the exclusion of fields of activity which are heavily reliant on earned income or government funding. To some observers this would represent an appropriate homing in on the true "core" of the voluntary sector (for example, see Ware, 1989c), and would bring us closer to the sector as defined under the current interpretation of international national accounting conventions (Kendall and Knapp, 1992; Anheier et al., 1993). But it is significant — even after narrowing the definition — that private giving is still outweighed by both government support and earned income, and that the ranking of sources — with earned income most significant, then government, and finally private giving — holds whichever definition is employed.

4.4 Employment, expenditures and volunteering

How do these aggregated, sector-wide statistics break down between fields of activity? Tables 4.2 and 4.3 show respectively the distribution of paid employment and operating expenditures by ICNPO category in 1990. Table 4.2 separately identifies the shares under both broad and narrow definitions, while Table 4.3 shows the broad UK sector's operating expenditures, and puts them in international context by comparing them with the seven-country averages.

In the broad sector, education and research (group 2) is the single largest field of activity on both counts, a characteristic that it shares only with Japan in the seven-country study. The employment figure for group 2 — around one-third of all full-time equivalent paid employees — includes paid university staff; staff employed in charitable "independent" schools funded prim-

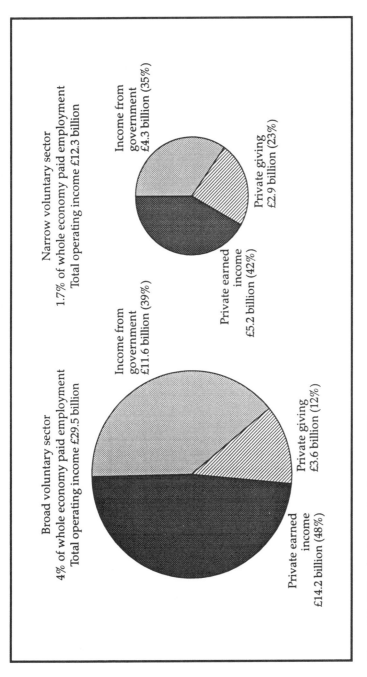

Broad voluntary sector
4% of whole economy paid employment
Total operating income £29.5 billion

Income from government
£11.6 billion (39%)

Private giving
£3.6 billion (12%)

Private earned income
£14.2 billion (48%)

Narrow voluntary sector
1.7% of whole economy paid employment
Total operating income £12.3 billion

Income from government
£4.3 billion (35%)

Private giving
£2.9 billion (23%)

Private earned income
£5.2 billion (42%)

Figure 4.1 UK voluntary sector income, 1990

Table 4.2

FTE employment in the voluntary sector

	Broad voluntary sector		Narrow voluntary sector	
	000s	%	000s	%
Culture and recreation	262	27.7	56[a]	14.4[a]
Education and research	330	34.9	16[b]	4.0[b]
Health	43	4.6	43	11.1
Social services	146	15.4	146	37.4
Environment	17	1.8	17	4.3
Development and housing	74	7.8	74	18.8
Civic and advocacy organizations	9	0.9	9	2.3
Philanthropic intermediaries and voluntarism promotion	7	0.8	7	1.8
International activities	23	2.4	23	5.8
Business and professional associations, trade unions	35	3.7	–[c]	–[c]
Total	946	100	390	100

a Excludes recreation (primarily sports and social clubs) but includes culture and arts, service clubs.
b Excludes primary, secondary and higher education (all universities, most independent and maintained voluntary schools) but includes other education and research.
c All excluded under narrow definition.

arily through fees paid by parents; charitable special schools catering for students with special needs; and staff in voluntary-aided and special agreement (mainly church) schools. The figures also include employment in the handful of schools which, by 1990, had opted out of local authority control for charitable grant-maintained status, and the new city technology colleges — a subsector which has expanded significantly since that date (albeit not to the extent the government would have liked; see Chapter 6).

Social services (group 4) have traditionally been regarded as the centre of gravity of the UK voluntary sector, and these agencies are indeed the largest employers in the sector if our

Table 4.3

The UK voluntary sector: operating expenditures in
international perspective

	Broad voluntary sector (%)	Seven-country average (%)[a]
Culture and recreation	20.6	16.5
Education and research	42.7	24.0
Health	3.5	21.6
Social services	11.6	19.6
Environment	2.2	0.8
Development and housing	7.9	5.0
Civic and advocacy organizations	0.7	1.2
Philanthropic intermediaries and voluntarism promotion	0.7	0.5
International activities	3.7	1.2
Business and professional associations, trade unions	7.1	9.2
Total	100	100

a   From Salamon and Anheier (1996a).

narrow definition is used. Table 4.2 shows that organizations
in this field were employing just under 150,000 full-time equivalent paid staff in 1990, almost two-fifths of the total for the
narrow sector. Many of these organizations provide residential
or nursing home care for adults or children, but increasingly
the voluntary sector is concentrating its activities in day, domiciliary and short-term care, support programmes for carers, and
user advocacy.

The culture and recreation field actually employs more paid
workers than social services under the broad definition, reflecting
relatively large numbers of paid staff in working men's clubs,
ex-servicemen's clubs and other non-profit social clubs, often
employed on a part-time or temporary basis. Moving from the
broad to the narrow definition, we exclude these paid employees
as well as those staffing the estimated 150,000 amateur sports
clubs in the UK. The remaining 56,000 employees shown in
group 1 under the narrower definition are then primarily those

working in the culture and arts "industry". Most of these are employed in the "professional" end of the sector — including such vast charitable organizations as the national museums and the English National Opera with, unsurprisingly, far fewer in the amateur culture and arts field. For example, the amateur music societies, choirs, brass bands and "independent" museums in the voluntary sector, which are all subsumed within our aggregate figures, typically have no or few paid employees.

In the fourth largest category — development and housing (group 6) — a significantly sized sector is the direct result of support from government. Considerable amounts of capital and revenue funding have been passed from central government to housing associations, and over half of the 74,000 employees in group 6 work in these organizations in housing provision. In terms of expenditure (Table 4.3), only Germany has a relatively larger development and housing subsector than the UK (although if corresponding data were available for developing countries, these would probably also have particularly strong sectors in this field). Central government has also been a major funder of voluntary sector employment and training projects. We describe the dynamics of government funding of housing associations and training providers in more detail in Chapter 5. Like culture and arts, development and housing also includes a major contribution from unpaid workers. For example, located here are over 11,000 urban community centres and rural village halls, most of which employ no, or just one or two (often part-time), staff.

Taken together, these four fields — education and research, social services, culture and recreation, and development and housing — dominate employment in the UK voluntary sector. Other parts of the voluntary sector are nevertheless still qualitatively important. In comparison to other countries in the study — particularly the US and Germany — the UK health subsector is relatively small because of the dominant, public sector National Health Service. The largest single subcategory of the voluntary health sector in the UK is the "other health" field, with more paid employees than the small number of independent, voluntary hospitals. Particularly prominent are the hospice movement and services for people with HIV/AIDS, or alcohol or drug problems.

Although the environment and international activity sectors

account for quite small proportions of the overall total — 2.2 percent and 3.7 percent respectively — these fields are far larger in relative expenditure terms in the UK than in the other countries in the study. The environmental voluntary sector has grown rapidly in this country in recent years as reflected in the mushrooming membership figures reported in *Social Trends* (Central Statistical Office, 1995; and see Pinner et al., 1993). Only Hungary shares with the UK an environment sector accounting for more than 1 percent of national whole sector expenditure. As far as international activities are concerned, Germany ranks second after the UK, but even here the proportion of total voluntary sector expenditure accounted for by this field is far smaller, representing 1.5 percent of the German sector's total.

As we have already noted, our mapping strategy did not generate data on volunteering under the definitions that we have adopted, but we can call on the rich and timely national household survey conducted by the Volunteer Centre UK. The survey defined volunteering as "any activity which involves spending time, unpaid, doing something which aims to benefit someone (individuals or groups), other than or in addition to close relatives, or to benefit the environment". A great deal of volunteering is directed "informally" — that is, not through organizations — and some volunteers work in public or private sector bodies, but there is no doubt that organizations in the voluntary sector are enormous beneficiaries of the time, expertise and other contributions of volunteers.

Half the survey respondents had been involved in some formal, organized voluntary activity and three-quarters in informal volunteering (Lynn and Davis Smith, 1991). The survey did not structure activities or organizations in such a way as to make it possible to project volunteer inputs onto each of the ICNPO groups, but the main fields in which volunteers were regularly active were:

- religion (28 percent of volunteers)
- sports and exercise (25 percent)
- children's education/schools (25 percent)
- youth/children (outside school) (25 percent)
- health and social welfare (21 percent)
- hobbies/recreation/arts (21 percent)

Examination of the patterns of volunteering by age, gender, income group and other individual and household characteristics reveals a range of motivations, opportunities and constraints (Knapp et al., 1995, 1996). In later supplementary work, the Volunteer Centre estimated that formal volunteering through organizations was worth about £25 billion in 1991, although estimates of this kind are fraught with conceptual and practical difficulties, and new research at Loughborough University is addressing this important question.

4.5 Sources of revenue

The three major subcategories of voluntary sector income to which we have referred are described in more detail in Box 4.3. While private giving is a smaller source of revenue than commercial income or government funding for the sector as a whole, Table 4.4 shows that this aggregate figure conceals large variations between constituent parts of the sector. We now describe the types of income in more detail, being careful to attend to these intra-sectoral differences.

Private earned income

Income from commercial activities is considerable in the fields of culture and recreation, and education and research in particular. Figure 4.2 illustrates how this earned income is made up. In both these ICNPO groups, a large proportion comes from charges paid for services, ranging from net income generated by bars attached to sports and social clubs to private fee payments to charitable independent schools (£1.6 billion in 1990, some 60 percent of all fee payments to the voluntary education sector). Also rather striking is the large concentration of fee income in culture and arts, primarily reflecting net box office earnings. Fee income is also a particularly significant source of revenue in the development and housing field, where it mainly comprises rent paid by housing association tenants (from private funds; housing benefit, sponsored by public finance, is classed as "user subsidy" income from government — see below). Charges are also important in health and social services, indeed disproportionately so to the

Box 4.3   Subcategories of sources of income

Private earned income:

- gross income from mission-specific *fees and client charges*, i.e. payments directly relating to organization purpose;

- net income from *sales of products and business income*, i.e. proceeds from products and services ancillary to organizational mission, and proceeds from for-profit subsidiaries, and net trading income;

- *dues*, or membership fees;

- *income from endowments and investments*, including interest on savings and temporary cash investments, dividends and interest on securities, net (non-mission specific) rental income, and capital gains; and

- other income not elsewhere classified.

Income from government:

- funding from all tiers of the state, whether "grants", "contracts" or "service (-level) agreements", including revenue from *central government* (Whitehall departments, territorial government, non-departmental public bodies (NDPBs) or quangos), and all tiers of *local* government;

- *user subsidies* — publicly-funded "demand-side" payments channelled through clients; and

- *other income*, including funding from supranational government (including the European Commission) and foreign governments.

Income from donations:

- direct contributions by *individuals*;

- gifts from *companies* (including sponsorship which, although commercial in character, are inseparable from giving in our data); and

- income from *grant-making trusts*, primarily including organizations located in ICNPO group 8, philanthropic intermediaries, other than *federated fundraising* (such as from Children in Need, Telethon, media appeals etc.), which is separately identified.

Table 4.4

Broad voluntary sector sources of income, £ billion, 1990

Field	Private giving		Earned income		Government		Total operating income	
	£ billion	%	£ billion	%	£ billion	%	£ billion	%
Culture and recreation	435.3	7.4	4761.8	81.2	665.9	11.4	5863.0	100
Education and research	528.0	4.6	3626.4	31.4	7380.5	63.9	11534.9	100
Health	270.3	26.3	520.5	50.7	235.6	22.9	1026.4	100
Social services	1314.0	39.7	1142.5	34.5	852.9	25.8	3309.4	100
Environment	227.9	36.1	282.6	44.8	120.4	19.1	630.9	100
Development and housing	126.7	4.3	1010.8	34.2	1816.4	61.5	2953.9	100
Civil and advocacy organizations	13.1	7.2	65.2	35.7	104.2	57.1	182.5	100
Philanthropic interventions and voluntarism promotion	245.0	26.9	633.3	69.7	30.2	3.3[a]	908.2	100[a]
International activities	422.3	41.5	246.9	24.3	402.3	39.5	1017.5	100
Business and professional associations, unions	31.8	1.6	1951.9	97.3	22.0	10.9	2005.7	100
Broad voluntary sector total	3614	12.3	14242	48.8	11630	39.4[a]	29486	100

Source: GUSTO mapping strategy: estimates built up individually for each ICNPO group (see Appendix 1).
a Excludes £306.7 million public funding passed through charitable arts quangos (Arts Councils and boards etc.), which also appear as part of group 1 income.

acute hospital sector, whose £277 million fee income accounts for two-thirds of ICNPO group 4's fee income. In social services, some £360 million were paid in private fees in 1990, including payments for residential and domiciliary care services.

Dues or membership subscriptions are prominent in the funding of professional associations and trade unions (group 11), but were slightly exceeded by subscriptions to recreational organizations, which totalled some £800 million in 1990.

There were also significant concentrations of endowment and investment income. The grant-making trust sector dominates, reflecting the UK's rich and long tradition of accumulated wealth in this area. But there are also large amounts of revenue from this source to be found in social services and education and research, where many of the country's oldest and wealthiest charities are found. Significantly, half of the endowment and investment income in the higher education subsector is attributable to the colleges of Oxford and Cambridge Universities, generated by land and property accumulated since their establishment in the 13th century.

Government income

Income from government may originate from a number of organizational tiers (Figure 4.3), and may be transferred along various routes (Box 4.3). It is important to note that these figures do not include the hidden support from the state that comes through tax concessions (whose inclusion would add around £1 billion to the value of public support, as we noted in Chapter 1).

Direct government funding of the broad voluntary sector is dominated by quasi-contractual funding of higher education by central government, and of primary and secondary education by local government. In fact, payments to these ICNPO subgroups accounted for 62 percent of all direct public statutory support for the broad voluntary sector. These sources have historically been at high levels and have exhibited considerable stability over time. £3.6 billion of funding for higher education from government primarily came in the form of monies channelled through the recently reformed Funding and Research Councils. State resources for primary and secondary education mostly comprise local education authority funding of maintained

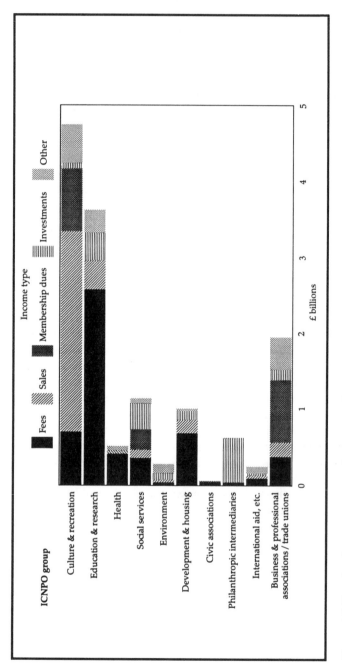

Figure 4.2 Broad voluntary sector private earned income, 1990

Some income from dues is included under "other" income.

voluntary schools (although local authority fees paid to special schools in the sector are also significant). The maintained voluntary sector is dominated by Catholic and Church of England schools, perhaps the most obvious reflection of the UK's rich heritage of religious endeavour in the voluntary sector (see Chapter 6). These churches had embarked on major school-building programmes in the 19th and early 20th centuries in particular. Unlike the voluntary hospitals, which were nationalized by the social legislation of the 1940s, these schools remained semi-autonomous bodies funded by local government as a result of the so-called "dual system" settlement between the churches and the state — although since 1990 a number have opted for "grant-maintained" status, replacing local government with central government as their paymaster.[9]

If local authority support for maintained voluntary education is disregarded as wholly within the "state system" then, under the narrower definition, social services departments emerge as the most significant local government funders of the sector. Figure 4.3 highlights other important contributions from local government, particularly to civic and advocacy organizations which, under our use of the ICNPO, is predominantly accounted for by subgroup 7 200 — law and legal services (including citizens' advice bureaux, independent advice agencies and law centres, all heavily dependent on a combination of local and central government money). Similarly resourced are the generalist local intermediary bodies, or local development agencies, a small but prominent subcomponent of ICNPO group 8.

A significant input is made by *central* government to housing and development (including training provision), and is also contractual in nature. It has come to prominence only over the past couple of decades and has been subject to considerable fluctuation over that period. During the 1980s, over £10 billion of public funds were allocated to the housing association movement — over and above user subsidies in the form of housing benefits — and nearly £4 billion was invested under a variety of employment and training schemes. The next most important single funding programme for the sector — and the biggest single source of "grant" for general organizational activities rather than specific contracts — was the Department of the Environment's Urban Programme, which allocated more than £700

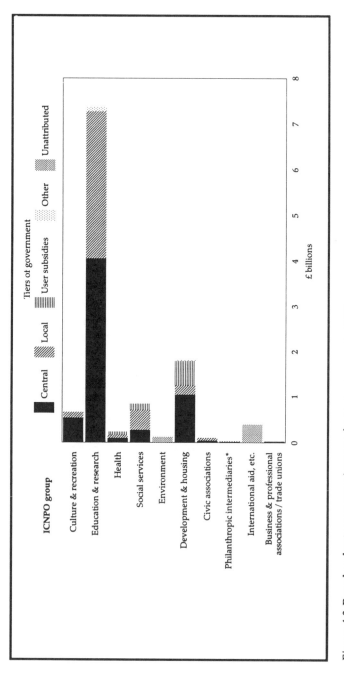

Figure 4.3 Broad voluntary sector income from government, 1990

* Excludes central government funding of charitable quangos to avoid double-counting.

million to fund a range of social, economic and environmental activities to combat inner-city decay. The Urban Programme is now being phased out, replaced by alternative measures including the single regeneration budget (see Chapter 5).

Figure 4.3 also identifies the scale of two other categories of income from government. "User subsidies" have primarily benefited housing associations through housing benefit — of which we have estimated that £542 million was used to subsidize rent in this sector in 1990. In the form of "income support", user subsidies were also supporting clients (mainly elderly people) in voluntary sector residential and nursing homes, totalling some £187 million. The global budgets for both programmes (which have, of course, also supported services delivered by the private sector) witnessed rapid expansion during the 1980s. Both were subject to growing policy attention because of their implications for public expenditure, and responsibility for these funds has now been mainly transferred to local government, accompanied by the formalization of needs assessments alongside means-testing.

Finally, the category "other government income", primarily funding from non-UK governments, totalled nearly £160 million in 1990, a small amount in comparison to the aggregates from other tiers, but obviously significant to its recipients. Over half of this funding was channelled to the "old universities" in the higher education field. Other noticeable examples of supranational and foreign government support include the European Social Fund's support for voluntary sector training projects (ICNPO subgroup 6 300) administered via UK central government in cooperation with the NCVO; the Northern Ireland-based International Fund for Ireland (funded jointly by the EC, Canada, New Zealand and US governments) giving support for economic development; and EC and foreign government support for international activities (although it has not been possible separately to identify the scale of this support in our data, and the £160 million does not include this).

Private giving

Although smaller in aggregate than commercial and government income, overall private giving in the UK (including from individuals, trusts, companies and federated fundraising) is a relatively large proportion of total operating income in comparison to most of the countries in the study: only the sectors in Hungary and the US secured a larger share from this source (Salamon and Anheier, 1996a). Across the seven countries, only international activity has private giving as its largest single source of income.[10]

Within the UK, social services also has private giving as the largest single category of the three broad income categories (Table 4.4), largely because of the sizeable youth development sector (whose location within group 4 appears a little odd in the UK context, but is a convention adopted for the purposes of international comparison). Other areas of voluntary organiz-ation social service are far more dependent on statutory income; for example, voluntary organizations oriented towards multiple user groups and those for people with learning disabilities receive most of their income from government, mainly local authorities (see Chapter 7).

There is recent evidence of stagnation in contributions (Half-penny and Lowe, 1994), but *individual* donors remain the sector's most significant source of private donations, giving £1.9 billion in 1990, equivalent to 6.5 percent of total operating income. This proportion is outdistanced in the international study only by the US, with 14.4 percent. After international aid and social services, which are the major beneficiaries of direct donations from individuals, health organizations and philanthropic inter-mediaries come next in terms of the amounts given (Figure 4.4). The latter primarily reflects the fundraising efforts of grant-making medical research charities and federated fundraising campaigns, which we have included in group 8 (see section 4.2 above).

Interesting complementary evidence on individual giving based on a survey of donors is available for 1993 from the CAF Individual Giving Survey (IGS). Like the volunteering data reported earlier, the baseline is a survey of individuals rather than organizations, and so covers giving to organizations in *all* sectors. The type of recipient organization most often cited by non-tax-efficient donors — who account for nearly 90 percent of the total — was "health and medicine". Out of twelve forms of "philanthropic donation" identified in the survey, this was the single most cited recipient field in nine categories, *inter alia* accounting for 100 percent of donors who said they gave via phone appeals, 59 percent via shop counter collections, and 50 percent via appeal adverts (Halfpenny and Lowe, 1994). Although we do not know from this survey the relative *amounts* donated by field of activity, the findings underline the importance of medicine and health to the donating public. However, looking at this in conjunction with our own data would suggest that the average size of donation must be relatively small compared with the fields receiving larger amounts: international activities and social services. On the other hand, the significance of this field is reinforced in another part of the IGS survey, which found that "health and medicine" was the only charitable aim regarded as "very important" by individual donors. This may be linked to disproportionate coverage from the press, as this type of agency gains more attention from the printed media than any other (Fenton et al., 1993; Deacon et al., 1995).

The 1993 IGS also reported on the popularity and amounts raised by 22 separate methods of giving, revealing a number of interesting features. It shows, for example, the continuing significance of giving through the churches. In addition, only around one-tenth of the population are actually involved in tax-efficient giving, which accounts for 13 percent of all "giving", with traditional covenants still much larger than the newer Gift Aid and payroll giving alternatives. The IGS also illustrates that the most popular and highest profile methods for giving do not necessarily raise the largest amounts. Transactions with a mixed commercial/donative character (quasi-commercial giving or quasi-donative purchases) are important, with almost half of the UK population involved in this type of "giving", accounting for 44 percent of the overall total.

Individual giving is but one form of private donation. Among the others, *corporate funding* at £848 million outweighed trust support, totalling £725 million.[11] With active encouragement from umbrella and promotional bodies who have pushed it hard as "enlightened self-interest" rather than charitable generosity, and also with encouragement from government and the royal family, both financial and in-kind corporate giving has certainly expanded over the past two decades.

However, for the very largest companies — the only corporate givers for whom time series data are available — giving has

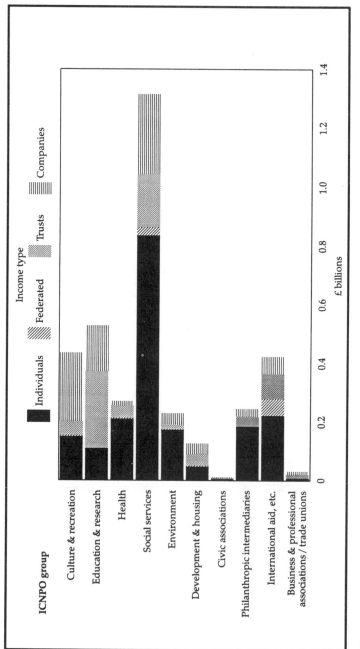

Figure 4.4 Broad voluntary sector private giving, 1990

tended to average only around 0.2 percent of current pre-tax profits, comparing poorly with the US in this regard, and there is evidence of stagnation in overall giving levels in the early 1990s (Lane and Saxon-Harrold, 1993; Lane, 1994; Passey, 1995). This may be linked to recessionary pressures, although profit margins alone cannot "explain" company giving; other factors include the availability of tax breaks, even if the effect is small (Fogarty and Christie, 1991), company size (Narendranatham and Stoneman, 1989) and the myriad managerial and organizational characteristics which make up a company's culture or "corporate identity" (Mayer, 1989).

Grant-making trusts have tended to characterize themselves as making qualitatively significant contributions over and above their measured impact, especially through their support for innovative, pioneering and unpopular causes, although there is little available evidence to substantiate this claim. Our figures show that education and research, and social services were the main beneficiaries of trust support in 1990. Finally, the relatively small contribution of federated funds is also noteworthy: despite their high media profile, the funds raised by events such as the ITV Telethon and BBC Children in Need appeals are actually rather small when compared with other modes of private giving, let alone with government. This is certainly not intended as a criticism, for these appeals have benefits beyond the funds raised, but rather to put the size of their contributions into perspective.

4.6 Voluntary sector market shares

Another way to describe the voluntary sector's contributions is in terms of "market shares": the proportion of a defined field of activity (or "market") for which it accounts. In many activity areas the sector is operating alongside, and competing or cooperating with, both for-profit and public bodies in a variety of "mixed economies". Some examples are given in Table 4.5. Market share ranges from under 2 percent for acute hospitals to around four-fifths for pre-school day care, widely defined.

In considering these data, it should be borne in mind that, just as the "voluntary sector" embraces a huge variety of organizational types and forms, so the label "private" or "for-profit"

Table 4.5

Voluntary sector market shares in key fields of activity, 1990

Field and measure	BVS	For-profit	Public	Total
Primary/secondary education[a]				
Pupil headcount (000s)	1,660	70	5,830	7,560
Market share (%)	(21.9)	(0.9)	(77.2)	(100)
Acute hospitals[b]				
No. beds x occupancy	2	4	143	149
Market share (%)	(1.6)	(2.5)	(95.9)	(100)
Nursing homes[c]				
No. of staffed residential places (000s)	12	115	155	282
Market share (%)	(4.2)	(40.8)	(55.0)	(100)
Residential homes[c]				
No. of staffed residential places (000s)	53	169	142	364
Market share (%)	(14.5)	(46.5)	(39.0)	(100)
Pre-school daycare full-time[d]				
No. of places for under 5s (000s)	16	42	28	86
Market share (%)	(18.3)	(49.1)	(32.7)	(100)
Pre-school daycare all groups[e]				
No. of places for under 5s (000s)	406	61	30	497
Market share (%)	(81.6)	(12.3)	6.0)	(100)
All housing[f]				
No. of completions (000s)	17	156	17	190
Market share (%)	(8.9)	(82.2)	(8.8)	(100)
All housing[f]				
No. of occupants aged 16 or over (000s)	1,170	28,930	9,380	39,090
Market share (%)	(2.9)	(74.0)	(23.9)	(100)
Rented housing				
No. of occupants aged 16 or over (000s)	1,170	3,130	9,380	13,680
Market share (%)	(8.6)	(22.9)	(68.6)	(100)

Sources: See Appendix 2.

a   Includes primary, secondary and nursery education.

b   Non-psychiatric in-patient beds only.

c   For main adult client groups: Elderly people (including psychogeriatrics) and younger (16+) physically handicapped, people with mental health problems and people with learning difficulties.

d   Full-time day nurseries only.

e   As d, plus part-time groups, including playgroups, parent and toddlers groups and under 5 groups.

f   Includes owner-occupied properties.

conceals as much as it elucidates, covering sole traders, partnerships, and private and public companies. Furthermore, in order to understand the market context in which voluntary organizations are operating, we really need to go beyond this snapshot to examine *trends* in market shares: how the relative contributions of each sector have changed over time. This is one of the themes explored in the chapters that follow.

4.7 Conclusion

This chapter has summarized some of the key characteristics of the voluntary sector in terms of numbers of organizations, paid employment, volunteering, expenditures and income, and market shares. It is clear that the sector is a significant player within the wider economy as measured by these indicators. Thus far, we have had little to say about the sector's wider contribution in the more qualitative, intangible sense of its political role in shaping public discourse and contributing to the fabric of "civil society" (see, for example, Ware, 1989c; Wuthnow, 1991). Thus, it should be borne in mind that this is still a partial and economic (in the narrow sense) sketch, even if it does provide the most comprehensive statistical map to date of the UK voluntary sector.

We have endeavoured to describe some of the diversity across the sector, but we should now move down to the level of individual fields and programmes to gain a fuller understanding of the nature of the sector's activities. In Chapter 5, we consider some recent developments in the sector and include a focus on particular programmes. Chapter 6 is devoted to education, the largest single field under the broad definition, while Chapter 7 deals with the largest fields of activity under the narrow one — social services — alongside health, which is peculiarly small compared to some countries. These fields are currently facing some of the most interesting challenges in terms of evolving government policy.

Notes

1 The Employment Department have noted three difficulties in asking employers about their sector: "respondents may not know which sector they belong to, we would have difficulty in verifying replies and there is the additional problem of sectoral migration" (Chief Statistician, Employment Department, personal communication, October 1991). It should also be noted that, although described as a "census", a sample is drawn for employers with 25 staff or fewer (except in Northern Ireland, where a separate full census is undertaken). This would obviously have implications for the accuracy of any voluntary sector estimates even if a sectoral identifier were included in the survey, because most voluntary organizations employ just one or two paid staff.

2 In fact, the only ICNPO categories in which we directly used information from the census for our statistical mapping were for ICNPO group 11 (business and professional associations, and trade unions) and for subgroup 1 100 (culture and arts). In the former case there was a match between our ICNPO category and the SIC (code 963) as used in the census, and it could safely be assumed that the "market share" of the sector was 100 percent. In the latter case the census figure provided an indicative upper limit because the voluntary sector does not have a 100 percent market share (for example, many museums are directly run by local authorities or owned by private individuals, and arts centres and festivals are often organized under local government auspices). The other category where the ICNPO matches the census category and 100 percent market share could be assumed was group 10, religion, corresponding to SIC 966, "religious organizations and similar associations". Like the theoretical treatment of group 10 in our methodology, this excludes the service provision activities of these bodies, which are treated under their appropriate other industry heads. For the record, in 1989 this category included 16,800 full-time and 12,500 part-time clergy and other paid employees (Department of Employment, 1991, p.218), which are not included in our broad sector estimates given below. Assuming this converts to 21,800 full-time equivalent employees, the inclusion of these staff would increase the sector's share of employment from 4.0 percent to 4.1 percent of the whole economy total, with group 10 employing a similar number of full-time paid staff to group 9 (international activities; see below).

3 Appendix 1, Table A.1 (on page 269) identifies with an asterisk

those types of organization for which we were unable to collect data. Probably the largest gaps in our figures relate to tenants' associations, residents' associations, and "other health" and "other education" organizations which were not linked to the national federations or associations from which we sampled. We probably also failed to identify all intermediary and support bodies working in each specific field, although many were covered. The net effect, however, is likely to be very small, probably less than 0.1 percent of the broad voluntary sector income total, because, although the numbers of organizations involved *may* be large (although we do not know this), they are generally small in terms of financial resources, and rarely have paid staff.

4 An additional, if partial, cross-validation check was to gross up Family Expenditure Survey (FES) data on fees paid to "independent" schools, expenditure on particular recreational activities, and membership subscriptions to trade unions, professional associations, etc. This could only be a crude check, as the former two categories would also include spending on private, for-profit bodies, and many of the difficulties which apply to using the FES to chart individual donations (Lee et al., 1995) would also apply to its use to catalogue commercial transactions with the sector.

5 Our estimate of the total operating income of all philanthropic intermediaries thus defined and including government funding was £1.2 billion, or £0.9 billion excluding direct income from government. The latter figure has been used in our tables and figures (see Appendix 1). This compares with an estimated income *from* trusts across the whole sector of just over £0.7 billion. The difference arises primarily because grant-making bodies, of course, do not deploy all their income in order to make grants to voluntary bodies (some funds are re-invested, or retained for administration and other internal purposes), and because some grants are made to bodies wholly outside even the broad voluntary sector (including NHS facilities and maintained county and voluntary controlled schools).

6 The financial resources of public sector agencies attributable to voluntarism are extremely significant in the UK. Based on umbrella body information, in the key subsectors of health and education alone, in 1990 over £265 million in private donations and £93 million in investment income was generated by fund-raising activities or trust funds linked to specific NHS facilities, while parent teacher associations linked to state schools probably raised over £50 million in that year.

7 The estimated numbers of organizations are also broadly consistent with information supplied to us confidentially on the number of bank accounts held by "clubs, associations, charities and other societies" in the UK by one of the leading High Street banks, which also gave us an estimate of its own (banking) market share for such organizations' accounts.

8 We use paid staff as our index of the voluntary sector's contribution to the UK economy because, while we collected data on *operating* expenditure, we did not pick up the full information on the nature of the sector's financial transactions to determine its *final* expenditure, which is the appropriate comparator for ascertaining the sector's contribution to GDP in expenditure terms (see Box 4.1 on page 101).

9 Of the three categories of maintained voluntary school recognized by the Department of Education and Employment in England and its equivalents in the rest of the UK, we have included only voluntary aided and special agreement schools as sufficiently independent of government to be regarded as part of the sector (see Chapter 6).

10 In the UK, the income proportions for this particular field are heavily influenced by the inclusion of the huge charitable British Council in our figures — an agency existing to promote exchange, friendship and cultural programmes usually thought of as a quango despite its constitutional independence from the state.

11 It should be noted that our figures unavoidably overstate the corporate contribution in terms of "donations": the data we employed meant that we were not able to separate sponsorship income from gifts. This may be hard to do at the best of times, but much of £725 million shown should probably be treated as earned or commercial income for the voluntary sector. For example, a large proportion of the £234 million flowing from private business to culture and arts is essentially commercial in character.

Chapter 5

RECENT DEVELOPMENTS IN STATE/VOLUNTARY SECTOR RELATIONS

5.1 Introduction

Historically, the activities and scope of the state have had many and major implications for the nature and scale of the voluntary sector, through interaction in the political realm, provision of legal frameworks, and the development of financial relationships. Our statistical mapping of the sector in the previous chapter underlined the continued significance of state funding. This chapter examines recent developments in the *dynamics* of state-voluntary sector relations more broadly.

Description and analysis of these developments is not straightforward. There are problems of heterogeneity and conceptualization. The voluntary sector, under either of our definitions, is a "loose and baggy monster", characterized by a multeity of structures, activities and orientations (Kendall and Knapp, 1995). Government support varies enormously in both scale and nature between fields of activity, and government is itself a multifaceted entity. Today, the "state" comprises a bewildering array of central departments and ministries at Westminster and their regional outposts, territorial offices outside England, quangos or non-departmental public bodies, traditional local government functional departments, and numerous quasi-autonomous local entities (Rhodes, 1988; Gray, 1994). Many of these central and local state agencies have relationships with voluntary sector agencies.

Other difficulties arise in trying to understand trends in state-voluntary sector relationships. Substantial advances in charting the sector's statistical profile have been made in recent years, particularly by the Charities Aid Foundation. Yet large gaps in information remain, and there are serious problems of quality, reliability and definition with much of the data that relate to changes over time. Moreover, in seeking to understand the available quantitative data, there is a paucity of qualitative information and interpretive perspectives. In the UK, political scientists, economists and sociologists have devoted remarkably little theoretical attention to the dynamics of voluntary-government relations (notable exceptions are Ware, 1989a,b,c; Wolch, 1990; Beckford; 1991). The academic field in the UK in recent years has been dominated by social policy analysts working within or close to the Fabian tradition, and by management scientists (useful overview volumes have included Brenton, 1985 and Johnson, N., 1987; and Batsleer et al., 1992 respectively).[1]

In the next section we offer a broad overview of the ideological context that provides a backdrop to the recent evolution of intersectoral relations. However, the rhetoric of central government support for voluntary organizations has limited explanatory power in understanding the reality of this relationship because of the many political, economic and social factors that intervene between rhetoric, policy intention and outcome (Ham and Hill, 1993). We need a narrower focus, concentrating on specific components of the state. We therefore include a survey of the nature of central government contributions in the three major programme areas in which the voluntary sector has benefited most from tangible financial support (section 5.3); then turn to the nature of relations with local government (section 5.4); and finally look at territorial government in Wales, Scotland and Northern Ireland (section 5.5). The concluding section tries to identify the themes emerging from this extremely diverse body of evidence. We draw both on the available research literature and on the policy interviews undertaken between 1990 and 1992.

5.2 The ideological context

Developments before Wolfenden

From the 1950s to the 1970s, the state was firmly entrenched as the "senior partner" in formal social welfare provision following the spate of post-war social legislation (see Chapter 2). The senior players that were to emerge alongside the state in what has often been characterized as a "corporatist" era were not voluntary organizations but the trade unions and business associations, whose legitimacy as "partners" with government tended to be taken for granted. This did not preclude a role for the voluntary sector, but rather viewed voluntary organizations as incidental "allies" to the state and its dominant partners — provided they had the appropriate democratic and professional credentials. The influence of trade unions as corporate players in this context is illustrated by the attitude of the Aves Committee (1969), whose recommendations had provided the impetus for the development of the structures of support for volunteering. This was careful to allay trade union concerns about the potential impact of the expansion of volunteering on paid employment. While highlighting the importance of training for volunteers, it also went out of its way to suggest that the distinction between volunteers and professionals should not be "blurred" and that the "unique" contribution of volunteers should be safeguarded by not using them as substitutes for paid staff, but rather as complements (Sheard, 1992, 1995).

How do we explain the reluctance of Conservative administrations in the post-war era to carve out a distinctive ideological position, consistent with the traditional antipathy of the right towards the state? Voters' empathy with the growth of the state appears to be the most obvious single factor. Prompted by the electoral popularity of policies which expanded the role of government — whose activities tended to be equated with social progress following the evident achievements of the state during war-time — post-war Conservative administrations had little incentive to destabilize the *status quo*, and those ideologues who raised objections had little effective influence (Deakin, 1994, pp.46-7; Mullard, 1993, chs 3, 5; but see Glennerster, 1995).[2] Several influential academic commentators from the 1950s onwards even argued that a "welfare consensus" had emerged during this period which de-emphasized or even denied the ideological character of empathy with the *status quo*. For some of these observers, the "fundamental conflict between capitalism and socialism ... had been transcended and that transcendence institutionalized in the welfare state" (Holmwood, 1993, p.99; and see Johnson, N., 1987, pp.27-8).

Dominant "welfare consensus" thinking, then, afforded un-questioning primacy to a welfare system directed by the state, recognition of the trade union movement as legitimate defenders of workers' interests, and with professionally-run local govern-ment as the senior "partner" in service delivery. In this essentially "welfare statist" or "collectivist" model (Taylor and Lansley, 1992), it was widely accepted that central government funded, controlled and delivered income maintenance and health services and should continue to do so; and it was assumed that the bulk of local authorities' statutory responsibilities in education, social housing and personal social services would be met by the expan-sion of their own, directly-run services. Although the voluntary sector did continue to have major roles in education and personal social services, as described in Chapters 6 and 7 below, its contributions had a relatively low political profile and, with the exception of the universities and schools, were dwarfed by the sheer scale of public sector provision.

By the early 1970s, the voluntary sector was to be given some general recognition through the government's provision of finance for a national Volunteer Centre, and this was followed by the initiation of a small Voluntary Services Unit at the Home Office. Yet it is important to emphasize that, in the broadest terms, the sector's political profile was not high when compared with that of the dominant partners to which we have referred.

Wolfenden and after

Although published just a year before Mrs Thatcher became Prime Minister, the Wolfenden Committee report, *The Future of Voluntary Organisations*, reflects a world view falling squarely within this "welfare consensus" tradition. There was, for example, little ac-knowledgement of the ideological critiques of either the new left or new right. While some "major shortcomings" in statutory ser-vices were catalogued — including unresponsiveness, inflexibility and failure to encourage participation — Wolfenden did not argue for major structural reform, but both predicted and advocated that statutory services "continue to occupy something like their present dominant position over the next quarter century". The *status quo* was "on the whole ... desirable, granted the need for major collective intervention if adequate social services are to be assured for the whole population" (Wolfenden Committee, 1978, pp.25-6).

The tenor of the report was to increase awareness of the sector's actual and potential contribution within this context, while offering only limited and low-key criticism of the dominance of directly-run local authority services. The voluntary sector was to continue to be a "partner" in "pluralism" (terms whose meanings were not clearly developed), whose cost-effectiveness, innovativeness, flexibility and pioneering nature had supposedly been demonstrated by research sponsored by Wolfenden. However, the sector's role in service delivery was still defined in essentially residual terms *vis à vis* other provision, being "best seen in terms of the ways in which it complements, supplements, extends and influences the informal and statutory system" (ibid., pp.26-7). Three specific contributions were emphasized: to *extend* provision; to *improve* the quality of government provision; and in some (but, by implication, relatively few) cases to act as *sole or principal provider*.[3]

Significantly, Wolfenden was also dismissive of the commercial, for-profit sector, whose involvement in social welfare services was equated — naively — with the use of uncompensated demand and vouchers. The Committee stated simply that this sector was "unlikely to grow to any significant extent before the end of the century" because the "many objections and obstacles to the voucher system" were "unlikely to be overcome" (ibid., p.24). As the market share statistics referred to in the previous chapter imply, this was to prove a serious misjudgement. In particular, in residential care this sector was to expand dramatically during the 1980s for reasons that are explained in more detail in Chapter 7.

Critics of the *status quo* on the centre and left, while welcoming Wolfenden's stamp of approval for the voluntary sector, suggested that the cumulative "failures" of the state were actually so severe that nothing less than radical restructuring would suffice. An important component of the proposal of these "welfare pluralists" was a significant rebalancing of power between the statutory and voluntary sectors in favour of the latter (Gladstone, 1979; Hadley and Hatch, 1981). For these observers, while decentralization and participatory initiatives within statutory services were crucial, the benefits of pluralism and citizen participation, mutual aid, proximity to need, flexibility, responsiveness and empowerment were particularly closely associated with the activities of voluntary organizations. By encouraging the transfer of service delivery responsibilities, these advantageous attributes of voluntary action could, it was argued, be harnessed, while the state continued to provide the necessary regulatory and financial frameworks.

Some of this thinking undoubtedly informed the enthusiasm for voluntary action associated with left-wing local authorities over the coming years, but — like the rhetoric of the new left and the new right over the previous two decades — its impact at the national level was minimal. Although "welfare pluralism" was briefly adopted as a cause of the fledgling Social Democratic Party (Beresford and Croft, 1983), this was soon to fade into electoral oblivion, while social policy analysts and critics from the left soon developed influential critiques of the project (Box 5.1).

Within this overall context, however, it is widely accepted that, in the wake of the Wolfenden report, and the debates around

---

Box 5.1   Critiques of "welfare pluralism" in the early 1980s

In the academic world, a number of social policy analysts were quick to develop arguments to challenge the assumptions and evidence of the new "welfare pluralist" position. It was held up as chronically naive, being strong on the former and weak on the latter; quick to recognize the "failures" in the state while not recognizing those of voluntary organisations, many of which, it was pointed out, were still "old-style" agencies (paternalistic, oligarchic and controlled by the middle classes, and so on); not providing details of how the redefined "partnership" could be operationalized; and failing to describe how the power relationship could be satisfactorily rebalanced in practice against the backdrop of an "unjust" society (Brenton, 1985; Johnson, 1987; Webb and Wistow, 1987).

"welfare pluralism" that followed it, there was a noticeable increase in interest in the voluntary sector by government. Although Brenton (1985) links renewed enthusiasm for voluntarism to the fiscal crises of the late 1970s under a Labour administration, social policy analysts have traditionally stressed how it was the Thatcher administration in 1979 whose stance marked a radical shift in the ideological climate (for example, Lawrence, 1983). There was continuity with Wolfenden in the sense that the voluntary sector continued to be labelled as a "partner" in the pursuit of welfare goals, and there was a proliferation of rhetoric to this effect; but there was a sharp change in attitudes towards the state itself, and the other major participants in policy. Drawing on new right arguments, the growth of the state was now seen as problematic, trade unions were portrayed predominantly as malign distorters of market processes, and local authorities as profligate "overspenders". Characterized more as adversaries than as partners, these were now charged with responsibility for much that was wrong with the UK economy (Marsh and Rhodes, 1992, p.171). It was within this overtly conflictual climate that the development of voluntary-state relations during the 1980s and early 1990s needs to be located.

5.3 Recent trends in central government support

In moving from rhetoric to reality, we consider here two programmes in which voluntary organizations have delivered clearly specified services to the state (housing and special employment), and one area of significant central government spending on more generalized "grant" support, the Urban Programme (UP). Comparable year-on-year data for overall central government funding are available only for 1983/84 to 1990/91 and, under a restricted definition, we are only able to chart the actual state finance of the sector with any degree of confidence from several years into the "Thatcher revolution"[4] (Kendall and 6, 1994). Figures 5.1 and 5.2 below demonstrate how funding for housing and employment programmes in particular have completely dominated central government support of the sector (thus defined) in recent years.[5]

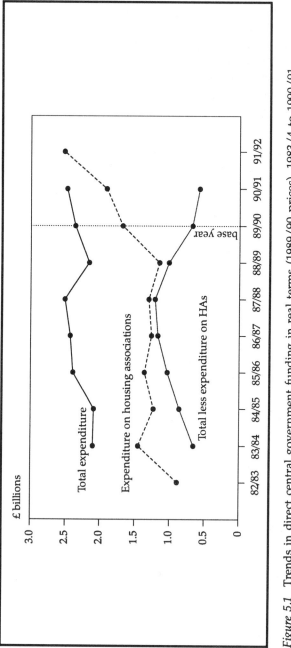

Figure 5.1 Trends in direct central government funding in real terms (1989/90 prices), 1983/4 to 1990/91

Source: Kendall and 6 (1994) using data reported in *Hansard*.

* Principal funders only under restricted definition; see endnote 2.
Comparable data not available prior to 1983/4 and after 1990/91 (other than for housing associations).
Deflated using GDP deflator supplied by the Treasury (adjusted to remove distortions caused by domestic rates abolition).

Housing associations

Housing policy has probably witnessed more radical change than any other area of British social policy since 1979, and the voluntary sector has been a major beneficiary of these developments. The government's aims of controlling public expenditure, weakening the role of local authorities and increasing home ownership were successful due to electoral popularity, appeal across both wings of the Conservative Party and administrative feasibility (Kemp, 1992). However, another goal — that of expanding the private rental sector — was not accomplished. Rather, the "market share" of non-local authority rented housing has been expanded through the deployment of the voluntary housing association movement (Table 5.1).

In the housing market, the sector's share trebled between 1971 and 1988, representing an increase from 1.9 to 8.2 percent of *rented* housing stock over the period. This growth was made possible largely through the financial support provided by the

Table 5.1

Housing tenure in England and Wales, 1971-1992 (percent of dwellings)

Year	Owner-occupiers	Rented from local authority	Rented from housing association	Rented from private landlord
1971	52.1	28.2	0.9	18.8
1981	57.9	28.5	2.2	11.4
1982	60.3	26.8	2.3	10.6
1983	61.6	25.8	2.4	10.2
1984	62.6	25.2	2.4	9.8
1985	63.6	24.5	2.5	9.4
1986	64.5	23.8	2.6	9.1
1987	65.5	23.1	2.6	8.8
1988	66.6	22.0	2.7	8.7
1989	67.2	20.9	2.9	9.0
1990	67.4	20.0	3.1	9.5
1991	67.5	19.5	3.2	9.8
1992	67.6	19.2	3.4	9.8

Source: Hills (1990); Department of the Environment (1993, table 9.3).

Housing Corporation,[6] which was (and is) unique in being simultaneously both a large, powerful centralized national regulator and a funder of voluntary sector activity (Day, 1992). It tightly controlled the pattern of new development, aiming to ensure economy and efficiency in management, and that national social policy objectives such as ethnic mix and tenant participation have been realized. As well as the supply-side stimulus provided by the Corporation's programme of quasi-capital grants, demand-side means-tested housing benefit, administered first by central government but subsequently transferred to local authorities, put low-income tenants in a position to pay rent. The housing association's market niche developed in catering for people on low incomes, and for those with special needs, including disabilities or age-related needs.

The housing association movement's growth, and government's enthusiasm for it, can partly be understood by reference to the failures or limitations of, and difficulties associated with, the other rental sectors. Many for-profit landlords left the housing market following the development of extensive restrictions and regulations in this field in the post-war period, originally prompted by successive governments' unease about both the inefficiencies and inequities of an unregulated market. Investment in municipal housing stock after the war had initially aimed to fill the gap in the rental market: as local government was undertaking the post-war demolition and slum clearance, it was simply assumed to be "natural" that they should not only rehouse those who had lived in these properties and rebuilt on the cleared areas, but also own the new housing developments (Hills, 1989, p.250). But publicly-owned rented housing was soon itself vehemently criticized, apparently exhibiting many of the problems identified by welfare pluralists and others described above — including over-centralization, over-bureaucratization and a lack of responsiveness. These "failures" created a window of opportunity for voluntary sector social housing, which appeared to offer

variety and organisational style [which have] given them a good reputation both for innovation and good management. They harness[ed] the enthusiasm and expertise of large numbers of voluntary management committee members while using professional staff to run their day-to-day operations (op. cit., p.264).

The growth of the voluntary housing sector must also be seen in the context of central government antagonism towards local authorities and its objective of limiting the latter's expenditure. While there was certainly already a significant input of public funds into the voluntary sector during the 1970s (following the establishment of the housing association grant system in 1974), the dynamic of voluntary sector growth *at the expense of* local authority housing did not emerge until the Thatcher and Major administrations. Social housing suffered the most dramatically of all public services from the constraints on public capital expenditure implemented first in response to the late 1970s' fiscal crisis and subsequently accelerated by the Thatcher administration. In this context, even when spending on housing associations was being limited, the voluntary sector's market share of rented housing still expanded because economies in overall public capital housing expenditure were primarily achieved by dramatically curtailing local authorities' own new building programmes (Hills and Mullings, 1990).

Legislation permitting shifts of property from local authorities to housing associations added to the momentum from the mid-1980s onwards. 1985 legislation allowed voluntary transfers for the first time at local authorities' own initiative; and the 1988 Housing Act facilitated the transfer of housing previously let by local authorities to existing or new voluntary sector landlords through an "opting out" voting process, as well as revolutionizing the overall system of Housing Corporation finance. This Act also introduced another mechanism for taking housing stock out of direct local government control, the Housing Action Trust. These were "public-private partnerships" for which the central government provided additional resources, and hoped would then be passed on to full private or voluntary control.

Special employment measures

It has been argued that voluntary organizations pioneered opportunities for unemployed people before government became involved, delivered specialized services, performed advocacy, campaigning and research roles, and delivered innovative and flexible services (Moon and Richardson, 1984). Over many years, a number of special government programmes have provided job

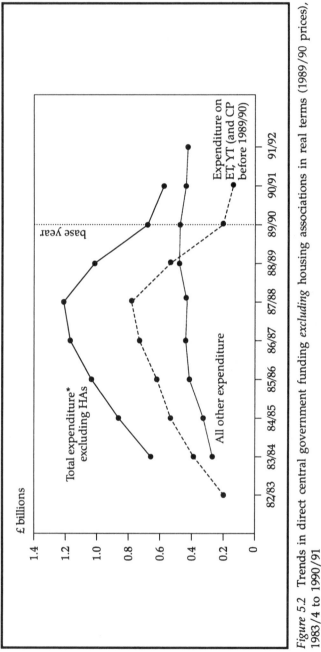

Figure 5.2 Trends in direct central government funding *excluding* housing associations in real terms (1989/90 prices), 1983/4 to 1990/91

HA = housing associations; ET = employment training; YT = youth training; CP = community programme.
Source: Kendall and 6 (1994) using data reported in *Hansard.*
* Principal funders only under restricted definition; see endnote 2.

and training opportunities for unemployed people. Figure 5.2 traces out the funds allocated to the voluntary sector under the two largest schemes during the 1980s.[7] Central government expenditure on the narrow sector *apart from* housing increased significantly in the early and mid-1980s, before slumping dramatically in the early 1990s, largely due to trends in the resources made available under these programmes.[8]

The changing availability of funds in this field has been the direct result of central government's labour market strategy in response to its interpretation of the problem of unemployment. A rapid increase in unemployment was the inevitable outcome of the Thatcher government's anti-inflationary and "hands-off" labour market macro-economic strategy. (For the government, this was the pain before the gain.) Investment in the voluntary sector on a huge scale provided an opportunity for the government to act quickly to "contain" a phenomenon which was still regarded by the electorate as a social problem worthy of its attention — even if some members of the government regarded this expenditure as profligate (Clark, 1993, p.40). Whether or not it was genuinely believed that these expenditures would help to "solve" the problem of unemployment, the schemes certainly provided government with a cost-effective way to meet the *political* imperative of keeping down the headline unemployment figure. "Trainee" positions were not included in this figure and, as the trade unions and others pointed out, received low rates of pay.

Many national and regional voluntary bodies felt unable to pass up opportunities for growth presented by huge inputs of public funds, despite ideological reservations. Indeed, ideological tensions and organizational conflict were commonplace as schemes were implemented over the heads of local trade unions (Addy and Scott, 1987), and were often virtually monopolized by large voluntary organizations at the expense of small, local organizations (Rankin, 1987). But by the mid-1980s, Moon and Richardson were arguing that voluntary organizations were in such a strong position in implementation that they had effectively rendered themselves indispensable to central government within the policy process by virtue of their role as sponsor and agent of key programmes. Having surveyed evidence on the sector's wide-ranging pattern of participation, they concluded

A system of exchange relationships exists and a genuine policy community appears to be evolving, within the loose network of groups, in the business, voluntary, local government and MSC spheres ... Groups have not only come to play a significant part in the implementation of schemes for the unemployed, but they have also been invited to participate in policy-making and programme evaluation signifying their arrival as "insider groups" (1984, p.406).

However, as Figure 5.2 shows, the steady growth of public funds was to be dramatically reversed in the late 1980s. The stability of the policy community and the place of the voluntary sector within it therefore turned out to be less secure than implied by the tenor of Moon and Richardson's account. As the economy appeared to recover, and fewer young people entered the labour market after 1985, global public spending on training (across all sectors) was reduced. At the same time, the government changed the priorities of the special employment measures from "community benefit" projects towards an emphasis on measurable trainee achievement in the labour market (under the switch from the Community Programme to Employment Training), despite considerable opposition from many voluntary sector providers. The voluntary sector was less responsive than private providers to this change, experiencing a sharp fall in "market share" of the dwindling budget at the latter's expense (as measured by numbers of trainees; see Palmer, 1990). Further losses were incurred with the transfer of responsibility for Employment and Youth Training to quasi-private employer-led Training and Enterprise Councils (TECs). The process of transition to a TEC network (and the associated contractual funding regime) was particularly fraught for many voluntary providers (Bridge Group, 1991; more recently, see National Council for Voluntary Organisations, 1995). While a recent survey found that 60 percent of TEC chief executives viewed the voluntary bodies as "key non-employer stakeholders" (twice as many as gave this seal of approval to trade unions), there was ample evidence of continuing misunderstandings and frustrations in the relationship between TECs and voluntary groups (Haughton et al., 1995).

The Urban Programme

The third major source of central government funding in the 1980s was the Urban Programme. This was originally launched under Home Office auspices in 1969 to provide supplementary help to local authorities, strongly influenced by — among other things — the "rediscovery of poverty", the re-emergence of selectivity in the early and mid-1960s, the US poverty programmes, growing emphasis on area-specific policies, and the growing public concern over the issue of immigration and race relations. The UP was a joint scheme between central and local government, funded primarily by the former (providing 100 percent of capital and 75 percent of revenue funding) but administered by the latter. The UP was in fact only one of a complex and confusing mix of initiatives from various government departments aimed at combating inner-city decay, jointly attempting to mobilize statutory, private and voluntary resources in deprived urban areas (Deakin and Edwards, 1993). Although recently "tidied up" under arrangements for a single regeneration budget, throughout the 1980s the UP was by far the biggest central government resource for inner-city voluntary groups.

While funding for the voluntary sector under this scheme grew consistently up until the mid-1980s (Jacobs, 1989), from the late 1980s onwards it declined in real terms in England as earmarked inner-city expenditures were directed elsewhere. This affected the voluntary sector disproportionately. The priorities of the Department of the Environment increasingly emphasized economic and environmental activities over the social projects in which voluntary sector activity had traditionally been concentrated, and capital over revenue grants. As in employment and training, the private sector was to prove more responsive to realignments of central government priorities, and voluntary organizations lost "market share" to profit-oriented organizations.

The announcement of the Programme's phased abolition in England in 1992 was predictably met by a combination of horror from voluntary groups, many of which could not foresee securing replacement funds from an alternative source, and dissatisfaction with the way in which the announcement occurred. The absence of consultation preceding the decision was interpreted by many

---

Box 5.2   The VSU's ineffectiveness within government

Although the VSU had suggested that government departments "assess implications that policy changes might have for voluntary activity and the voluntary sector", this was interpreted differently by NCVO and the DoE. While the former felt this necessitated a formal impact assessment statement, the latter considered only discussion within the Department was implied. For an NCVO interviewee, this constituted an example of the VSU's inability to impact on government departments' modus operandi:

[This should have been a] very simple way of [the VSU] waving a mini stick around at least to say, "OK, you want to abandon the Urban Programme next week, we're not saying you can't do it, but where is the assessment about what the impact is, and how are you going to communicate that to organizations and try to explain why you've come to that decision?" That's an example of the rhetoric not being translated into resource availability and the practicalities of coordination across departments.

---

as symptomatic of the government's lack of commitment to meaningful "partnership" with the sector. It also provided an example, according to one of our umbrella body interviewees, of the inability of the Home Office's Voluntary Service Unit to exert influence within government when this would have been most useful (Box 5.2).

During its lifetime, this programme came in for a good deal of criticism for being over-bureaucratic, and for not incorporating effective monitoring procedures (Lawless, 1990); for lacking accessibility to the ethnic minority groups it was meant to be serving; and for the limitations of its consultation processes (Hodson, 1984; Munt, 1991). Despite these shortcomings, the decline and phased abolition of dedicated UP funding was still greeted as disastrous by many voluntary organizations, both because of the sheer volume of resources lost, and because it had been perceived by many in the sector as a relatively secure and flexible source of support, without being "too prescriptive" (Hodson, 1984).

5.4 Trends in relations with local government

While many voluntary organizations experienced close relations with the state for the first time under the major central government programmes described above, the primary point of contact for many groups was *local* government during the 1980s. For example, as we described in Chapter 4, in the key fields of social services, civic and advocacy associations and voluntarism promotion, local exceeded central government support in 1990. Moreover, in other ICNPO fields, such as health, while central government funding has been higher overall, local funding has nevertheless been a mainstay for many organizations. In addition, statutory "in-kind" support for the sector has come primarily from local authorities. Leat et al. (1986) estimated that this resource — including rental concessions, financial advice and payment of the salaries of seconded staff — could have been worth as much as 50 percent of direct funding in the mid-1980s.

Trends in local authority funding

Trends in local authority funding of the sector, like those relating to central government, are difficult to trace because of data limitations and problems of sectoral definition. Anecdotal evidence suggests increases in local authority funding of the sector during the 1970s and early 1980s, but, as with central government, relatively reliable aggregate statistics are available only from 1983/84 onwards (Table 5.2). The estimates in Table 5.2, based on annual surveys undertaken by the Charities Aid Foundation, probably reflect an implicit definition of the sector reasonably close to our narrow definition (local authority funders are not offered a definition of "voluntary organizations" in the survey questionnaire). It should also be noted that these figures are thought to under-estimate local authority fee expenditure, and may under-estimate overall expenditure because of the grossing procedure employed (Mocroft, 1995).[9]

During much of the 1980s, local authorities were vocal in lamenting the scope and scale of cuts in their budgetary allocations from central government in the tense ideological climate that prevailed for much of the 1980s (see below), causing much anxiety among voluntary groups reliant on their support.

Table 5.2

UK local authority expenditure on the voluntary sector as a percentage of all expenditure over time in real terms (at constant 1989/90 prices)

Year	83/84	84/85	85/86	86/87	87/88	88/89	89/90	90/91	91/92
Total estimated LA expenditure on voluntary sector	484	563	536	485	572	507	570	na	689
LA current expenditure	38830	39133	38376	40529	41661	41666	42389	43706	46131
LA total expenditure	45260	45379	43644	45494	46133	45108	48655	48303	50960
Expenditure of voluntary sector as % of LA current expenditure	1.25	1.44	1.40	1.20	1.37	1.22	1.37	na	1.49
Expenditure of voluntary sector as % of LA total expenditure	1.07	1.24	1.23	1.07	1.24	1.12	1.17	na	1.35

Source: Taylor et al. (1993).

However, while in some individual cases these fears were un-doubtedly realized, in aggregate local authorites appear to have been remarkably successful in sustaining levels of spendable resources through increases in local taxation to compensate for falling levels of central government grant finance, the manip-ulation of financial information, and creative accounting (Stoker, 1991; Cochrane, 1993). In turn, they appear to have used these resources partly to protect their expenditure on the voluntary sector, with a real increase of some 42 percent between 1983/84 and 1991/92.[10]

Yet perhaps the single most striking feature about these fund-ing trends is the low proportion of *total* local authority expend-iture which was allocated to the sector — varying between just 1.2 and 1.5 percent over the period.[11] This underlines the con-tinuing extent to which welfare resources in the fields in which local government had lead responsibility were still very heavily tied up in funding local authority directly-run provision in the "welfare statist" tradition. The much-vaunted shift towards a "contract culture" at local government level, with the implication of a massive shift from local authority direct delivery towards contracting out, was not to emerge until the mid-1990s with the late implementation of the relevant legislation in personal social services (see Chapter 7).

In contrast to the tightly regulated or quasi-contractual payments which we have seen accounted for most central government funding in the 1980s, overall local authority grant funding consistently outweighed "contracts" and fee expenditure (although it is difficult to be certain of the extent because the surveys are thought to under-estimate fee payments). In 1991/92, £464 million (67 percent of the total) was estimated as "grant" support, compared with £224 million for "fees" (at 1989/90 prices; see Taylor et al., 1993). While anecdotal evidence suggests that funding specificity may have increased over the period *within* this "grants" total, there are no data to allow us to tease out this effect.

Why did overall local authority funding of the voluntary sector grow from the 1970s onwards, albeit to a very limited extent when compared to the scale of local authorities' own directly-run services? As with central government, dis-aggregation is vital to make sense of overall trends, and we focus on the links between local government and the largest recipient fields —education and social services — in the following two chapters. However, it is possible to suggest that increasing local authority awareness of both the limitations of their own services, and the perceived advantages of voluntary action spelt out by the Wolfenden Committee were of some import. A critical facilitatory factor in this process was probably the increased *opportunities* for mutual learning made possible by what Stoker (1991) refers to as the "opening up" of local government. From the mid-1970s onwards, there was certainly a growing diversity of voluntary organizations linked to local authorities (Unell, 1989). Specifically, growth in interaction between the sectors was evidenced by

- the appointment in many social services departments of full-time voluntary sector liaison officers (Johnson, 1981);
- voluntary groups' involvement in joint planning for community care and other coordinating mechanisms, mandated by central government (Challis et al., 1988; Wistow et al., 1994);
- many authorities' increasing consultation with ethnic and women's groups as a plank of equal opportunities policy; and
- the impact of central government's Urban Programme (see above).

Joint activities of this sort not only fostered greater familiarity and understanding, but also allowed identification of shared values and goals. Interpenetration of key personnel was also increasingly likely, with local authority officers and members often sitting on the boards of voluntary agencies, or otherwise involved in running or directing them. Drawing on research undertaken for the Widdicombe Committee's enquiry into local government in the early 1980s, Stoker suggests that increasing "consultation with interest groups", formalized through the creation of new consultative committee structures and the increased use of coopting into existing committees, helped to transform many previously "oligarchic and inward-looking" authorities, changing the attitudes and the practices of both officers and members.

During the 1980s, it is also important to be aware of the impact of local authority support for the sector of ideological tensions between central and local government (Carter and John,

1992). Just as central government looked to the voluntary sector in part as as ideologically desirable alternative to local government in housing (see above), so some on the left saw political advantage in supporting the voluntary sector.

Particularly prominent in this regard were authorities associated with the so-called "urban left" (see Box 5.3). Wolch (1990) describes, somewhat dramatically, how the archetypical authority of the "urban left", the socialist-dominated Greater London Council (GLC), actively sought to encourage "radical"

Box 5.3   The new urban left and the voluntary sector

While the ideological stance of central government shifted to the right in the early 1980s under Thatcher's premiership, at local government level a new brand of radical politics came to prominence in some local authorities controlled by the left. This resulted in a marked polarization of views between central and local government and a degree of intragovernmental conflict unprecedented in developed countries (Carter and John, 1992). The position of these authorities represented a deliberate departure from the "traditional labourism" which had characterized post-war central government Labour administrations. This had seen Parliament as the primary or core mechanism for achieving socialist goals, with local authorities seen as the "handmaidens of parliamentary socialism" (Gyford, 1985). The urban left, on the other hand, gave "priority to extra-parliamentary struggle and campaigning" (Hain, 1980) as a means of pursuing socialist goals. Alongside general dissatisfaction with the *status quo*, this development was prompted by social and generational changes leading to new values, and perceptions of fiscal, ideological, social and electoral crises (Gyford, 1985).

The forging of alliances with disadvantaged groups and the voluntary organizations that purported to represent them was a key element in a strategy seeking to "build...a new coalition which could simultaneously attempt to reunite divided communities while also creating a broader political constituency for the Labour Party than that represented by its traditional supporters alone" (op. cit., p.84). The relevant groups included trade unions, claimants' unions, "community organizations", ethnic minority, women's, and gay and lesbian groups, single-issue and protest campaigns, and tenants' and residents' associations. These often had local authority membership, and were heavily reliant on local government funding.

campaigning and social rights groups, partly through grant aid, as a tactical weapon in the conflict with central government. Central government responded by simply abolishing the GLC and metropolitan councils, overtly on the grounds of their wastefulness and inefficiency, including their supposedly profligate expenditure on "loony left" causes.

However, it is important not to overstate the extent to which grant aid strategies for voluntary groups were pursued for such overtly ideological reasons, even among the more radical authorities (which in any case constituted a minority of Labour authorities; Cochrane, 1993). While ideologically-inspired grant aid made interesting news for some parts of the media, we know from research conducted with social services departments in the late 1980s and early 1990s (Wistow et al., 1994) that most local funding programmes by this tier of the state were driven by the much more mundane, apolitical rationales identified by the Wolfenden Committee. This included a desire to capitalize on assumed advantages in terms of cost-effectiveness, specialist expertise, flexibility and so on, within the context of local needs and institutions. These less newsworthy rationales almost certainly had more general applicability throughout the 1980s and across other departments. Indeed, Wolch (1990) herself notes that even in her London sample at the height of the GLC's supposedly radical phase, most grant recipients were "established charity" service providers rather than radical campaigning groups. Many relationships between local government and the voluntary sector most likely also reflected the influence of tradition and habit which may be rather harder to explain in either "rational" or political terms (Judge and Smith, 1983; Mocroft, 1989; and Chapter 7).

5.5 Territorial government

Links between the state and voluntary organizations in England have clearly been varied and multifaceted. Further layers of diversity stem from the impact of different cultures and traditions of public administration and voluntary action in Scotland, Wales and Northern Ireland.[12] For these three countries we briefly sketch the scope and scale of central and local government links with

Table 5.3

Total expenditure on the voluntary sector as a percentage of local authority expenditure, UK, 1991/92

Expenditure/country	England	Wales	Scotland	Northern Ireland	UK
	000s	000s	000s	000s	000s
Total estimated LA expenditure on voluntary sector	663	27	99	4	794
LA current expenditure	44809	2800	5411	127	53145
LA total expenditure (current plus capital)	58981	3318	6251	160	58708
Expenditure of voluntary. sector as % of current expenditure	1.5	1.0	1.8	3.3	1.5

Source: Kendall and 6 (1994).

voluntary organizations. (Of course, much of the discussion of statutory-voluntary sector relations earlier in the chapter applies equally to the consituent countries of the UK, and we should stress that all statistics reported earlier relate to the whole of the UK.) Table 5.3 compares expenditure on the voluntary sector with total local authority expenditure in each country in 1991/92 (under a narrower definition consistent with that used in Table 5.2).

Wales

Local authority financial support for the voluntary sector in Wales has traditionally been low compared to the rest of the UK. In 1991/92 only 1 percent of total Welsh local authority current expenditure was allocated to the voluntary sector, compared with 1.5 percent for England and for the UK as a whole (Table 5.3). Spending by local authorities in Wales appears to have typically been around half the equivalent figure for England, although this had increased somewhat by 1991/92. We should treat such comparisons with caution because the huge variation in spending patterns *within* England limits their usefulness. However, the Wales Council for Voluntary Action (WCVA) has been quick to argue that the sector has suffered from "historic under-funding" in Wales. This can be partly explained by ideology: the relative predominance, until relatively recently, of authorities in the "welfare statist" mould. One of our interviewees commented in 1991:

> You have some very statist local authorities who have ... a total grasp of power of the area and a very monolithic approach to life. Meaning that, if a service is worth running or something's worth doing, then the council [local authority] should do it and if it's not, then it's not worth spending money on anyway ... It might take you five years to convince any Welsh authority to fund something.

In the early 1980s, this attitude was evidenced both by relatively low levels of direct funding and a tendency for local authorities to use UP funds to support their own directly-run projects, rather than voluntary projects. Following WCVA lobbying, the Welsh Office issued circulars in the mid-1980s urging local authorities to reprioritize their submissions in favour of the voluntary sector, and mandating consultation (Williams, 1984). Yet despite Welsh local authorities' apparent general lack of ideological empathy with the voluntary sector, they still allocated £27 million to the sector in 1991/92 (Table 5.3). For example, the traditional, established UK child care voluntary sector provides extensive services under contract to Welsh local authorities, fulfilling an important role as specialists and innovators in that field.

Although responsible for allocating only one-quarter of statutory support in the form of direct grants (just under one-third if the UP is included), the Welsh Office dominated voluntary-statutory sector relations during the 1980s and early 1990s. It also provided a single focus in Wales in a way not matched in England (where we have seen that the Voluntary Services Unit of the Home Office is politically weak). A relationship emerged between the Welsh Office, the WCVA, and the 150 or so organizations in receipt of significant direct funding, described variously as "symbiotic", "close" and "cosy". Close personal relationships, including overlapping committee membership, developed between Welsh Office staff and the larger voluntary organizations, with local authorities and other voluntary groups effectively often excluded from the evolving cliques.

Scotland

Voluntary organizations in Scotland, as in Wales, have operated in different cultural, historical and political contexts from their "typical" English counterparts, but, unlike Wales, there is also a separate legal system (see Chapter 3). Most Scottish local authorities were controlled by the Labour Party or Scottish National Party, but, unlike Wales, local authority expenditure on the voluntary sector as a proportion of total expenditure is significantly *higher* than the UK national average (Table 5.3). This may be linked to Scotland's strong tradition of encouragement for voluntary community development initiatives and "grass-roots" organizations. Many organizations have owed their existence to local authority funding, and have long been heavily reliant upon this source. Local government reorganization in the 1990s raises similar concerns for such organizations to those experienced by GLC-funded groups in London in the mid-1980s.

One particularly clear distinction from the rest of the UK emerges from considering patterns of overall statutory funding in Scotland. The UP has been particularly important in Scotland, accounting for around one-quarter of the sector's statutory income. This may have reflected a combination of local authority enthusiasm for voluntary projects, and the provision of incentives by central government in favour of this sector over schemes directly run by local authorities.

In terms of the provision of direct grants to the sector, the Scottish Office's contribution has been relatively small. In fact, relations between the Scottish Office and voluntary organizations in Scotland were not well developed during the 1980s, although this situation seems set to improve with the establishment of a "voluntary sector branch" in the Scottish Office in the early 1990s.

Northern Ireland

The civil disturbances in and unique political culture of Northern Ireland have added a further sharply contrasting dimension within the UK (Oliver, 1992). As in Scotland, there is no Charity Commission to frame the regulatory environment (see Chapter 3). Because of perceived sectarian abuse of local government powers, responsibility for the key human services has operated under central government auspices since 1972, administered by the local civil service but directly accountable to the UK government at Westminster. Some three-quarters of statutory funding for the sector originates from central government, making the latter uniquely powerful in the UK in Northern Ireland.

Oliver has identified nine contextual features which differentiated the sector in Northern Ireland in the early 1990s from the rest of the UK and the Republic of Ireland (see also Acheson and Williamson, 1995). *Inter alia*, these included: constitutional uncertainty; the "troubles" and sectarian violence; long-term and systematic deprivation, resulting in a mood of "both bitterness and resignation"; the suspension of civil rights, providing both an issue for and restriction on the sector; and the use of Northern Ireland as a test-bed for British legislation: rubber and plastic bullets, and political vetoing of recipients of government grant aid have all been "pioneered" in Northern Ireland. These features created a dynamic unique to the province, in which Oliver argues that a stultified state and atmosphere of stalemate led to a vacuum in which the "community development" wing of the sector in particular was able to flourish, seeking to foster non-partisan tolerance and mutual understanding (although prejudice and polarization also found expression under traditional sectarian voluntary organization auspices). The last two of Oliver's contextual features provided catalysts for the formation of single-issue civil rights groups probably unique in the UK to Northern Ireland. Many of these operated under the umbrella of the Committee on the Administration of Justice (CAJ), disseminating information and campaigning for change on such issues as plastic bullets, prisoners' rights and road closures in border areas (personal communication, 1994). Finally, the relationship between the Northern Ireland Office and the sector's national intermediary, the Northern Ireland Council for Voluntary Action (NICVA), compared favourably with the other countries. In particular, the Northern Ireland Office was responsive to NICVA's concern to include community development as a key part of the agenda in the development of central government-voluntary relations, in a manner not seen in other parts of the UK. One tangible outcome was a document, published in 1993, discussing community development strategies at some length (Northern Ireland Office, 1993).

5.6 Conclusion

While the rhetoric of "partnership" between the state and the voluntary sector in the early 1990s represented a strand of continuity with the 1970s and 1980s, many aspects of the general ideological climate in which voluntary organizations operated changed during the course of the latter decade. By the 1990s, the configuration of power within the "partnership" had changed markedly in a fashion unanticipated by the Wolfenden Committee. Driven at least in part by a commitment to new right ideology, central government had acquired new powers, local authorities were the target of sustained criticism and were subjected to new constraints from the centre, and trade unions were successfully marginalized. These changes were pushed through by a government often appearing to pride itself on its abrasive and *dirigiste* style (Marsh and Rhodes, 1992), and voluntary organizations, like other actors in the policy process, were often on the receiving end.

In reviewing relationships between the state and the voluntary sector, we have sought to capture some of the diversity that has characterized recent developments. A fascinating mix of interrelated ideological, political, social and economic factors was at play. It is clearly important to get beneath the ample rhetoric of "partnership" to develop an understanding of how the voluntary sector has actually experienced links with government. This is not to discount the symbolic function of rhetorical support, which has undoubtedly grown, for it helps to confer the legitimacy that is important in getting the sector onto the agenda as a recognizable and identifiable "island of meaning" (Zerubavel, 1991). For political parties, attempts to project an image of a coherent and consistent position towards a "voluntary sector" may also be an important tactical campaigning weapon (Kendall and 6, 1994), and may resonate nicely with ideological themes.

Yet our survey of the major funding programmes of central government suggests that — unsurprisingly, perhaps — the generalized rhetoric of "partnership" should certainly not be taken at face value. A fuller understanding of the recent relationship between government and the voluntary sector needs to deconstruct both, and deal with the particular political, economic and social circumstances that apply at the level of field of activity or policy community. There is no single over-arching explanation for state support, whether it is from central or local government. As far as *central* government is concerned, the provision of resources in the two largest programmes appears to have been motivated by different mixes of factors. In housing, the perceived ability to innovate and the opportunity to secure added value through the contribution of volunteer management committees appear to have been important. But the decision to invest so heavily in the sector has not been made in an ideological vacuum. The voluntary sector provided central government with the means to disempower local authorities in the housing field, and to broaden its own ambit of influence through the development of a tight regulatory regime.

In the case of special employment measures, important reasons for funding the voluntary sector have included perceived cost-effectiveness and specialist expertise. In addition, the German political scientist Wolfgang Seibel's characterisation of the sector as a "shunting yard" for "unsolvable" social problems (cf. Chapter 1, p.14) appears to have particular relevance here (although, of course, those of a more optimistic Keynesian persuasion would take issue with the argument that unemployment fell into this category). It would certainly be naive to interpret the government's motivation for injecting huge sums of money into this area in the early and mid-1980s as independent of political advertising or "statecraft". The relative importance of this motive is suggested by the speed with which the government was prepared to withdraw financial support in the late 1980s and early 1990s or switch it to the public sector as the political and economic climate changed, in spite of the insistence of many voluntary organizations that the need for their contribution remained. This experience, together with the problems created by the withdrawal of Urban Programme funds, created considerable resentment and cynicism among many voluntary organizations. It also suggests that, in these particular fields, voluntary organizations remained very much at the behest of government, to the extent that the "partnership" label appears at best an innocuous distraction and at worst dangerously misleading.

We explore the specific factors that apply in the fields in which local government incurs most expenditure — education and social services — in the chapters that follow. But we can reiterate here that, despite fiscal constraints from central government, *local authorities* did manage to protect and nurture a diverse — albeit patchy — tradition of both "grant" and "contract" funding in the 1980s. Yet it should always be recalled that the vast bulk of services continued to be delivered according to the "welfare statist" model of state funding and delivery. The most recent survey of funding trends — for 1992/3 (Mocroft, 1995) — shows that this patterns appears to have been preserved in the year prior to full implementation of the radical reforms in social services.

A widespread feeling current in the early 1990s was that the diversity of funding that existed in the 1980s would be increasingly hard to sustain moving into the late 1990s. In a climate of fiscal uncertainty — aggravated by moves to restructure local government — attempts by local government and voluntary bodies to plan and develop long-term strategies could, it was feared, be undermined. For example, there were very real concerns that grant funding which we have seen has mostly come from local, not central government — might be regarded as a "soft target" in times of fiscal retrenchment. In contrast, Wilson and Game were more optimistic, arguing that the extant infrastructure of support for voluntary organizations "will not be easily dismantled: It has a dynamism and strength of its own" (1994, p.292). Until further surveys of local authority funding trends are undertaken, we do not know whether extensive infrastructural and grant support has continued to survive into the late 1990s.

As we shall describe in Chapter 7, in the mid- to late 1990s voluntary organizations are being presented with new opportunities to secure contract funding from the state in "quasi-market" situations in the field of social service provision in particular. While this represents a new departure from the previous decade in this field in terms of the dramatic increase in the extent to which voluntary sector providers are now delivering mainstream welfare services, it is also important to recognize that this has been preceded by the extensive recent history of state funding that we have charted in some detail here. Batsleer and Paton (1993) point out that the UP and special employment programmes of the 1980s generated many tensions for organizations "forced" into a close relationship with the state. The new emphasis on contracts in social care, they argue, "may throw the issues of autonomy and dependence in statutory-voluntary relations into sharp focus, but they are certainly not *new* issues". It would be surprising if the experiences of the 1980s do not hold at least some lessons for organizations confronting similar challenges in the late 1990s, albeit in rather different contexts and fields of activity.

Notes

1 The polemical style of some of the UK writing in this field has strengths and weaknesses compared to the drier North American academic analyses, dominated by economists, whose paradigms have come to dominate the international research scene in recent years (cf. Chapter 1; Evers, 1993, 1995).

2 "New left" and then "new right" structural critiques were important *undercurrents* throughout the 1960s and the early 1970s (Holmwood, 1993). References to a welfare state "crisis" were beginning to call existing assumptions and institutional arrangements into question, portraying the state as inappropriately "paternalistic", and marshalling evidence that major problems of poverty, need and social exclusion persisted. Many on the left and right alike railed against the sense of "dependency" supposedly induced by reliance on "bureaucracy", often uncritically equated with the "grey uniformity" of state provision. Yet radical critiques of this sort made relatively little impact on the political mainstream and the approach taken by national governments up until the late 1970s, when the ideas of the new right in particular were to come to prominence.

3 No mention was made in the report of voluntary providers' continued major presence in education (see Chapter 6) — as these institutions were ruled out under the Committee's narrow working definition.

4 These trends *exclude* large elements of public funding of the broad voluntary sector, most importantly the financing of universities and maintained voluntary schools. The figures also exclude funding provided by arts quangos and the National Health Service, for which data are available for some years only. It should be noted that whereas the former funding is excluded under the narrow definition identified in Chapter 1 and deployed in Chapter 4, the latter is included, and represented the major components of central government funding of culture and arts, and health, in 1990.

5 In our explorations of the available data on housing associations, we came across a very large difference between the amount actually received by housing associations in housing association grant (HAG) according to the Housing Corporation data which we used to map the sectors in 1990 (see Chapter 4 and Appendix 1); and the year-on-year data reported in *Hansard* which underpin Figure 5.1. This is thought to be primarily because the latter figures include funds committed over several years but not actually spent ("forecast approvals"), and possibly also private matching funding for the HAG. This finance is excluded from the government funding figures in Chapter 4.

6 The Housing Corporation operates in England; Wales and Scotland have their own housing quangos, Housing for Wales and Scottish Homes, while the movement's funding in Northern Ireland is administered by the Department of the Environment in that country.

7 The Manpower Services Commission (MSC), delivering the Community Programme and Youth Opportunity Programme, was the first agency to channel public finance towards the sector, and presided over the major expansion of government funding in the early 1980s. It evolved into the Training Commission, and then the Training Agency, delivering renamed Employment Training and Youth Training, which aimed to give more emphasis to training for re-entry into the labour market, rather than simply creating jobs *per se*. The new network of Training and Enterprise Councils (TECs) (Local Enterprise Councils in Scotland) took over responsibility in the early 1990s.

8 Data are not available after 1990/91, when a network of 82 TECs were established in England and Wales by government (see below).

9 The figures below do not include central government's 75 percent contribution to revenue costs and 100 percent contribution to capital costs in those local authorities which received Urban Programme funds (see above).

10 Problems of non-response bias mean that we should probably not set too much stall by year-on-year changes but, taken as a whole, the evidence does suggest considerable growth. It should also be noted that National Council for Voluntary Organisations surveys in England in the early 1990s appeared to show that local authority funding across the country was actually falling (Mabbott, 1992b, 1993). However, the methodology of these surveys is open to considerable doubt and the sample sizes were small. While there are problems with the CAF survey, it still remains the best source of information available on local authority

funding as a whole, although separate information is also available from statutory sources on funding by SSDs and LEAs. (Chapter 7 uses these statutory sources — returns made by local authorities to the Department of the Environment — in noting the scale of SSD expenditure alone in 1990/91.)

11 If funding of maintained voluntary schools were included, the figure would be closer to 8 percent.

12 Outside England, the territorial ministries — the Scottish Office, Welsh Office and Northern Ireland Office — take local responsibility for implementing central government policy, sometimes performing some functions of local government. They add a layer of complexity to central-local government relations (Hampton, 1991). As Rhodes (1988, p.143) observes, although these "cannot be described as the governments of the peripheral nations", as their heads are members of the British Cabinet which leads the British government, they do operate with a significant degree of policy discretion as a result of their access to a variety of legal, organizational, informational and political resources. However, it also needs to be emphasized that they remain "a constituent unit of [UK] central government", and it has been shown that "concurrent policies" account for the overwhelming bulk of public expenditure and employment (Rose, 1982, cited in Rhodes, 1988).

Chapter 6

EDUCATION

6.1 Introduction

In Chapter 4, we noted that the largest single field of broad voluntary sector activity in the UK is education and research, but the schools and universities that account for the bulk of this activity are usually not considered to be part of the "voluntary sector" in the taken-for-granted usage of that term. Furthermore, it is also clear that *within* the "mixed economy" of educational provision, the sector has a highly signficant presence — accounting for practically all higher educational provision, and more than one in five of all pupils in primary and secondary education (see Table 4.5, p.128).

This account is much more weighted towards historical description than our other chapter with a specific field focus, Chapter 7, which deals with health and social care. There are three main reasons for this relative emphasis. First, our general historical account in Chapter 2 was oriented more towards the narrow definition of the sector, and thus devoted relatively little attention to education. Second, while research on the sector's role in social services in particular has proliferated in recent years, as evidenced by the extensive evidence we are able to marshall in Chapter 7 below, modern research on schools *qua* voluntary bodies has been extremely thin on the ground. Third, voluntary education provision is still dominated by entities with deep historical roots. If there is a single industry where a case can be made that the legacy of history weighs particularly heavily, then it is undoubtedly the education field. We concentrate here on primary and secondary education.[1]

6.2 Historical development: medieval origins to the 19th century

In the education field, a number of institutions still operating today can claim origins stretching back well into medieval times. Prominent examples include the King's School, Canterbury, which has some claim to being the oldest school in the country and even the world. Co-founded as part of St Augustine's mission to England in 597, it was acting as model for other schools by the late 7th century (Maltby, 1993). Winchester and Eton colleges — prominent "public schools" (see discussion of the 19th century below) — were established several centuries later in the 14th and 15th centuries respectively.

Yet these high-profile institutions were by no means isolated examples of medieval educational endeavour. As early as the second half of the 13th century, elementary and grammar school education was being provided in 60 places in England under both secular and Church auspices (Hibbert, 1987). By the 15th century, there were between 300 and 400 grammar schools in England. New schools were often established by successful local entrepreneurs and relied on endowment income to support "free" provision, or provision for poor students for whose education they were specifically founded. Yet even when it was private benefactors rather than the church which founded schools, the latter's influence was pervasive, reflecting the penetration of religious thinking as an animating impulse deeply ingrained in medieval belief systems. Gay maintains that the church effectively "retained an absolute control of education", manifested in practical terms through control of the licensing of teachers — and most teachers were clergymen (1985, p.5).

The Church of England was to remain hegemonic well beyond the medieval era, reflecting its constitutionally prescribed role as the state religion. It exercised control over the teaching profession until the 18th century, when restrictions on dissenters' rights to teach were first relaxed and then repealed (Smelser, 1991). "Free places" in these schools were often only provided for the poor on the condition that they were members of the Church of England (Gay, 1985). In practice, they were usually not limited to providing "free" education to those of limited means. Hibbert (1987) suggests that, as with medieval foundations, many of these schools actually charged at least nominal fees, and some had complex pricing regimes linked to the social status of parents. By the end of the 16th century, there was evidence that the most famous institutions, including Eton and Winchester, were predominantly catering for the relatively wealthy, despite the spirit of their founding constitutions (Moffat, 1989).

While the state Church dominated the educational scene, it did not have a complete monopoly. For example, 30 "dissenting academies" founded by puritan clergy dispelled from the church were operating by the end of the 16th century, and 15 Quaker boarding schools had been established by 1671. In the early part of the century, these schools struggled to operate both because of the general legal restrictions on non-Anglican entities that existed at the time (Picarda, 1995), and the Anglican Church's control of the teaching professions. By the late 18th century, however, many middle-class Anglican parents had joined their dissenting peers in sending their children to institutions run by dissenters, which were able to expand in the more tolerant political environment that had emerged. Although dissenters still only accounted for a small minority of the population, they were to make a disproportionate impact in the educational world, since their establishments had apparent advantages over many of the traditional endowed Anglican grammar schools in terms of cost, curricula, respectability and discipline (Sutherland, 1990).

Yet while many in the middle class had begun to seek a different style of secondary education, an elite group of nine Anglican foundations (including Eton and Winchester) now stood out as providers of schooling for the very highest echelons of society. Although true to the wishes of their founders in concentrating on the provision of an Anglican, classically-based education, their constitutional commitments to educate the local poor were widely ignored, and most had developed into boarding schools attended predominantly by the wealthy from all over the country.

The largest area of actual growth in the charitable sector in the 18th century occurred through the innovation of collective support by the middle classes for schooling targeted purely on the working classes (Owen, 1964). This associative philanthropy, given institutional expression first through the charity school and then the Sunday school movement, tended not to rely on individual endowments (although this was an important resource for some schools), but rather on the collective contributions of the thousands of subscribers who made up the membership of local committees. The charity school movement has been characterized as a response by the Anglican and dissenting middle classes to the perceived threat posed by irreligion and Catholicism to the existing social order (Owen, 1964, p.24). The schools were to be "pious nurseries of godly discipline", combating improvidence and irreligion through the inculcation of appropriate Protestant moral attitudes. The movement was given particular impetus by the establishment of the Society for the Promotion of Christian Knowledge (SPCK) in 1699, comprising an "effective fusion of bishops, lower clergy and laity" (ibid., p.23). By 1729, 1,419 charity schools were providing for over 22,000 pupils in England alone (the movement also had an impact in other parts of the UK). However, the schools never achieved universal coverage. Although the SPCK gave the movement a national focus, the schools themselves were essentially local in character, and their foundation and operation were largely dependent upon the availability of local middle-class leadership and patronage, as well as a ready supply of local teaching staff.

The Sunday school movement was the other major example of 18th century associative philanthropy, emerging towards the end of the century and mushrooming well into the next. Like the charity school movement, these schools had narrow curricula by modern standards, concentrating on religious instruction and reading. They also had a national intermediary body, the Sunday School Society, run as an ecumenical venture with board membership split evenly between Anglicans and Nonconformists. By the middle of the 19th century, 23,135 schools were educating over two million children: three-quarters of all working-class children aged between five and fifteen (Brown, 1991a).

While educational provision was structured by, and served

to exaggerate, status distinctions prior to the industrial revolution, as the latter gathered momentum during the early 19th century this became more clearly the case than ever before. While status distinctions are important in all societies, sociologist Neil Smelser has commented that education in 19th century British society is of particular interest because

education [was] probably as finely and self-consciously differentiated by social class as [it] has been at any other time or place...the idea of class hierarchy was — and has been, and is — central as a primordial principle and organizing basis in British society (Smelser, 1991, p.2).

As "primordial dimensions", both class and religion can be regarded, not as the "sole determinants" of the structure of education, but as "constitut[ing] 'givens' within which Britain's educational system evolved". The notion of primordiality seeks to convey the idea of their essentiality within dominant systems of belief, and the subsequent deployment as organizing concepts within that society; they acted as "fundamental cultural values or beliefs that [were] the first premises for organizing and legitimizing institutions, roles and behaviour" (ibid., p.39).

By the middle of the Victorian era, the "fact" of status differentiation in schooling was so taken for granted that it was formalized in the agendas of the various education commissions. The investigation of each was focused on the education of a specific social class or classes. This was also very much a "mixed economy" of education, to use current jargon, and one in which the voluntary and private sectors were the major players. The only direct state provision prior to the introduction of board schools under the 1870 Education Act (see below) was in workhouse schools for paupers. "Dame schools", for example, were effectively private sector entities (small for-profit businesses run by women) operated alongside charitable sector day schools in providing for the working classes. Below, we consider developments in voluntary sector provision for the working classes, before looking at its role in school education for middle and upper classes.

19th century provision for the working classes

Into the early 19th century, the existing provision of working-class education in charity and Sunday schools was supplemented and then gradually superseded by full-time day schools.[2] Significantly, education was the first field of voluntary sector endeavour to attract large-scale inputs of state funding, and it was this particular set of institutions which was the primary beneficiary of governmental largesse.[3] However, the path to the partnership between central state, local state and voluntary sector in elementary educational provision which was to be given legislative force by the 1902 Education Act was halting, ideologically fraught, politically highly charged and extremely complex.

It was halting in the sense that Britain was relatively slow compared to other countries in Europe, and to the US, in establishing universal tax-funded compulsory education. And it was fraught and complex because it involved conflict and compromise between the state, the state church, the various Protestant Nonconformist groupings and the Roman Catholic Church. All the denominations saw elementary education as a fundamental component of their wider strategies for preserving or enhancing their own influence within society, and plans for educational expansion often emerged as a direct and explicit response to the activities of rivals. Commentaries on this period are replete with references to antagonism, bitterness and squabbling between the various denominations and the state, and disputes over education tended to "spill over" from the vexed religious controversies that dominated political debate at the time (Smith, 1936; Sutherland, 1990; Smelser, 1991; Pugh, 1993).

The most significant development at the start of the century was the foundation of two national organizations, the British and Foreign School Society (BFSS, in 1811) and the National Society for Promoting the Education of the Poor in the Principles of the Established Church (in 1814). Like the national bodies of the previous century, they existed to provide "stimulation and assistance" to schools, which in turn relied on a ready supply of local middle-class enthusiasts for most of their sponsorship. Both viewed moral and religious education as at the core of their curriculum, although with different emphases (Francis, 1993).

These networks initially grew entirely independently of any financial support from public funds. However, despite this apparent success, by the second quarter of the century the case for a more proactive state was being promoted by reformist individuals and pressure groups across the religious divide. *Inter alia*, surveys of provision in the north west of England appeared to show that the combined efforts of the voluntary and private sectors had left large swathes of the working class entirely untouched or with wholly inadequate provision (as measured by the surveyors' own standards). These arguments were bolstered with opinions among many middle-class commentators that the *status quo* in the UK was characterized by underinvestment in human capital, and that efficiency gains would result from public funding, following the example of foreign governments (Smith, 1936). Many of the arguments, in modern terminology, amount to contemporaries' recognition of the pervasiveness of "voluntary failures" — especially philanthropic particularism and insufficiency (cf. Salamon, 1987; see Chapter 1).

However, there was by no means consensus on this issue. Some saw any education as a dangerous enterprise likely to destabilize society, echoing critics of 18th century charity schools. Across the denominational divide, many still felt that the state had no business in "interfering" with the "moral and religious matter" of education; Nonconformists in particular were often dedicated "voluntaryists", adhering to the doctrine of *laissez-faire* in education as in other areas of social policy (cf. Chapter 2). They feared that state funding would inevitably be used to perpetuate the existing strength of the state church in education.

The net result of these pressures for continuity and change, played out within and outside Parliament, was a rather timid initial contribution of just £20,000 by the state in 1833. Moreover, funds were initially provided purely in support of the two existing societies, came with very few strings attached, and involved no attempt to rectify the insufficiency and particularism which characterized the existing pattern of supply. If anything, the scheme made matters worse, since support was provided "in aid of private subscriptions" (what today would be described as "matching funding" for capital projects). The result was that the National Society accessed four-fifths of the available funding

— a *de facto* favouring of Anglican provision which appeared to confirm Nonconformist voluntaryists' reservations. The latter were further aggravated by Anglicans' success in blocking reform in 1839, when the established church exploited its bishops' votes in the House of Lords to frustrate legislation that had passed through the House of Commons successfully (Gash, 1965).

This was, however, to prove a relatively short-lived victory for reactionary Anglicanism. A central government body with responsibility for national education was established, which succeeded in reforming the existing system through initiating the principle of inspection in publicly-funded schools; introducing measures to rationalize the grant-making system; and negotiated access to state funds for an enlarged grouping of denominational coordinating bodies, including those representing Methodists and Catholics. The inspectorate was to occupy an extremely powerful position in the late 19th century with the introduction of an incentive payment scheme, in which schools were partly funded according to the rate at which their pupils were able to pass exams set by the inspectorate itself. Yet the availability of these funds from the state, albeit on these apparently harsh terms, was critical in enabling the denominations to sustain their expansive school systems.

During the early 19th century, the country underwent the transition from a Confessional state characterized by Anglican hegemony to pluralist denominationalism (Brown, 1991b). Connected with this trend was the opening up of access to political office to non-Anglicans (although the Anglican Church was to remain the "established church" in England, and has retained certain constitutional privileges to this day, including its representation in the House of Lords). With the state now less obviously purely the instrument of the Anglican establishment, the way was clear, particularly in the eyes of Nonconformists, for the promotion of a proactive state as a force for the national good. Furthermore, the widening of the electoral franchise was seen as requiring that all voters be appropriately educated (Thane, 1982); human capital or "nation-building" arguments were restated with renewed vigour in the face of foreign competition; and in this context the official Newcastle Commission, published in 1861, reiterated the problem of "areas of educational destitution", directing attention to the existence of geographical unevenness once again. Legislation designed to address this problem finally came into force with the 1870 Education Act. Gladstone's Liberal government guaranteed continued central government funding for voluntary schools, but also allowed for the creation of schools run on a statutory basis by boards controlled by central government. These schools, the first to be fully controlled by the public sector in mainstream provision, were to be funded by both central and local government (through local taxation) in order to fill the gaps where existing voluntary provision was insufficient, thus ensuring universal coverage.[4]

A final shift to the "dual system" — involving not only central government and the main churches, but a leading role for elected local government — took place with the 1902 Education Act of Balfour's Conservative administration. Voluntary schools retained considerable autonomy, but also accepted increased influence from the new local authorities, with one-third of schools' managers (i.e. governors) now to be local education authority (LEA) appointees. The remaining two-thirds, "foundation managers", were to continue to be appointed in accordance with the founding trust. In return for accepting local state representation, schools received a significant boost in funding. Local government, supported by a population- and attendance-based specific grant from central government, was to finance voluntary schools' running costs in full. The specific aim was to make up the quality deficit which appeared to have emerged between the new gap-filling local authority schools and voluntary schools since the 1870 Act (Thane, 1982).

Yet again, reform was to create intense denominational squabbles and bitterness, this time between Anglicans and the Catholics on the one hand, and Nonconformists on the other. In the late 19th century, the Catholic community had rapidly built up its own extensive network of schools with the support of the central government grant programme, and Anglican and Catholic schools now dominated voluntary provision. Many Nonconformists objected vehemently to "subsidizing" these schools through taxation "on the grounds that public funds, in meeting so preponderant a part in the financing of voluntary schools, were in effect being used to subsidize the propagation of the dogmas of particular churches" (Cmd 6458, 1943). While the children of Nonconformists who had no choice but to attend an

Anglican or Catholic school because they were in "single school areas" were legally entitled to opt out of religious education and corporate worship, teaching staff were still typically required to be members of the relevant denomination, and the law effectively allowed schools to cultivate a denominational ethos.

19th century middle- and upper-class education

With the growth of denominationalism, the 19th century also witnessed a proliferation of non-Anglican schools for the middle classes, including those linked to other faith groups (most conspicuously, the expanding Catholic and Methodist Churches), as well as schools run on secular lines. Yet while the Anglican Church may have lost considerable influence during the course of the 1800s in society as a whole, it was to remain the dominant religion for the elite, and this had implications for the education system. The nine "classical public" schools continued to operate, as in the 18th century, as providers of very expensive — predominantly boarding — Anglican education for upper-class clienteles, and the endowed (also primarily Anglican) "grammar schools" established in previous eras provided education for the local middle classes.

A major 19th century development in education was the foundation of a new generation of schools, partly modelled on the prestigious elitist Anglican foundations. In many of these schools a combination of high fees and social selectivity aimed to sustain schools' reputations for exclusiveness, thus ensuring parents got the "product" they required. As far as the new Anglican foundations for the middle class were concerned, there was no equivalent to the National Society and its coordinating role in educating the poor. The Anglican schools catering primarily for the middle and upper classes were not formally linked to the church's infrastructure in any way (Gay, 1985, p.22); instead, individual moral entrepreneurs (cf. Chapter 2), or groups of like-minded individuals with strongly-held Anglican convictions, tended to act autonomously in founding and running individual schools, or attempting to develop networks of schools. A particularly prominent example in boys' education was Nathaniel Woodard, who saw his schools as principled responses to the ongoing structural changes in British society (see Box 6.1). Woodard and others sought to bolster the strength of their own particular strand of

---

Box 6.1   Nathaniel Woodard, a 19th century "moral entrepreneur" in middle-class charitable education

Nathaniel Woodard, an Anglo-Catholic, had the extremely ambitious plan of establishing nationally a "triple hierarchy" of schools, with each layer corresponding to a tier of the middle class to supplement the existing provision for upper-class Anglicans historically provided by Eton, Winchester and Harrow in particular. Rhetorically, the explicit objective was to "get possession of the Middle Classes, especially the lower section of them" (cited in Bamford, 1967, p.30), fashioning his pupils into "instruments of national salvation". The ongoing forces of change associated with the Industrial Revolution were seen as potentially catastrophic, particularly the perceived secularization of society. His antidote — Anglican regeneration in the high church mould — was to be achieved via his pupils. These would become "cells of influence" within the increasingly powerful middle classes. In reality, Woodard was rather more pragmatic, accepting and tolerating pupils from other traditions into his schools, although catechism-based religious education occupied a central part of the curriculum, and high church ritual and even confession all featured in his schools.

Anglicanism and saw control of middle-class education as at least as important as control of education for the working class.

While state intervention in schooling for the working classes had taken the form of increasingly specific grant support, its interest in middle-class provision was initially purely regulatory. The Endowed Schools Act of 1869 was significant in pioneering large-scale state regulatory intervention in the charitable field where this was deemed to be "in the national interest". Extensive powers to "rationalize" the system so as to create a coherent system of middle-class education were granted to government officials. Broadly, the aim was to encourage schools to so "modernize" as to meet the perceived demands of particular subcategories of the middle class, if necessary by allowing state appointees to remodel their constitutions. Schools for the upper middle classes (including professionals) were to retain a strong bias towards classical education, while those in the lower middle class were to orient themselves towards modern subjects and the basic education deemed appropriate for tradesmen, farmers and clerks, for example. The "modernization" involved a long and drawn-out rolling programme of schemes introduced on a school-by-school basis.

Yet while the 1869 Act and subsequent legislation had been framed with the hope that a national secondary school system for the middle classes could be moulded merely by regulation and without recourse to public finance, by the end of the century it was widely accepted that this had not been achieved. The successes of the joint attempts by regulators and the voluntary and private schools themselves were acknowledged to be patchy at best, and incomplete in terms of geographical coverage (Sutherland, 1990, p.151). Balfour's 1902 Education Act therefore made secondary education a statutory responsibility, although fees were still charged. As with elementary schooling for the working classes, the purpose was to capitalize on the existing efforts of the voluntary sector, with the state acting primarily in a "gap-filling capacity" in terms of its own direct provision. Existing secondary schools in the voluntary sector had the option of either remaining entirely independent of state funding (though subject to its regulatory oversight), or receiving local and/or central state funding.

6.3 The early to mid-20th century

At the start of the 20th century, the voluntary sector was still the principal provider of primary and secondary education.[5] But by the outbreak of the Second World War, the picture had changed dramatically. Outside of the elite educated in the charitable public and preparatory[6] schools, direct "gap-filling" provision by the state overtook voluntary sector supply at both the elementary (or primary) and secondary levels in the early years of the 20th century (Cmd 6548, 1943).

As far as *primary* education was concerned, the pattern of development in the voluntary sector was, however, very different according to denominational auspice. The falling overall contribution of the sector was largely a reflection of the closure of Church of England facilities, or their transfer to the local state: the number of Anglican schools fell by 25 percent, from approximately 12,000 to 9,000 between the start of the century and the outbreak of war (Howard, 1987, p.112).

During this period the churches were apparently experiencing increasing financial difficulty in sustaining their school networks (Francis, 1993). While able to rely on local government to fund their current expenditure, schools were struggling to fund the capital and repair programmes which both politicians and civil servants regarded as increasingly urgent. The precise cause of the financial problems is unclear. It can be conjectured that recessionary pressures in the wider economy (most prominently in the early 1930s) and the expansion of the state's tax base would have made their mark through affecting church members' disposable income and thus their ability to give. In the case of Anglicanism and Nonconformity, the ongoing decline in church membership and the fading of Evangelicalism within Protestantism (Obelkewich, 1990) presumably had a major effect. As their membership base contracted, the number of potential Anglican and Nonconformist supporters would have fallen, and the waning of Evangelical enthusiasm among those who continued to adhere to Protestantism may conceivably have affected their willingness to give.

The position of the Catholic Church, was very different in the early part of the 20th century: their provision actually *increased* from approximately 1,000 to 1,200 schools between 1900 and the outbreak of war. The growth of the Catholic school network was a direct response from the church authorities to the continued expansion of the Catholic working-class population, contrasting sharply with the experience of the Protestant denominations. This was driven primarily by the influx of Irish immigrants into urban locales in the north of England. Norman (1985) argues that the administrative skills of the clergy leadership were critical in enabling the church to build up this segregated system. Since the mid-19th century the Catholic Church in England, following guidance from Rome, had seen the development of a separate network of schools as an integral part of Catholicism and imperative for ensuring the protection of Catholic identity. This was assumed to be a direct corollary of Catholic social theory, wherein access to Catholic education was regarded as a "right" of Catholic parents under "natural law" (Coman, 1977). Schools were controlled by Catholic orders or came under diocesan bishops' trusteeship, with management boards typically chaired by the local parish priest. However, notwithstanding the apparently heroic fundraising programmes of the Catholic community, by the 1930s their contributions, like those of the other denominations, were still proving insufficient to allow them to maintain and modernize their schools along the lines favoured by politicians and civil servants.

Secondary education was still only experienced by a minority in society in the early 20th century. At this level, the expanded "public" school elite, now numbering somewhere between 30 or 40 (primarily boarding) schools,[7] was socially prominent. These schools remained formally almost completely free of direct state control. The only involvement with the state was the one-off investigation recommended by the 1918 Education Act, but this was a "timid affair" (Bamford, 1967, p.287) and the schools operated without any regular inspection or regulation. A further noteworthy feature of the inter-war period was the development of a coherent ideological critique of these institutions. The leading social theorist of the Labour movement, R.H. Tawney, set a precedent for the left by criticizing the role played by the "comically misnamed" public schools in perpetuating inequality, privilege and class antagonism, and advocated their abolition (Thane, 1982).

A major innovation in the early years of the 20th century was a massive expansion in the physical provision of state-funded secondary day schooling for those outside the privileged elite. At the political level, the growth of the Labour movement was an important force for change, and the widening of educational opportunity for the working classes was a key element of the Labour Party's programme during the 1920s and 1930s. Local education authorities exploited their new powers under the 1902 Balfour Act to build up their own secondary provision (later to become known as "county" schools), or fund voluntary sector establishments to do likewise. However, most schools (in both sectors) still charged fees, and the middle classes were the main beneficiaries. Working-class access was typically dependent on free or low-cost provision, and this could be secured (in either state or voluntary schools) only through their own academic scholarships, or state subsidy, usually predicated on pupils' abilities to pass competitive scholarship tests.

In 1926, circular 1381 ruled that voluntary schools could receive grant funding either as "direct grant" schools from central government, or as "maintained schools" from local government, though not from both tiers. The "financial difficulties" of many schools meant that this state funding was regarded as a welcome lifeline, although many expressed fears that this would "compromise their independence" or "dilute" their social character, which remained a key feature of their "product" (Smith, 1936). In particular, the fact that support from public funds was contingent on accepting a certain percentage of children who had previously attended a local authority-funded elementary school, and were often from lower-class backgrounds, was of great concern in some schools.

The years between the Second World War and the late 1970s were to witness unprecedented growth in public expenditure on all tiers of education as the number of full-time pupils (across all sectors) in primary and secondary education increased. The voluntary sector schools were to be beneficiaries of this state largesse, but the direct provision by the local state that had come to dominate prior to the war was to expand still further at the expense of voluntary sector provision. Figure 6.1 shows the dramatic increase in pupil numbers that occurred during this period, and how these were differentially absorbed by each sector.

The 1944 Education Act was benchmark legislation for the school system as a whole, and the place of the sector within it, setting the parameters within which it would operate for the next 45 years (Box 6.2). Voluntary schools were presented with the option of either receiving continued funding, but on modified terms, or of complete financial independence from the state. In

---

Box 6.2   The 1944 Education Act

This Act "was a continuation and completion of the considerable inter-war changes" (Thane, 1982). It allowed for schools directly controlled by the churches and other voluntary bodies to be funded by the state within the "maintained" system, as well as permitting the continuation of private fee-funded "independent" education. The churches also ensured that religious worship and education were mandated in *all* maintained schools, although in county (local authority-run) schools, "neither the corporate act of worship nor the religious instruction required to be given [could] include any catechism or formulary distinctive of any particular religious denomination". The syllabus for religious education was to be decided jointly in each authority by representatives of the churches, teachers and the local authority.

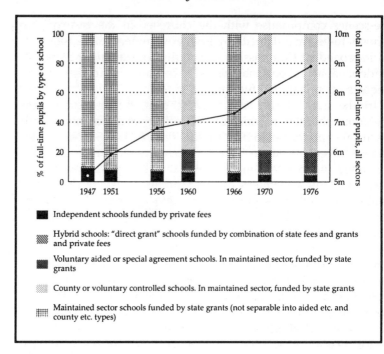

Figure 6.1 Full-time pupils by school type, England, 1947-1976

Sources: Totals for independent/direct grant schools for 1966-1976 from DES (1991, table A30/90). Maintained sector totals, 1947-1976 from DES (1991, table A30/90). Split outside maintained sector between independent and direct grant school pupil numbers for 1951-1976 estimated using Walford (1990, table 1). England and Wales ratio of independent sector: direct grant sector pupils for 1961 and 1971 used to estimate ratio for England only for 1960 and 1970. Split within maintained sector between school type from DES (1982, table A12/81). Proportion in independent and direct grant schools for 1947 from Glennerster and Wilson (1970, table 2.1).

effect they could choose to operate either within a tax-funded "maintained" sector in close cooperation with local government, disallowed from charging fees; or they could opt for private or quasi-private status, as part of an "independent sector" still predominantly dependent upon private resources. The politician responsible for creating the new system, Conservative R.A. Butler operating within the context of a war-time coalition cabinet, had adopted a very different strategy in his negotiations to secure reform with existing providers in each case. He opted for behind-the-scenes compromise with the churches in the case of the schools to be "maintained" by local government, but appointed an independent Commission of Enquiry to examine the case of "independent" schools that wished to continue relying to varying degrees on private fee funding.

In the case of the *maintained* schools, Butler devised an ingenious solution in which a trade-off between autonomy and financial support was to be offered to each school. Schools could choose to become either "aided" or "controlled". Aided schools remained independent in the sense that the governing board, dominated by appointees of the founding trust, retained full control of admissions policy, staff appointments, curricula (in secondary schools), religious education and use of school buildings. The price they paid for this autonomy was a major contribution to capital costs (initially 50 percent, subsequently reduced in response to church lobbying), although current costs were to be fully funded by the local state. Alternatively, controlled schools could have both their capital and current costs borne by the state, but at the price of a huge loss of operational autonomy and effective absorption into the local state. If this option was pursued, the founding trust lost its majority representation in the school's governance, and decisions with regard to pupils, staffing, curricula and use of buildings were to be matters for the local education authority, although governors did retain some residual rights as far as staffing and religious education were concerned.[8]

While Butler's proposal secured the support, with relative ease, of the Anglican Church and then Nonconformists with whom he confidentially discussed the matter in the first instance, it was strongly opposed by the Roman Catholic Church to whom it was presented, some months later, as a *fait accompli*.[9] In spite of these protests, Butler's proposals eventually reached the statute books substantially unmodified. This "typical British compromise or more bluntly, muddle" (Howard, 1987, p.111) was to operate relatively free of political controversy over subsequent decades, at least in comparison to the heated debates over fee-paying education (see below). Despite local tensions between schools' rights to determine their own admissions and local authorities' plans to phase out academic selectivity in the context of the introduction of "comprehensive education" in the maintained sector from the 1950s onwards, the issue rarely surfaced in national debate as concerning these schools *qua* voluntary bodies; rather, the discussion tended to be couched in terms of arguments for and against academic selection, regardless of institutional sector.[10]

In addition, the relatively low political profile of aided schools reflected their reduced contribution within the maintained sector as a whole. The "market share" of the maintained voluntary sector as measured by pupils and schools was now much lower than it had been historically: by the 1960s and early 1970s its share of all full-time pupils was fluctuating between 14 and 15 percent (Figure 6.1). However, as with trends prior to the 1944 Act, it is vital to distinguish between the two principle denominations in interpreting these figures.

Over the period 1940 to 1970, the proportion of pupils in aided (or special agreement) Church of England schools fell from approximately 20 percent to below 6 percent. This partly reflects the absorption of most of its existing schools into the local state, since two-thirds of schools opted for voluntary controlled status, in which, as we have seen, the church exerted only a residual influence through minority representation on relatively weak governing bodies. In contrast, Catholic aided school provision witnessed sustained growth well into the latter half of the 20th century, including the creation of an extensive network of secondary schools.[11]

What factors explain these very different denominational trends? While the relative decline of Anglican schools may be in part linked to continued decline in church membership (see Kendall and Taylor, 1996), three other points are worth noting. First and most obviously, Anglicanism was, in the immediate post-war years at least, itself part of the dominant culture and value system. With Anglican values less distinctive within British society than Catholic values, the imperative of separate schools as protectors of identity was seen to be less relevant in the former case. Second, the social composition of each denomination may have had implications for the relative demand for maintained (tax-funded) and independent (fee-funded) school places. The concentration of Church of England membership in higher socio-economic groups suggests that proportionately more Anglican than Catholic parents may have chosen to opt out of the "maintained sector" entirely, and send their children to fee-paying schools, particularly at secondary level.

Third, Anglican leaders sought to exert influence in the educational field through means *other than* through their schools. While those Church of England schools which acquired voluntary controlled status were essentially transferred to local state control, some denominational input into religious teaching was still permitted under Butler's plan. Moreover, the church managed to ensure under the 1944 Act that *all* maintained schools — including those run entirely by the local state — should conduct a daily act of worship and provide religious education, to be determined locally through joint consultation. While worship and syllabi could not be denominational (see Box 6.2), Lankshear has suggested that in the case of religious education

no sophisticated distinction existed between the churches' confessional teaching and the schools' non-confessional teaching of religion. Many Anglicans therefore felt that the rationale behind teaching religion in county schools was so close to their own objectives that there was less need to retain church schools (1993, p.160)

The Catholic case was very different. Most obviously, the number of Roman Catholic adherents continued to rise into the 1950s and 1960s. The continued expansion of Catholic education in the mid-20th century, and the development of a secondary education system to supplement primary provision, was a response to the continued, perceived need by the leaders of that community to provide segregated education for its members right up until school leaving age.

As far as *independent* schools were concerned,[12] the 1944 Education Act was a landmark in leading to the introduction of a system of registration, which sought to establish minimum standards with regard to premises, teaching and staffing, although this was not fully operational until the late 1950s. However, the most significant potential effect of the Act was indirect, for at least three reasons. First, in upgrading the maintained sector and funding its expansion through taxation, the reforms threatened independent schools' viability by affecting disposable incomes, and hence parents' ability to pay private fees. Second, and less tangibly, numerous commentators have argued that the shared experiences of war, including evacuation, led to aspirations towards an amelioration of class divisions (cf. Goodin and Le Grand, 1987). Given the widely-made association between private fee-funded education and inequalities in society as a whole (theorized by Tawney and his successors, but more widely felt by the broader population), it was scarcely surprising that the schools felt apprehensive. Third, an improved and expanded maintained sector created new competition.

Over the thirty or so years that followed the Education Act, these schools experienced mixed fortunes. Figure 6.1 shows the proportion of all pupils attending independent and direct grant schools over the period. Overall there was a loss of "market share", with the percentage of all children educated independently falling from 10.2 in 1947 to 5.7 in 1976. However, as with the maintained voluntary sector, overall time trends data tend to conceal wide variations according to school type. In this case, it is not possible to analyse trends according to religious affiliation, but clear differences are apparent between the schools according to whether they were "public" schools, direct grant schools or other schools. The number of recognized "public" schools had swollen to 273 by the mid-1960s, and the number of places rose as admissions went up and sixth forms expanded. Direct grant schools also weathered the post-war storm, with the proportion of pupils hovering around the 1.5 percent mark. The casualties of change turned out to be schools *other than* the "public" and direct grant schools. Some 2,000 schools closed between 1951 and 1965 (Glennerster and Wilson, 1970), and there was a further net fall of over 1,000 establishments over the period to 1976 (DES, 1991, table A30/90, sheet 2). Glennerster and Wilson (1970, ch. 2) suggest that the third factor we noted above — "rising standards in the state schools" — was one of two key reasons for the relative decline of these schools. It has also been argued that "progressive" maintained primary schools in particular successfully diverted students into the state sector who would otherwise have attended independent schools (although significant numbers of these later transferred to the latter, particularly in the sixth form) (see Walford, 1990). The other effect highlighted by Glennerster and Wilson was central government's new regulatory regime, which may have forced some schools out of business, as well as presumably imposing additional costs on those that continued to operate.

Pressure for further reform was building up from the mid-1950s onwards. The apparent continued role of "public" schools in the perpetuation of the elite's privileged position in society — and consequently, the bolstering of class divisions — meant that they had become an "obsession" with the political left (Glennerster, 1995, p.179). Within the labour movement, some wanted to make the "public" schools, or independent schools as a whole, illegal, and then take them over — as had been done with most of the voluntary hospitals (see Chapter 7). Others felt that abolition would be electorally damaging, that their right to exist should be respected, with the way forward to move them from "isolation" into a relationship of "integration" with the maintained, putatively comprehensive sector (op. cit., p.179). In the event, proposals to secure this foundered in part on the grounds of cost and complexity. Furthermore, the charitable status of the schools themselves and the associated tax advantages they received as organizations were unaffected despite intense criticism of the inappropriateness of this privileged treatment.

The Labour Party's most significant reform was to come with regard to the quasi-private direct grant schools. With its formal commitment to comprehensive education, it was illogical to continue to support selective academic education in these schools with state funds. In the mid-1970s they were to be given the option of becoming fully funded by the local state — but reorganized comprehensively — or of retaining their selective character but losing direct state financial support.

Of the 172 schools with this status in 1975, 118 chose the independence option while 54 opted to become maintained voluntary aided comprehensive schools. Practically all the schools opting into the maintained system were Roman Catholic ones. This was to be expected since, as a group, they were far more reliant on state funding than the other direct grant schools, and tended to be less selective as far as academic criteria were concerned (Glennerster and Wilson, 1970, ch. 5). They therefore stood to keep more and lose less than other direct grant schools by retaining close links with the state. Furthermore, as aided voluntary schools, they were to continue to exercise control over the aspects of their operations that mattered most to them: the religious allegiance of pupils and teachers.

6.4 Recent developments: from the late 1970s to the mid-1990s

1976 was a turning point for two principal reasons. First, this was the year in which limiting public spending came to the top of the political agenda. Education was an obvious target. Second, the overall demand for school places across all provision fell back from this point onwards, although renewed growth began to emerge in the early 1990s (Figure 6.2). These factors were, of course, related. As Glennerster and Low comment, "education entered the bargaining arena in a poor strategic position. Whether in terms of a pure rational planning model or vote-loss mini-mizing, demography was not on its side" (1990, p.37). The other key turning points for the sector during this period have been 1979 and 1988. The former year saw the replacement of a Labour government ideologically hostile to private fee-paying education and generally against academically selective education with a Conservative government broadly supportive of both. More significantly, the Education Reform Act of 1988 and subsequent legislation introduced the most radical reforms since the 1944 Education Act, with major direct implications for the maintained voluntary sector and, more indirect but important, effects on independent schools.

As Figure 6.2 shows, the sector's share of the declining pupils total gradually crept up until 1990. By 1993, the figure had either fallen back or risen, depending crucially on whether grant main-tained schools and city technology colleges are treated as part of the voluntary sector or part of the state sector (see below).

At first sight, the relative growth of the voluntary sector's contribution appears somewhat surprising, since membership of both the Anglican and Catholic Churches –– the prime movers in voluntary sector education historically — has declined over this period. In the maintained sector, some aided schools did close where their traditional role was rendered unsustainable by a lack of denominational pupils or staff. There was a net decrease of over 600 aided and special agreement schools between 1976 and 1990. Yet others managed to survive while continuing to adhere, to varying extents, to an essentially denominational model. As far as Catholic schools were concerned, the church's leadership continued to argue that these

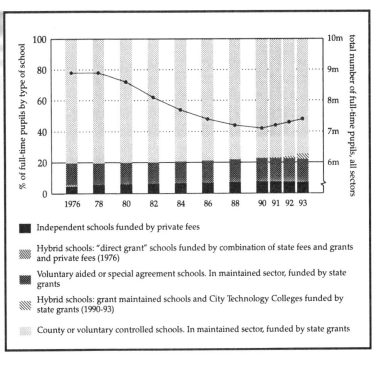

Figure 6.2 Full-time pupils by school type, England, 1976-1993

Sources: For 1976 see Table 6.1. Totals for independent schools for 1978-1983 from DES (1991, table A30/90); for 1984-1993 from DfE (1994a, table 2, adjusted to exclude CTCs). Totals for split within maintained sector for 1976-1981 from DES (1982, table A12/81); 1982-1986 from DES (1987, Table A13/86); and for 1987-1993 from DfE (1994b, table A13/93). Separate data for CTCs from DfE (personal communication).

schools should strive to be strongly denominational in character, and strive to preserve a distinct, Catholic, ethos. For example, as recently as the late 1980s, staffing and admissions policy in the diocese of the Archbishop of Westminster (the head of the Catholic Church in England) were both theoretically oriented towards this goal (Diocese of Westminster, 1988).

In the Church of England case, some schools, particularly at the secondary level, also retained an essentially denominational character through admissions and staffing policy (O'Keefe, 1986). However, many schools adapted to the changing social context by significantly softening their denominational objectives, an important factor in explaining the continued strength of the sector's presence in the face of declining church membership. This adaptation was reflected at the national policy level in the case of the Church of England through the National Society's promotion of a "neighbourhood school" model as appropriate for primary schools in areas with very few (or in some cases, no) Anglican families. These effected an explicit shift in orientation towards the multifaith and secular communities in which many were located. For example, in neighbourhood schools, "while religious education is in accord with the rites, principles and practices of the Church of England, these can be widely and liberally interpreted" (Brown, 1993, p.164). Gay's (1985) research on the independent sector provided complementary evidence in the case of Anglican fee-paying schools; while many were explicitly denominational foundations, religious activity was no longer as central to curricula as has been the case historically. The contrast with the Catholic Church's *formal* policy position is obvious. Yet even here, Brown's observation (1993, pp.164-5) that in some Catholic schools as many as two-fifths of pupils and staff are not Catholic suggests that there may have been a *de facto* shift in policy. This comes close to challenging the separatist *raison d'être* in some schools.

It is also important to attend to the impact of parental demand on the overall pattern of provision. Here, evidence comes from a small number of case studies of parental attitudes, which, although not derived on the basis of representative sampling (and hence not generalizable) can be treated as providing indicative evidence. O'Keefe's (1986) study of aided Church of England secondary schools and Johnson's (Johnson, D., 1987) survey across all types of school found a variety of factors influenced parents. For example, a quarter of the 139 parents interviewed in the former study claimed to choose Church of England secondary schools primarily because of their Anglican character, and a further 22 percent because of their "Christian education". Significantly, however, "academic reputation" was cited by 23 percent ahead of these factors (O'Keefe, 1986, p.38): a reputation apparently often predicated on their former status as grammar schools prior to comprehensive reorganization.

As far as parental choice of fee-paying schools is concerned, as with the maintained sector it appears that the sector's growth in "market share" — from 5.8 percent in 1976 to a peak of 6.6 percent in 1990 and 1991 (Figure 6.2) — is primarily linked to factors *other than* these schools' religious character.[13] While religious orientation may still be of relevance to many parents (Rae, 1981; Devlin, 1984; Dancy, 1984; Johnson, D., 1987), most UK commentators on the sector have stressed other factors, including a general desire to "get on better in life" and a wish to secure academic advantage, or develop character and discipline. Research has also linked choice to parents' own educational experience and family culture, as well as taken-for-granted assumptions about the inherent superiority of fee-funded education.

Explanations of the continuing role of fee-paying schools' during the 1980s also come from considering how perceptions of *relative* quality as between the independent and maintained sectors may have changed. The sharp cutbacks in capital expenditure on maintained schools and the further consolidation of comprehensive education by local authorities (despite central government's antipathy towards it under the Conservatives) are likely to be contributory factors, although there appears to be little evidence which might unambiguously establish causality.

The experience of the independent sector in particular also needs to be located within the changing political context in the early 1980s (over and above effects of constraints on maintained sector expenditure). The Labour administration in the late 1970s succeeded in translating rhetoric into action through the abolition of the direct grant scheme, but did not manage to implement a proposal to withdraw schools' charitable status, despite a commitment to do precisely this. The hostile attitude of the Labour government towards independent schools in general and public schools in particular was replaced in 1979 by a broadly sympathetic Conservative government. For the Conservative Party, encouragement for independent schools was a stance which appealed to a wide range of its natural constituencies (Chitty, 1992). In the late 1970s, enthusiasts had worked behind the scenes with the schools' pressure groups to devise a replacement, means-tested grant scheme (Salter and Tapper, 1985). The Education Act 1980 consequently introduced the assisted places scheme to pay day fees to many charitable independent schools, thus replacing in a different form the financial support provided under the direct grant scheme withdrawn under the Labour government. The stated aim was to provide a "ladder of opportunity" to academically-gifted children who would otherwise not have been able to benefit from these schools. Yet although undoubtedly of symbolic importance — and providing significant public funding for small numbers of individual schools — the assisted places scheme in reality only ever accounted for a very small proportion of independent school activity. For example, by 1990, only around one in twenty of all independent sector pupils were funded under the scheme (just 0.4 percent of pupils across all sectors), generating less than 4 percent of independent schools' total income, a sum actually outweighed by income from the state under other, existing schemes (Kendall, 1993a).

Of potentially more significance in explaining independent schools' relative success was the combination of the *indirect* effects of central government's broad economic and fiscal policy, and the preservation of the *status quo* with regard to these schools' tax privileges. The cutting of high marginal income tax rates from 1979 onwards increased the disposable income — and hence the ability to pay school fees — of high socio-economic groups, reversing the historic trend towards higher levels of direct taxation. Moreover, the government's switch to indirect tax to sustain public revenue through increasing the rate of value added tax (VAT) did not affect parents adversely, since fee payments to schools were exempted under existing regulations (a concession not available to charities in general; see Chapter 3). This hidden state support outweighed the value of direct public funding (see Robson and Walford, 1989, for a detailed discussion of the relative significance of the various tax concessions).

Notwithstanding the symbolic importance of the assisted places scheme and the beneficial indirect effects of economic and fiscal policy on the fee-paying sector, the period up until the late 1980s still represented a good deal of continuity with the post-war period. The introduction of radical changes in the education sphere, as with social and health care (see Chapter 8), were not to emerge until the end of the decade. The 1988 Education Reform Act was a landmark in attempting to alter the balance of power between the major players in education in place since the 1944 Act. Box 6.3 outlines the key changes introduced by the Act, and notes how these have been developed further in subsequent legislation.

In contrast to the negotiations that preceded the 1943 White Paper, *Educational Reconstruction*, the churches, as corporate players, appear to have had relatively little direct impact on the proposals (although Anglican bishops in the House of Lords were responsible for amending the legislation to ensure that a specifically Christian emphasis was mandated in religious education). Rather, the character of the reforms appears to have been the outcome of dialogue between two broad groups. Neo-liberal politicians and libertarian educational pressure groups lay behind the reforms' dispersal of power to consumers and local school management; while politicians in the Conservative authoritarian tradition, and senior DES civil servants, emphasized the need for tighter control from the centre, and promoted the idea of a national curriculum. DES civil servants had been arguing for greater central control of curricula since the 1970s, putatively in the interests of teacher accountability (Chitty, 1992). Glennerster and Low (1990, p.33) suggest that DES enthusiasm for the Act's centralizing measures can also be interpreted as part of their search to "justify their existence" as the decline in pupil numbers drove down the relative size of the education budget.

The most striking parallel with wider trends in the voluntary sector would appear to be in the housing field, because of the transparent shift of power away from local to central government (see Chapter 6). As with developments there, criticisms of local authorities' perceived "bureaucracy", "inefficiency" and "monopoly" were at the heart of the thrust to "shake up" the system. The main churches' general reaction to the reforms was cautious and conservative (Catholic Education Service, 1992; General Synod of the Church of England Board of Education, nd). There were many concerns about the appropriateness of market forces and competition in education, and the massive shift of power within the state from local to central government, typified by the response of the Catholic Church (Box 6.4).

Reactions to the national curriculum were also mixed. The Church of England did not object to the general principle, but wished to upgrade the status of religious education within it

---

Box 6.3   The 1988 Education Reform Act and after

The principal reforms to maintained school education contained within the 1988 Education Reform Act were:

- Mandatory delegation of financial control within the maintained sector from local authorities to schools.

- Forcing local authorities to link school funding more closely to pupil numbers than previously.

- The creation of two new types of school outside the purview of local authority control and eligible for exempted charity status: "grant-maintained" schools, being those that "opt out" of links with local government following parental ballots, and becoming directly funded by central government, an option available to all types of maintained school; and newly created "city technology colleges". The latter, despite being funded almost entirely by central government, are officially classed as independent schools and, unlike grant maintained schools, are not legally required to adhere to the national curriculum.

- The introduction of a national curriculum imposing uniformity in the teaching of certain "core" and "foundation" courses, and introducing consistent examinations across all schools, allowing for comparison of results and the construction of league tables.

Legislation in 1993 extended these reforms by moves to reduce drastically the remaining functions performed by local authorities: first, by encouraging a vastly increased rate of opting out, with grant maintained schools to be funded by a network of regional quangos whose members are appointed by the Secretary of State for Education; and second, by moves to reduce the numbers of surplus school places. Furthermore, the strict rules on academic selection in maintained schools introduced in the drive towards comprehensive education are gradually being relaxed in the aftermath of these reforms.

The legislation also sought to introduce a reinterpretation of the provisions of the 1944 Act with regard to mandatory religious education and collective worship in all maintained schools by emphasizing that these activities should have "proper regard to the nation's Christian heritage and traditions" (Cm 2021, 1992, para. 8.2). Religious education was, uniquely, described as a "basic" subject. Like core and foundation subjects in the national curriculum, it must be provided in all maintained schools, but unlike those subjects, its contents are still negotiated locally.

Box 6.4 The Catholic reaction to educational reform

Much of the flavour of the Catholic Church's attitude towards the reform is captured in the following quote, which was part of a submission in response to the 1992 White Paper, *Choice and Diversity*:

We do not believe that competition is a panacea for failings in education. Nor do we accept market forces as a fundamental principle in the provision of education opportunity. Both competition and market forces operate to some extent in education, *but we consider the emphasis given to these two processes to be inimical to true education.* Planned intervention is needed to protect those who are vulnerable. In place of an emphasis on competitiveness, market forces and autonomy (so easily giving the impression that education should be driven by purely utilitarian motives) we wish to place emphasis on the whole person growing within a community...the White Paper is severely critical of LEAs. *We do not accept this most blanket criticism.* Despite certain difficulties and occasional disagreements the record of our work and achievements together is one of genuine and valuable partnership. *It is a partnership not to be lightly set aside...we are deeply concerned that this partnership could be severely disrupted* (Catholic Education Service, 1992, paras 5.1-5.2, our emphases).

(General Synod of the Church of England Board of Education, nd, para. 11). By way of contrast, the response from Catholic Bishops was to object to the principle of subjecting its schools to a national curriculum because of potential conflicts between the "ideals and practice of Catholic education" and a curriculum "ultimately controlled...[by] secular authorities with no professional competence in the matter" (Catholic Bishops' Conference of England and Wales, 1987, cited by Arthur, 1993, p.179). The safeguard of "exception clauses" to allow Catholic schools to opt out in aspects "unacceptable on religious grounds" were dismissed as providing insufficient protection (op. cit., p.179).

The provisions of the 1988 Act also offered considerable financial incentives for aided schools to switch the statutory agency from which they received public funds. As local authority funded schools, by the late 1980s they were contributing 15 percent towards capital and repair costs. However, schools were guaranteed 100 percent funding from central government for these expenses if they opted to become "grant maintained", replacing their local authority funding with central government finance, while at the same time still being guaranteed that foundation appointees would continue to dominate governing bodies. Some church schools, after balloting parents, did decide to pursue this option (the 3.4 percent of pupils in hybrid schools in 1993 shown in Figure 6.2 includes pupils in newly grant maintained church schools). However, most schools chose not to do so, and the "opting out" rate appears to have been far lower than expected by the government; many schools preferred to retain valued links with local education authorities, despite the financial inducements to do otherwise. Moreover, a recent suggestion by the Prime Minister that church schools might be able to switch to grant maintained status *without* conducting a parental ballot was rejected by church leaders on the grounds that this would be potentially divisive between schools, and imply church schools were less concerned than other schools about parental choice (*The Guardian*, 13 September 1995).

As far as the independent sector is concerned, the stagnation in the early 1990s shown in Figure 6.2 is likely to be connected in part to economic recession. The primary impact on fee-paying schools of recent legislative upheaval has been indirect, as with the legislation of the 1940s. In particular, the reforms undertaken in the maintained sector affects the demand for places in fee-paying schools since, if parents perceive that the performance of their local maintained sector schools improve as a result of the Act's measures, they have less incentive to use the independent sector. There is potential for much more transparent competition for pupils to emerge *between* the fee-funded and tax-funded sectors, although children have always been mobile between these broad groups of schools (Johnson, D., 1987). Particularly if increasing numbers of maintained schools choose to revert to academic selection, one of the principal rationales for choosing a private fee-paying education will be undermined. If extensive overt academic selectivity within the maintained sector re-emerges, the market inhabited by independent schools would begin to resemble the situation prior to the expansion of comprehensive education, with one key difference. These schools' primary competitors would be maintained academically selective schools which are funded — and to a significant extent controlled — predominantly by central, rather than local, government.

6.5 Conclusion

This chapter has focused on primary and secondary education, just one subgroup of the largest ICNPO group in the UK under the structural operational definition, education and research. In Chapter 1, we noted that this group of establishments is typically filtered out of the taken-for-granted understanding of the voluntary sector in the UK. This is on the grounds of their reliance on the state (in the case of "maintained aided" voluntary schools), and their social exclusiveness or lack of public benefit orientation (with regard to so-called "independent schools" relying primarily on private fees). The issue of whether the latter establishments should legitimately benefit from the advantages of *charitable* status and the tax breaks associated with this has been a highly contentious and politically charged subject at least since Tawney described these schools as perpetuating privilege and inequalities in UK society in the 1920s (see also Chapter 3).[14] We have also seen that the issue of direct financial support from the state for these schools has, for similar reasons, been something of a political football — with a Labour government phasing out the direct grant scheme in the 1970s, only to be replaced by a new scheme for "assisted places" under Thatcher's incoming administration. The Labour Party's continued opposition to this form of state sponsorship remains one of the major issues separating the two political parties in the education field in the mid-1990s.

In Chapter 1, we noted a number of theoretical perspectives relating to the role of the sector. As we pointed out there, the data we have collected in this project do not allow us to test these theories, but our review allows us to make some comments. In seeking to understand the part played by these schools in UK society, the economic theory with most obvious purchase is clearly the work of Estelle James (1987) because it attends appropriately to both demand and supply factors. Unfortunately, while demand-side factors have received some attention in the literature on the modern role of these schools through surveys of parental attitudes and other qualitative research, this attention has tended to focus on the rationales for choice of schools outside the maintained sector, with little exploration of the significance of the "voluntary" or "charitable" label *per se*. On the supply side, we have summarized evidence about the sector's long-term historical development. The Church of England's major pro-gramme of school building for the working classes in the 19th century can, in James's terms, be seen as a "defensive reaction" to its ongoing loss of control and influence, and many of the schools established by individual Anglican entrepreneurs (like Nathaniel Woodard) bear a similar interpretation in the case of middle-class schooling. And moving into the 20th century, the expanding Catholic Church's primary purpose in building schools was certainly to socialize children and retain adherents to the Catholic faith. However, in contrast to social care settings, suprisingly little appears to be known about the motives and orientation of providers in the late 20th century.

James's perspective therefore appears to provide the most helpful starting point within economists' own terms of reference, but it is clear that a fuller understanding of the sector's evolving *social* role requires us to supplement abstract economic analyses with a focus on the particular cultural and sociohistorical context. For example, Smelser (1991) argues convincingly that the development of education for the working classes in 19th century England can only be adequately understood by attending to the extent to which that society was organized along class and religious lines at that point. It is also clear that the activities of the state have been more important in determining the sector's pattern of development than might be implied by purely market-oriented interpretations. Even in the case of the independent schools, operating with relatively little direct government financial support or regulation, we have seen that the political decisions of the state with regard to the funding, structure and nature of the maintained sector have been extremely significant in shaping the overall environment in which these schools have operated.

In the case of voluntary schools within the maintained system, the state and the voluntary sector clearly developed in tandem, and it would be tempting to characterize the "dual system" arrangements that prevailed in the 40 years after the 1944 Education Act as "corporatist" at both national and local levels. Power was effectively shared between central government, local government and the voluntary schools. Diocesan Education Committees (DECs) liaised with the appropriate local authorities and the central government Department for Education on school closures and openings, reorganization or any changes directed at church schools in their area, and provided individual schools with advisory and sometimes financial support (for capital projects). In as much as corporatism implies a high level of dependency by the state on its "partners" to enable policy implementation and service delivery, this is a useful metaphor.

However, while mutual dependency has been an important feature of this relationship, the corporatist model is best seen as an "ideal type" for two reasons. First, it implies more effective control by the DECs and national bodies over individual schools than actually existed.[15] Second, it tends to suggest an absence of conflict between these schools and the local authorities in whose areas they operated, but there was some evidence of significant tensions arising from schools' religious character and autonomy. In particular, some local politicians objected in principal to church involvement in education, characterizing the system as anachronistic and questioning its appropriateness in an increasingly secular society. It has also been argued that voluntary secondary schools were in a position to frustrate attempts to pursue equality-related goals by covertly "cream-skimming" or "poaching" pupils (Francis and Lankshear, 1993, p.476). This debate had most obvious relevance in the context of the shift towards comprehensive education. While only one in twenty voluntary aided schools were still *formally* designated as "grammar schools" by 1990, O'Keefe's study (1986) of Church of England-aided schools found evidence that many parents still regarded them as such. The net outcome of the interplay of parental preferences and schools' admissions policies could be social or academic — as well as religious — selectivity, an outcome which commentators in the educational establishment have purported to seek to avoid.

The 1988 Education Act and subsequent legislation marked the most radical restructuring of the education world since 1944. As with that earlier Act, the effects on the independent sector thus far have been more indirect than direct. For maintained voluntary schools, the rhetoric is still that of "partnership" between church and state, but it is a relationship premised on a very different balance of power between the partners than has prevailed historically. In contrast to the post-war settlement, the churches appear to have had relatively little impact on the direction taken by these reforms. Into the mid-1990s, church schools within the maintained sector find themselves dealing with an increasingly powerful central state and operating in a more market-like environment, while the role of local government, with whom these schools have traditionally worked closely, has been drastically curtailed. It is as yet too early to ascertain whether these schools, collectively, will flourish or suffer in this radically altered situation.

Notes

1 See Shattock (1989) and Salter and Tapper (1994) for interesting recent social and political analyses of the higher education field.
2 The other main varieties of voluntary sector provision for working-class children included industrial schools for the unemployed; reformatory schools, formed to deal with young offenders; and ragged schools, supported by Charles Dickens among others, and aiming to reach children too poor to attend ordinary schools. Mechanics' institutes were also established by middle-class philanthropists to provide technical education for working-class adults.
3 This funding had been preceded by the pioneering case of state-voluntary partnership in the field of education for offenders in the late 18th century; and the ragged schools also received some funding from government. While these were important precedents in establishing a model of joint working, the amounts of money were relatively small compared to the scale of investment in day school education for the working classes that developed during the course of the mid- to late 19th century.
4 The further principle that this universal elementary education should be free was not to become law until the 1891 Fees Act.
5 The private for-profit sector (through the "small business" provision of dame or private adventure schools) appears to have ceased to play a major role by the turn of the century. Sutherland (1990, p.145) cites evidence that the provisions of the 1870-80 legislation effectively "killed off the bulk" of private sector provision in working-class elementary education.
6 Up until the early 19th century, elementary education for the upper classes was traditionally provided at home or in the public schools themselves. However, a distinct network of fee-paying "preparatory schools" had developed by the end of the 19th

century, with the specific aim of preparing both upper- and middle-class pupils for secondary education (Walford, 1990, pp.9-10).

7 The exact total depends on the criteria adopted for identifying a school as a "public school": see Bamford (1967, ch. 10).

8 It was also possible to choose "special agreement" status, an intermediate option initially offered to support schools under earlier (1930s) legislation, but not widely adopted. For further discussion of the essential characteristics of each type of school, see Cmd 6458 (1943), O'Keefe (1986, p.14) and Nice (1992). The different statuses made available to schools had later parallels in the way that the government brought children's homes into the regional "community homes" system (see Chapter 7).

9 The case was forcibly made by the head of the Church in England, Cardinal Hinsley, in a letter to *The Times* (Howard, 1987, pp.128-9). The Catholic media were also instrumental in raising general Catholic awareness of the issue and, at the local level, priests and Catholic Parents and Electors Associations were formed to support the Archbishop's position (Coman, 1977, pp.52-9).

10 The 1944 Education Act had abolished fee payments in maintained secondary schools, but the system initially remained pre-dominantly academically selective. The view that this was not leading to appropriate educational opportunity gained currency from the 1950s onwards (Walford, 1990, p.28). In response to these and other pressures, an increasing number of local authorities switched to comprehensive education, under which access to secondary school education was to be determined "without reference to ability or aptitude" (DES, 1991, p.2). The shift to predominantly comprehensive schooling did not end selectivity, but formally restricted the part played by purely academic criteria. In maintained comprehensive schools, selection on these grounds was formally replaced with selection according to other factors deemed appropriate by local education authorities — most importantly, where people lived — and also according to religious criteria in the case of aided comprehensive schools.

11 From educating 8 percent of maintained sector pupils in 1,200 schools in the early 1940s (Howard, 1987, p.112), by 1976 some 2,562 Catholic aided (or special agreement) schools were educating some 770,000 pupils — an increase in its share of maintained sector pupils to 9.1 percent, thus actually expanding faster than the dramatic overall increase in pupil numbers that occurred during this period (Figure 6.1).

12 The time trends data with regard to the independent sector referred to in what follows and reported in Figures 6.1 and 6.2 relate to all non-maintained schools (other than special schools), and thus include those run on a for-profit basis as well as establishments with charitable status. (In contrast, all maintained voluntary schools are charitable, either registered or excepted from registration.) The data are not available to separate the contributions of the two "independent" sectors consistently over time. The only reliable source on this division comes from Posnett and Chase's (1985) one-off survey, which found that 56 percent of respondents were registered charities by the early 1980s. However, charitable schools on average tend to be much bigger, and as a consequence it can be estimated that close to 90 percent of pupils in the independent sector are in schools with charitable status (Kendall, 1993b). It is this ratio which was used to estimate the split between the broad voluntary sector and the for-profit in the summary market share statistics reported in Chapter 4. It should be noted that all the "public schools" and schools participating in the assisted places scheme (see below) now have charitable status, although some of the former were originally established in the 19th century as for-profit companies.

13 There are exceptions. The growth in the Muslim population has been accompanied by the establishment of independent Muslim schools, which have controversially failed to achieve voluntary aided status; and other schools for religious minorities and Evangelical Christian groups have also been founded (Walford, 1990, 1991). But since these schools are relatively few in number, these trends are unlikely to be sufficient to explain the strength of the overall upward trend.

14 Whether these schools allow parents to "purchase privilege" remains an open question (see Walford, 1990). See Salter and Tapper (1985, ch. 4) for a review of party political positions with regard to these schools' charitable status up until the 1980s, and an interesting analysis of the political importance of this status.

15 While the national bodies provided guidance on admissions and staffing policy, in the Church of England case at least this has not been legally binding, and not necessarily adhered to by individual schools. Decisions were ultimately taken by school governors, subject to the constraints implied by trust deeds (O'Keefe, 1986, pp.19-20).

Chapter 7

HEALTH AND SOCIAL CARE

7.1 Introduction

Many of the oft-trumpeted strengths of the UK voluntary sector have long been claimed and celebrated in the health and social care fields. These are also quantitatively important fields: not only are many health and social services provided by the voluntary sector, but a sizeable part of the sector is engaged in these activities. For example, between them, health and social care organizations account for 20 percent of employment in the broader voluntary sector, and 14 percent of the sector's £29 billion total income.

Many health and social care bodies have long-standing and substantial links with the state. Many are heavily reliant on income from public grants and contracts, and in the late 1980s and early 1990s the sector also received significant funding from the state via user subsidies, predominantly in the form of income support payments for residential and nursing home care. Some have other contacts with local and central government, participating in formal planning procedures and consultation mechanisms, and are prominent members of local and national policy communities (Ham, 1992; Wistow et al., 1996). As with education, the role of the state is therefore central to an understanding of voluntary sector health and social care activity in the UK today.

As we saw in Chapter 2, the voluntary sector's contributions pre-date government action by many centuries. Tracing these historical roots offers pointers to many of today's arrangements and questions. The cross-sectional statistical description of the sector in 1990 also illuminates many issues. In this chapter we look across all health and social care fields, and then consider four areas in more detail: residential care for elderly people, child care services, hospitals and mental health services. This is followed by an examination of the impact of the so-called "contract culture". We start, however, with the important legislation of 1989 and 1990, both to summarize the present policy environment and to locate the voluntary sector's scale, scope and roles in their broader contexts.

7.2 Health and social care reforms

The welfare state legislation of the 1940s markedly changed the complexion of voluntary health and social services, but their own influence on the purpose, design and implementation of the 1940s legislation was also considerable (see Chapter 2). Beveridge's report on *Social Insurance and Allied Services*, the 1948 National Assistance Act, the 1946 National Health Service Act and the 1948 Children Act were all influenced by successful features of charitable provision (see below). The 1945 Labour government was less hostile towards the voluntary sector than the pre-war pronouncements of some leading Labour supporters may have suggested. Nevertheless, the post-war legislation had to overcome the inadequacies of a voluntary sector comprising thousands of small, independent organizations, often uncoordinated and conflicting (Finlayson, 1990). In the face of growing demand, their resources of revenue and volunteer labour were — as now — less than fully predictable (often gloriously so) and frequently inadequate, and their services were spread unevenly across the country (Packman, 1968; Hatch and Mocroft, 1977). Many of what Salamon (1987) has referred to as "voluntary failures" — particularism, insufficiency, amateurism, paternalism (see Chapter 1) — were clearly evident in pre-1945 UK voluntary sector activity in these fields.

Not surprisingly given the enormity of the legislative changes of the 1940s, the post-war development, orientation and character of the voluntary sector have been considerably shaped by the formal and informal actions and attitudes of the state (see Chapters 2 and 5). Other forces were at work, including changing social values, "the rise and fall of professionalism", manager-ialism and economic pressures (Deakin, 1995, pp.63-4), each of them clearly evident in health and social care as in the wider sector. However, the sector's activities and contributions in the post-war period have varied quite markedly from client group to client group, and from service to service, as we describe in section 7.4. Recent legislation will change it further. In 1990, the base year for our cross-sectional statistical mapping, Parliament approved far-reaching reforms to health and social care (or "community care"), introduced by the 1990 National Health Service and Community Care Act, and local authorities began to implement the 1989 Children Act. This small burst of legis-lation in fact introduced the most sweeping changes to health and social care since the 1940s.

One interpretation of the recent health and social care legis-lation is to see them as the extension of Mrs Thatcher's zeal for markets, consumer-led services and personal responsibility, and her intention to "roll back the frontiers of the state". Another interpretation is that they were the expedient, if delayed, political reaction to numerous social and economic problems that had gathered weight during the 1980s, including some well-publicized cases of community neglect, limited user choice, and (especially) runaway social security expenditure on residential and nursing homes. The 1990 Act encouraged movement along four "strategic dimensions" (Wistow et al., 1994):

- to alter the balance of care from institutional to community care, including running down long-term hospital provision, discouraging residential and nursing home placements in favour of domiciliary care, and creating incentives for com-munity-based rather than in-patient treatment;

- to move away from supply-led towards needs-led decisions and service arrangements, better assessment of needs, and with more attention to be paid to users' and carers' prefer-ences;

- to promote the mixed economy of care, specifically creating incentives to greater pluralism in provision; and

- to give much more responsibility for community care decision-making and funding to local authorities, and away from the NHS and central government. This was effected in part by giving local authorities substantial additional funds, formerly held by the (central government) Department of Social Security to purchase residential and community social care.

The most visible manifestations of the reforms to health care were in primary health care, where larger practices could become "general practice fundholders" with their own budgets and the freedom to purchase many secondary care services, the division of health authorities into purchasers (commissioning authorities) and providers (NHS trusts[1]) in a new "internal market", and the final stage in the shift from local to central government control. Proportionately, the NHS spends substantially less in contracting out to private and voluntary agencies than do local authorities: less than 2 percent of its hospital and community health services budget.

Encouraging choice and diversity in the provision of health and social care was a broader policy thrust during the 1980s (see Chapter 5), and chimed with thinking in social care about "patch" systems (Hadley and Hatch, 1981), care *by* the community (Bayley, 1973; DHSS, 1981), community social work (Barclay, 1982) and, indeed, with some of the early thinking about case or care management (as reviewed and extended by Davies and Challis, 1986).[2] Much of the debate as it related to the voluntary sector was a reaction to Wolfenden, and gave rise to various forms of "welfare pluralism", an amorphous term used to cover a multitude of arguments and approaches to the provision of social services (see Chapter 5; and Brenton, 1985, ch. 8). Significantly, most of these discussions in the early 1980s, at least as they related to social care, paid most attention to voluntary sector and informal providers and to the likely consequences for political pluralism (cf. Hadley and Hatch, 1981). In contrast, the 1990 Act and subsequent discussions have tended to focus rather more on the private sector and the empowerment of the individual user in the context of a more strategically-aware state.

The main feature of the 1989 Children Act was quite different: to alter and clarify the balance between the responsibilities of parents, the rights of children and the duties of the state to intervene. Child care principles were laid out, and regulation and guidance arrangements clarified with the aim of raising care standards. As with the 1990 Act, the Children Act emphasized the desirability of family-based care rather than institutional provision and tidied up the legislative framework, but there were few other similarities. Certainly there were no changes to the balance of sectoral responsibilities, no "hallmarks of That-cherism" (Packman and Jordan, 1991, p.315).

Although radical in many respects, the 1990 and 1989 Acts were thus not as antagonistic towards the general thrust of the "welfare state reforms" of the 1940s as might have been expected of Mrs Thatcher's governments, nor had earlier legislation brought major changes. The bedrock of post-war reform — universal services funded largely from general taxation — remains substantially intact, despite growth in user charges over the last 50 years, incremental narrowing of the range of social problems and health needs addressed by the state, and (somewhat gentle) encouragement of private insurance. However, the latter day reforms offer both opportunities and limitations for the voluntary sector. They can now play a greater provider role and can participate more in strategic planning. On the other hand, their financial links with the state have been tightened up, a competitive environment has been fostered in which private organizations may play a larger part, and they may feel they have greater need but fewer opportunities to lobby for change and improvement, either for individual service users and their carers, or for "group action".

7.3 A statistical profile

Providing a statistical description of health and social care is no more straightforward than describing other parts of the voluntary sector.[3] A summary of the statistics produced by the mapping demonstrates the enormity of the sector (and indeed the enormity of the research task), as well as marked differences between client groups and service types (Table 7.1). There were many thousands of social services voluntary organizations, with total expenditure of £3,029 million. Full-time equivalent employment was 144,000, and we know from other research than an estimated 3.5 million people gave their time as volunteers across all provider sectors in this field (Lynn and Davis Smith, 1991). Total income stood at £3,062 million, a quarter of which came from government, a third from commercial activities and two-fifths from donations. Differ-

Table 7.1

Operating expenditures, paid employment and income in social services (subgroup 4 100), 1990

Client group	ICNPO code	Operating expenditure £ million	FTE employment 000s	FTE employment %	Total operating income £ million	Income from govt %	Private earned income %	Private giving %
Children and families	4 110	280	16.0	11.1	282	43.6	17.4	39.0
Elderly	4 120	424	25.8	17.9	476	39.9	50.4	9.7
Learning disabilities	4 130	93	9.2	6.4	98	73.5	8.2	18.3
Physical and sensory disabilities	4 140	380	21.9	15.3	399	43.9	20.3	35.8
Women's groups	4 150	28	0.8	0.6	24	33.3	41.6	25.0
Carers' groups	4 160	8	0.5	0.3	8	75.0	12.5	12.5
Pre-school playgroups	4 170	133	50.1	34.9	203	4.9	91.1	3.9
Youth development	4 180	1,359	6.1	4.3	1,315	7.9	31.3	60.8
Multiple client groups	4 190	250	13.0	9.1	257	59.9	11.7	28.8
Total	4 100	2,955	143.5	100.0	3,062	27.5	33.1	39.4

See Chapter 4 for definitions of revenue categories. Youth development is usually treated as part of the education field in the UK, but is included here for consistency with this project's classificatory conventions. This table covers only subgroup 4 100, social services, of the wider ICNPO group 4, also referred to as "social services". The latter also includes emergency and refugee services, and income maintenance (subgroups 4 200 and 4 300). Data on these subgroups are included in Appendix Tables A.4 and A.5.

ences within the social services sector are marked: two areas (services for people with learning disabilities and support for carers) were reliant on statutory support for around three-quarters of their income, compared to only 5 percent for pre-school playgroups and 8 percent for youth organizations.

As far as the health field was concerned, organizations in the sector spent £926 million in 1990 (90 percent of income), with the largest fields being hospitals and rehabilitation (income of £343 million) and "other health" (£447 million). Overall, it is not possible to give precise breakdowns of income sources, as public sector payments could not be separated from patient fees; but at least 23 percent of income came from the NHS or other government bodies, 51 percent from commercial activities, and 26 percent from private giving (see Appendix 1). Mental health organizations were the most heavily reliant on public sector funding (58 percent).

Funding the voluntary sector's social care activities has always been an important, albeit quantitatively small, element of local authority expenditure — as, for example, Mencher (1958) describes for the early 1950s, and Judge and Smith (1983) showed for the late 1970s — but has assumed greater importance since full implementation of the 1990 Act. Many local authorities allocate significant sums in grants and contracts to the voluntary sector. Analysis of English local authority financial data for 1990/91 demonstrates the volume of support before implementation (Table 7.2).[4] These figures relate only to expenditure by social services departments, and therefore do not represent the sum of all support from local authorities, which show up in our income data. They exclude (the usually relatively small) payments from housing, education and other departments.[5] Nevertheless, expenditure described as payments (interpretable loosely as "contracts") dominates general contributions ("grants") as far as social services departments are concerned. Social services department support for the independent sectors combined amounted to just over 6 percent of social services expenditure in 1990/91, the same as in 1988/89, but was 8 percent in 1978/79 (Judge and Smith, 1983).[6]

In the last few years, such funding has taken a new direction and has grown significantly. This has been not only because the former social security payments to residential and nursing

Table 7.2

Local authority social services expenditure, England 1990/91: payments ("contracts") and general contributions ("grants") to voluntary organizations by user group and service type

| User group | Expenditure going to voluntary organizations as a percentage of total expenditure on the corresponding user group and/or service type | | |
| | Payments "contracts" | | General contributions |
	Residential care %	Other services %	All services %
Elderly	2.2	1.0	0.7
Younger physically disabled	40.3	8.0	5.3
Mentally ill	14.1	2.8	5.4
Adults with learning disabilities	16.8	2.1	0.8
Children with learning disabilities	12.8	n a	n a
Other children	8.9	n a	n a
All children	n a	3.9	1.6
Mixed client group	1.6	1.7	8.4
All user groups	3.5		1.4

Source: Local authority RO3 returns (PSS General Fund Revenue Account, 1990/91) as analysed by Wistow et al. (1994, Tables 3.1-3.3).

homes have been added to local authority budgets with stipulations to spend 85 percent on independent sector services as part of the reforms described in section 7.2, but also because some authorities have sold or floated off services to voluntary bodies and then funded them under contract. In a study of 17 organizations providing "welfare services" in one locality, Russell et al. (1995) found substantial growth in total income between 1989 and 1993 (averaging 40 percent), and a leap of 26 percent in the following year (when the 1990 legislation was fully implemented). Almost two-thirds of total income was coming from statutory sources in 1993/94. However, Russell also concluded that statutory funding was more volatile in the later year, did not always cover the costs of service expansion, and was sometimes accompanied by non-statutory income itself subject to unpredictable changes. But decision-making over local authority funding in many areas has become more coherent and better coordinated, with fewer payment channels and tiers. The price of this coherence for voluntary bodies may be some loss of control (see section 7.5).

Every description of local authority propensities to contract out reveal wide variations between user groups, local authority types and areas of the country. Conservative-controlled local authorities have traditionally contracted out more than authorities controlled by other parties, as we found to be the case across England in 1990. But there were no links between political control and (non-contract) grant-giving (Wistow et al., 1994, ch. 3). In fact, it is a complex web of interconnected political, social and economic factors which explains social services department support for voluntary sector providers, as for overall local government expenditure on the sector as a whole (see Chapter 5). Judge and Smith (1983) argued that "the beliefs and prejudices of local decision-makers and the historical experience of different patterns of welfare provision in particular areas" were more important than technical arguments based on specialization, choice, cost-effectiveness or innovation. A later study of residential child care, which was able to include measures of voluntary sector prices among the potential explanatory factors, however, concluded that local authority placements were certainly significantly influenced by relative cost considerations, and that voluntary sector providers also adjusted their prices in response to local market conditions (Knapp, 1986).

Central government health authority support for voluntary organizations is more modest in scale, but also varies widely across the country. Most NHS expenditure has concentrated on acute hospital care in the form of traditional service agreements with denominational hospitals. The post-reform policy emphasis on alternatives to hospital in-patient treatment might, over time, result in a higher level of NHS funding for voluntary bodies active in other, non-institutional types of care.

As late as the mid-1980s there remained public authority suspicion of the voluntary sector in some parts of the country (sometimes bordering on open hostility): encouraging the sector was seen in some quarters, for example, as a betrayal of Fabian principles (Challis et al., 1988). Attitudes have since changed. Two cross-sectional studies of a sample of 25 English local authorities in 1991 and 1993 included in-depth interviews with social services directors and the (political) chair of the social services committee (Wistow et al., 1994, 1996). In 1991 the voluntary sector was generally making a greater contribution than the private sector to day care, domiciliary support, self-help and other non-residential services, but was a much smaller provider of residential care (cf. Table 4.5, p.128). These contributions were widely welcomed by the statutory authorities. Services for ethnic minorities were seen by local authorities as a speciality of the sector, the flexibility and small scale of many organizations were approved, and campaigning and advocacy were identified as distinctive, if sometimes uncomfortable for authorities themselves.[7]

Two years later, 14 of the 25 sample authorities expressed a preference for voluntary over private providers, with no clear preference expressed by the other 11 authorities. Many reasons were given for this preference: commonality of values and ideologies; shared perceptions of social need; a marked degree of mutual trust built up over many years of close working; representation on joint planning groups; overlapping governance structures and membership; many years of grant aid and in-kind support; and the absence of the profit motive. Together, these considerations gave local authorities confidence that high standards of care could be achieved and control maintained if they contracted out to voluntary bodies, and also created an expectation of closer care networks and the further development of mutual respect and trust. In 1991 it was fairly common for local authority members and officers to describe the private and voluntary sectors as unprepared and unqualified to be able to provide *significantly* greater volumes of services, but fewer such concerns were expressed in 1993.

The importance of public sector funding should not divert attention from other income sources for voluntary health and social care bodies. Charitable support from trusts and foundations grew in importance in the early part of the 20th century, particularly because rapid industrialization enabled some individuals to amass vast personal fortunes. Many trusts were established in the early years of this century to address fundamental social problems and to encourage more systematic giving. However, by 1990, only a small proportion of income came in the form of donations from trusts and foundations (5 percent for social services bodies and 4 percent for health care bodies). Direct giving by individuals, on the other hand, remained important. For example, more than one in twenty adults in the UK in 1991 had volunteered at least once per month in the previous year through health and social welfare organizations (including some in the public and private sectors) (Lynn and Davis Smith, 1991). They volunteered for a host of reasons — including altruism, social adjustment aims, for therapeutic reasons, to gain knowledge and intellectual enrichment, and to acquire experiences or skills which could generate career opportunities — and the patterns of community care volunteering showed marked variations by social, economic, demographic and ethnic groups (Knapp et al., 1996).

7.4 Four health and social care areas

A more focused appreciation of recent health and social developments and current issues is gained by concentrating upon a few particular fields. Given the considerable diversity within the sector, this concentration allows us to tease out some quite different historical trends, statutory sector links and pressing issues. One of the most important issues today, however — the impact of the contract culture — does have a more general relevance, and this is considered in section 7.5.

Residential care for elderly people

Not surprisingly given the demographic make-up of the UK, elderly people loom large in any statistical or policy discussion of health and social care. Of all the voluntary social services for elderly people, residential care homes account for the lion's share: income of almost £400 million in 1990, about five-sixths of the total. (Many of these homes provide day care on the premises and some may act as the hub of a domiciliary care service, but residential services dominate activities.) The levels and sources of income, by service type, are summarized in Table 7.3. Only 1 percent of residential care organizations' income was the result of private giving, while 57 percent was earned commercially,

Table 7.3

Services for elderly people: total operating income and income sources, 1990

Service type	ICNPO code	Total operating income £m	Income from gov't %	Private earned income %	Private giving %
Residential	4 121	397	41.4	57.3	1.3
Domiciliary	4 122	4	0.1	97.9	1.9
Day care	4 123	26	54.7	0	45.3
Advice/representation	4 124	1	4.9	30.4	64.6
Multiple services	4 129	43	19.3	16.7	63.9
All other services	4 125-7	6	60.8	27.1	12.1
Total (all services)	4 120	476	39.8	50.6	9.6

See Chapter 4 for definitions of revenue categories. Significant amounts of day and domiciliary care, as well as advice services, are subsumed under "multiple services", but cannot be separately identified.

mainly from privately-funded residents. Four-fifths of the income from the state in 1990 came in the form of user subsidies paid by central government's Department of Social Security; today, following the recent reforms, relatively more would come from local authority contracts.

In the medieval period, the monasteries and convents had provided institutional care for elderly people, and almshouses (often referred to as hospitals or hospices) were also established by individuals and secular organizations. The Poor Law Act of 1601 had charged each parish, the relevant unit of local government at that time, with supporting those in need, allowing them to levy a local tax (the poor rate) to fund this relief (see Chapter 2). By the middle of the 19th century, the state's responsibilities had grown, and congregate care for elderly people was heavily reliant on the public workhouse, a symbol of impoverishment which lingered into the 1950s and conditioned the post-war Labour government's plans for widespread public provision. For example, the new local authority homes of the 1950s, established to allow local government to meet its new statutory welfare responsibilities under the 1948 National Assistance Act, were to charge residents a modest fee. Although this was reimbursed from the old age pension, it was intended to remove the stigma of "public assistance" and to create a "relationship between hotel resident and manager [rather] than inmate and master" (Cmd 7910, 1949, p.311).

A survey sponsored by the Nuffield Foundation in the 1940s — the first of its kind — found that the "public assistance institutions" (the name had replaced "workhouses" in 1929) were "structurally inadequate" and inferior in a number of ways to voluntary homes (Rowntree, 1947; Knapp, 1977). For those who could gain admission, the voluntary home was therefore often a welcome alternative, both before the 1948 National Assistance Act and for some years after. Certainly the level of demand for voluntary sector facilities greatly exceeded the supply (Rowntree, 1947). However, the same report also concluded that

the administration of many endowed charities is so confused, and the trust deeds under which many of them are administered so archaic, that the whole picture is one of chaos and of frustration of the spirit in which the charities were originally endowed (p.98).

Voluntary sector residential homes were often catering for particular religious, ethnic or national groups, or had been, and continued to be, established by occupational welfare or benevolent associations (such as the British Sailors' Society, the Linen and Woollen Drapers' Cottage Homes and the Retired Nurses' National Home). Today many of these "specialist" homes continue to function, but now under closer statutory regulation and (usually) with many (and often most) of their residents supported by statutory payments. While these tend to retain an orientation and cultivate an ethos reflecting their religious or occupational group focus, many, like schools (cf. Chapter 6), now admit at least some clients who lack an obvious institutional affiliation with their home (Wistow et al., 1996, ch. 6).

The Nuffield Foundation survey had concluded that the best residential care homes were the small, voluntary sector facilities originally pioneered by the Catholic and Anglican sisterhoods and the Salvation Army (National Old People's Welfare Committee (NOPWC), 1961), and when the state came to replace the public assistance institutions with so-called Part III homes, it partly modelled its provision on these small homes (Davies, 1968; Sumner and Smith, 1969). Few local authorities ran small homes before 1939. Many new voluntary homes were opened during the Second World War, stimulated by public sector subsidies tied to individual elderly people, and by 1948 the NOPWC (1961) estimated there to be around 600 old people's homes in the voluntary sector. In later years, local authorities continued to express positive views about the voluntary sector's actual and potential contributions, often attracted by their small scale and homely environments. This is still the case today, although the associated higher costs can make it harder to justify placements to auditors or local politicians (Wistow et al., 1996).

By 1990, there were well over 300,000 places in public, private and voluntary residential care homes for elderly people (and some younger disabled people) in the UK, total provision having grown by 50 percent over just ten years. Twelve percent of these places were in voluntary homes. In addition there were about 100,000 places in nursing homes, 11 percent provided by voluntary organizations. A survey of residential care and nursing homes in 1986/87 by Darton and Wright (1988, 1991) found that voluntary residential home residents had a mean age of 83 and that 81 percent were female, in both respects being similar to public and private sector residents. On the other hand, voluntary nursing home residents were younger and less likely to be female when compared to the private sector. Interestingly, voluntary sector residents in both types of facility were less dependent than residents in the other sectors with respect to mobility and use of the lavatory, less confused and less disruptive. In other words, the voluntary sector was filling a slightly different "market niche" than the two larger provider sectors.

The voluntary sector is also distinguished from the other sectors by its high degree of market concentration. In the private sector, just 3.6 percent of residential homes and 21.2 percent of nursing homes in 1994 were controlled by "major providers" — that is, organizations or partnerships running three or more homes. In contrast, 45.1 percent of voluntary sector homes (across both types of facility) were connected to major providers, representing a sharp increase from 34 percent in 1992, the first year in which market penetration data in the sector were available (Laing and Buisson, 1995). This increase in concentration in part reflects the transfer of blocks of accommodation previously run directly by local authorities to housing associations or not-for-profit trusts, retaining strong links with local authorities (Wistow et al., 1994, ch. 6).[8]

Most of the growth in both residential care and nursing home provision in the past 20 years — part government preference, part entrepreneurship, part policy accident — has been in the private sector. Broad changes in political attitude and economic means over the past 20 years may have changed preferences among elderly people and their families to leave them better disposed towards the independent sectors and less keen to use public services. Certainly, many more elderly people and their families now have the economic ability to satisfy preferences of this kind, because of the growth in occupational pensions, private care insurance, "equity release schemes" on owner-occupied property, and disposable income generally. More important, however — until arrested by legislation in April 1993 — was the widespread availability of social security payments[9] to fund private or voluntary sector care, and the tight constraints on local government spending. Local authorities rapidly reduced their own contracted-out placements as it became increasingly attractive to let the social security ministry pick up the bill: two-thirds of voluntary residential care home residents were funded by local authorities in 1975, but only 16 percent in 1990.

The growth in demand for residential care met with a mixed supply response. Local authorities had few resources to expand their own provision, and their residents were not eligible for the fairly generous levels of social security subsidies. Market shares altered dramatically during the 1980s: the public sector got smaller (a 40 percent fall in market share) and the private sector displaced it as the largest sector. The number of private home places grew by 300 percent between 1980 and 1990. Voluntary sector provision barely altered, and its market share fell from 19 to 12 percent of places in the ten years to 1990, and to 13 percent in 1995.

Setting up an independent sector home was relatively cheap, and tax exemptions cut voluntary organization revenue costs. In the competition to attract competent staff, voluntary organizations have a potential advantage if people are prepared to volunteer for low or zero wages. However, volunteering in residential care homes for elderly people may be less appealing than in other fields, and in fact few voluntary home workers are unpaid. (Ernst and Whinney, 1986, put the figure at less than 3 percent, and identified no systematic difference between voluntary and private homes.) The equity necessary to transform a low-priced supply of suitable premises (particularly small, vacant hotels in formerly popular coastal resorts) into care homes has generally been more readily available to private than voluntary agencies because they can offer the prospect of dividends to investors, while the voluntary sector is legally bound by the non-distribution constraint. Bradshaw (1988) even identified the emergence of a new entrepreneurial class prepared to make considerable investments in private residential care. Indeed, in the liberal social security environment of the 1980s there were few better investments. Of course, some voluntary homes may have access to donative capital, especially if they were being set up by established parent organizations, but this does not appear to have been widely used for this purpose.

What occurred during the 1980s was fully consistent with Hansmann's (1987) argument that the private sector's market share will grow faster than the voluntary sector's in a period of rapidly increasing demand. The voluntary sector nevertheless retained certain distinctive features. It continued to satisfy particular needs, offering a residential care service often differentiated from the private sector in quality, style and orientation. Second, it has been argued that the sector may have wanted to give more emphasis to domiciliary-based rather than residential care, in keeping with the philosophy of the time (Parker, 1990).[10] Third, there was often a higher degree of "trust" between the voluntary and public sectors, something which has yet widely to characterize local authority relations with the private sector. This is consistent with those economic theories which argue that demanders' perceptions of differential "trustworthiness" between the private and voluntary sectors are important in understanding the latter (see Chapter 1).[11]

Fourth, there has been some growth in voluntary sector provision in the early 1990s, reflecting new involvement by housing associations in residential care. As we described in Chapter 5, these emerged as major providers of housing in the 1980s with support from the Housing Corporation, and elderly people were major beneficiaries. However, this typically did not involve sufficient care staff input to qualify as registered residential care, although the boundary with much sheltered or very sheltered housing is blurred (Tinker, 1992, ch. 7). More recently, however, housing associations have diversified into registered "housing with care", with the benefit of supply-side financial support from the Housing Corporation. This has allowed these providers to borrow more cheaply than the private sector, at least partly correcting for the traditional advantage of the latter in terms of access to capital (Stevenson, 1994, cited in Laing and Buisson, 1995).

Child care services

Although the Thomas Coram Foundation was established as the Foundling Hospital in 1739, most of today's major national children's organizations — including Barnardo's, the Children's Society and the National Children's Home — were formed between the 1860s and 1880s (often under other names). Initially they provided residential care and outreach work, seeking to complement rather than substitute for statutory provision.[12] It gradually became accepted during the Victorian period that moral reform and deterrence were not the answer to poverty (cf. Chapter 2), and voluntary child care organizations were at the forefront of developing alternatives to the workhouse. Statutory powers to safeguard the interests of children were introduced towards the end of the century.

The activities of the pioneering voluntary organizations grew rapidly. Thomas Barnardo accommodated 33 children in his first home in 1870, but the number of children in the care of his organization had reached 9,100 by 1910. The National Children's Home opened its first home in 1869 (with 29 residents), but had 1,100 residents by the end of the century and almost 4,000 by 1946. New organizations emerged, often to meet the needs of particular industrial groups — the Southern Railwaymen's Home for Children, the British Seamen's Boys Home, the Actors Orphanage and a home run by the Society of Licensed Victuallers, to name but four — although organizations associated with the major religions have always dominated this field. Pooling data for all voluntary child care bodies in England and Wales, Roy Parker and Frank Loughran counted 25,000 children in voluntary organizations' care in 1954, falling to 3,700 by 1985.[13]

There was little chance 50 years ago that a war-damaged, debt-laden UK economy could completely replace voluntary sector activity with public services. Voluntary sector assets were essential to ensure sufficient provision, and many voluntary services were anyway rightly recognized as exemplars. It was no surprise that the legislation of the 1940s should recommend that the new local authority welfare and children's departments should encourage voluntary provision. The post-war legislation thus brought sweeping changes, but many voluntary sector homes offered high quality care, particularly in what were at the time small residential homes. The Curtis Committee report, which paved the way for the 1948 Children Act, explicitly recognized these qualities, recommending the abandonment of large institutions in favour of the voluntary sector model: small "family group" homes with twelve or fewer children under the charge of a married couple.

Nevertheless, a large number of small voluntary child care organizations disappeared in the 1950s. Small and large organizations alike continued the process of diversification into non-residential services, such as foster care and placements for adoption, family centres, programmes for young offenders, support for homeless young people, provision for children and young adults with special needs, and preventive and other work with "at-risk" families. In some localities, child protection work and community programmes for young offenders are provided exclusively by the voluntary sector, largely under contract to the local authority. The National Society for the Prevention of Cruelty to Children even has powers enshrined in child care legislation. Voluntary bodies were sometimes the initiators of change and sometimes followed a specific state lead. For example, voluntary organizations may well have pioneered community interventions for young people "in trouble", but it was the government's intermediate treatment initiative in the mid-1980s which greatly expanded community-based voluntary sector programmes for young offenders. This initiative pumped £15 million into the system over three years (at a time when total national annual expenditure was only £17 million), with funds only available to voluntary agencies. Relatively smaller but still important central government initiatives for the "under-fives" and for family support also injected funds into the voluntary sector.

In law, the voluntary and statutory child care sectors are seen as parts of the same system. With the growth of statutory powers and resources over the post-war period, voluntary services were often directly complementary to those offered by local authorities, the former continuing to specialize in terms of the behavioural, emotional, educational or physical needs of children, and by religion and ethnic group. Packman concluded from her interviews with seven leading voluntary child care bodies in the mid-1960s that

they described their role in terms similar to those outlined by Lord Beveridge, in *Voluntary Action*. That is, they did not wish to duplicate statutory services, but to pioneer new methods of dealing with old needs, and seek out new needs that had gone unrecognized (1968, p.101).

She described how voluntary organizations differed from local authorities in the 1960s in undertaking less "short-term" or crisis work, accommodating higher proportions of severely disturbed children and large families, and admitting a higher proportion of illegitimate children. There were also suggestions, although refuted by the seven voluntary bodies, that they tended more often "to help the stable and 'respectable' parent who had fallen on hard times" (ibid., p.103).

Of course, not all voluntary services represent particular specialisms; indeed, the existence in many areas of a sizeable voluntary sector providing high quality "generalist" care has for many years allowed local authorities to limit their own capital investment. One consequence has been intersectoral competition. In the residential care field, voluntary homes appeared to be adjusting the fees they charged for contracted-out placements in the early 1980s in response to different local authority circumstances (costs, placement policies, excess demand), although in almost all cases their fees were lower than their costs. The latter was a central and local government stipulation, the deficit to be covered from donative income.[14] By 1990, about a third of the income of residential child organizations and multiple service bodies came from donations (Table 7.4). Local authority placements were price-elastic: when voluntary home charges were higher, local authority placements tended to be lower (Knapp, 1986). These findings would be consistent with the existence of overlapping and competitive services.

Table 7.4

Services for children and families: total operating income and income sources, 1990

Service type	ICNPO code	Total operating income £m	Income from gov't %	Private earned income %	Private giving %
Residential	4 111	21	55.2	14.2	30.7
Domiciliary	4 112	4	82.9	1.2	16.3
Day care	4 113	10	4.6	58.5	36.9
Advice/representation	4 114	24	38.2	30.5	31.3
Multiple services	4 119	177	53.0	13.3	33.7
All other services	4 115-7	46	10.9	19.6	69.6
Total (all services)	4 110	282	43.6	17.2	39.1

See Chapter 4 for definitions of revenue categories.

Contracting-out levels varied markedly between authorities at that time, as they had in the 1960s (Packman, 1968; Davies et al., 1972), and as they do now (Department of Health, 1995).

Over recent decades, at least until the early 1990s, local authority demand for voluntary sector residential care has fallen. This has been because of demographic trends, falling numbers of children in care, the professional preference for family rather than residential care, a desire to keep local authority homes full, a preference to keep children in familiar locales (implying few out-of-authority placements), and fiscal pressure within local authorities combined with rising relative costs of voluntary sector provision.[15] This falling public sector demand for residential care followed policy decisions some years ago by most voluntary organizations not to admit children into residential care if they were not a local authority (funded) responsibility. In 1985, more than four out of five of all of the children in the care of voluntary sector children's homes were supported by a local authority, compared with one out of five in 1954. However, in some parts of the country, voluntary facility places are today heavily in demand, with some local authorities claiming that the providers can almost name their own fees.

In fact, diversification out of residential care has been marked, although a number of the major organizations in this field have long been providers of non-residential services. All of the national child care bodies now provide a range of support and advisory services for families. Multipurpose family centres were first provided by the sector, and a range of preventive services or programmes are now run by national and local groups. In the voluntary child care field, as in many others, there is strong evidence of a pioneering structure and quite wide respect for the quality of provision.[16]

Hospitals

Although some voluntary hospitals were established in the 12th and 13th centuries, the modern hospital ("infirmary") dates mainly from the early 18th century — first general hospitals, and later lying-in hospitals, dispensaries and fever hospitals. Between 1820 and 1860, the number of special hospitals trebled (Owen, 1964; Prochaska, 1988). Gradually, the old form of hospital became less and less relevant to changing times. With the rise of the public workhouse in the 19th century, the "least deserving" of its clientele were diverted into new, more punitive surroundings. But other functions were to be taken up by philanthropy. The Foundling Hospital, for example, attracted widespread support from subscribers during the 18th century, and hospitals for "fallen women" were supported through chapel collections and charity sermons. Fever hospitals, however, had little attraction for the general subscriber and were mainly supported by public funds or prosperous merchants. In the latter part of the 19th century, hospitals were beginning to compete with the friendly societies for charitable funds, and Saturday and Sunday hospital funds were set up which continued to operate until the inauguration of the NHS.

The First World War put a great strain on the resources of voluntary hospitals, and government began to subsidize them after the war, initially on a temporary basis. Legislation in the 1860s had already provided for Poor Law infirmaries to be set up independently of the workhouse but within the public sector. But it was in 1929, when the administrative structure of the Poor Law was dismantled and the infrastructure of the Poor Law infirmaries and fever hospitals were taken over by elected local authorities, that the state really began to develop its own hospital provision. Voluntary hospitals still provided 25 percent of beds between the wars (Thane, 1982). The Saturday and Sunday (donative) funds continued, but voluntary hospitals came to depend increasingly on user fees, local authority payments and subsidies. By 1938, about half their income came from charges to patients. Advances in medicine were outstripping the capacity and facilities of institutions set up to cater for the sick poor, but their significant capital and human assets ensured their continued significant contributions. Moreover, it was cheaper for local authorities to subsidize voluntary hospitals than establish their own. By the end of the 1930s, just over half of the in-patient treatments in England and Wales were provided by voluntary hospitals, and about 90 percent of out-patient treatments (Hollingsworth and Hollingsworth, 1989).

As in many other parts of the voluntary sector, the legislation of the 1940s brought the biggest changes, and once the 1946 National Health Act had set up the NHS in 1948, the roles of the non-statutory sectors in most aspects of health care funding and provision became quite modest. Most significantly, the vast majority of voluntary sector hospitals were absorbed into the NHS, and run — alongside the former local authority hospitals — by appointed Regional Hospital Boards. This represented a sudden and controversial centralization of state power. Some voluntary hospitals were "disclaimed", and survived as independent institutions, including many run by religious orders and of denominational character. These are now primarily fee-funded, although some do receive financial support from the NHS (see below). At the time, the endowments of the voluntary hospitals amounted to some £50 million (Prochaska, 1992). Those institutions designated as hospitals were able to keep their endowments, while others lost their endowments to a central pool. Charitable fundraising by NHS hospitals was permitted.[17]

The decision by the post-war Labour government to "nationalize" the voluntary hospitals rather than to grant-fund them or set up contractual links of the kind familiar in the 1990s was consistent with the earlier hostility which the Labour Party had shown towards these institutions. They were, a Labour Party document of 1922 averred, guilty of "hospital abuse" ("the admission of patients other than those for whom hospitals were intended"), understaffed and characterized by long waiting lists; they underpaid their nursing staff; and the choice of patients was influenced by "patronage ... to the exclusion of more urgent or more suitable cases". In fact, although some of the criticisms were valid, the voluntary hospitals were not performing as poorly as this polemic suggests. Indeed, using data for general hospitals collected in the *Hospital Survey* for 1938, covering all of England and Wales (Nuffield Provincial Hospitals Trust, 1946), Hollingsworth and Hollingsworth concluded that:

relative to hospitals in the public sector, those in the voluntary sector were somewhat more innovative, had a somewhat higher level of technological complexity, were much smaller, were somewhat less egalitarian in access to care, provided somewhat higher quality services, and spent more money on individual clients (1989, p.127).

However, there were widespread demands — across the sectors — to improve hospital provision and access, during a period in which constraints on income and rising costs left many hospitals in financial difficulties (Abel Smith, 1964; Pinker, 1966; Thomas, 1980).

Since 1948, the NHS has almost completely dominated hospital provision, and even today — with the greater policy emphasis on private medicine, and occasional signs of growth in sub-scriptions to private health insurance — it provides 95 percent of all acute hospital beds. Growth in independent provision has been confined to the private sector, which more than trebled in size between 1979 and 1990, in terms of bed numbers (see Table 4.5, p.128). The voluntary sector registered a discernible con-traction. Most voluntary provision is now to be found in London. In 1990, voluntary acute hospitals had total operating income of £343 million, total operating expenditure of £303 million and employed 13,000 people. An unknown proportion of the volun-tary hospitals' income came from the NHS (this revenue is included in the 81 percent from fees), with many contracted-out treatments provided at less than full cost. These payments ac-counted for only 0.5 percent of total NHS expenditure on hospital services in 1988 (National Audit Office, 1989).

Looking beyond hospital services, voluntary health care pro-vision may look modest alongside the enormous NHS, and may get less media attention than the small but fast-growing private sector, but its contributions are distinctive and highly regarded. As well as the well-known medical research charities, the voluntary sector's most conspicuous contributions to health care today are particularly in the areas of hospice and other care for terminally ill people, emergency medical services, health promotion, alternative medicine and medical research, where, unlike acute hospital care, voluntary organizations retain a significant, and often dominant, market position. For example, the hospice movement has flourished primarily under voluntary sector auspices by mobilizing a combination of private donations and growing NHS support, and there were almost 400 hospices in the UK in 1990 with a combined income of around £150 million. The sector is also a key player in those areas of long-term care which merge into social care provision, and it has a long tradition of provision for people with drug or alcohol problems (starting with the temperance movement of the 19th century).

Mental health care

From the late 19th century until quite recently, a lot of the hospital and community accommodation for people with mental health problems and learning disabilities was in the public sector, reflecting social concern about protection from these "dangerous" people (a view particularly associated with the Eugenics Society) and moral concern about promiscuity and "illegitimate" pregnancy which often led to incarceration. In fact, despite the state's growing responsibilities after 1945, Rooff's (1957) review of voluntary action found the sector to be a major player in mental health care. During the post-war period, voluntary organizations moved towards community development and "normalization" policies, building smaller community homes for people who had been institutionalized for years, and in so doing helped both to alter and to reflect changes in public attitudes. Then, as now, the voluntary sector often led new developments in treatment and care, involving the growth of special needs housing associations (Knapp et al., 1992, pp.244-53) and the diversification of general housing associations into the mental health field, a trend we have also noted has occurred more recently with residential care for elderly people.

Thus, long before the policy discussions which culminated in the 1990 NHS and Community Care Act, there had been moves to substitute community care for hospital provision for many people with mental health problems, learning disabilities (mental handicaps) and age-related needs. The hospital rundown policy was part medical preference, part public opinion, and part "hard political economy" (Korman and Glennester, 1990, p.11), although disentangling their respective influences is difficult. Lobbying had been influential: one eminent psychiatrist complained that the move to close hospitals was

> supported by a motley group of civil libertarians, who maintained in the name of various creeds and ideologies that mental hospitals were effectively prisons, depriving their inmates of "freedom" under an authoritarian medical regime from whose yoke discharge represented a release and a return to normal life (Shepherd, 1989, p.667).

One of the most important roles performed by the voluntary sector in this field has been to provide political muscle on behalf of people with mental health problems and their relatives, both for individual people in their day-to-day dealings with the health and social care systems, and for broader groupings of people. Half the national voluntary mental health groups responding to a UK survey conducted as part of this research were engaged in lobbying and campaigning (Schneider, 1994). Groups such as Mind, Sane and the National Schizophrenia Fellowship have been particularly influential in raising the profile of mental illness, and giving a voice to service users and families.

The number of mentally ill people in hospital in England and Wales peaked at 151,000 in 1954, but was down to 40,000 by 1992. The NHS continues to have a clinical responsibility for many of the discharged former in-patients (and for those who no longer get admitted), but this dehospitalization trend has shifted many responsibilities onto local authorities, voluntary and private organizations, and families. With care and treatment now more likely to be located in the community, the voluntary sector's contributions to meeting mental health care needs through service provision are larger today than at any time in the post-war period.

The trend towards community care has a long pedigree, so that the provision statistics illustrated in Figure 7.1 tell only part of the story, but they clearly illustrate the recent growth in independent sector provision. In fact, the full voluntary sector contribution is not clearly identified, as hospital statistics do not

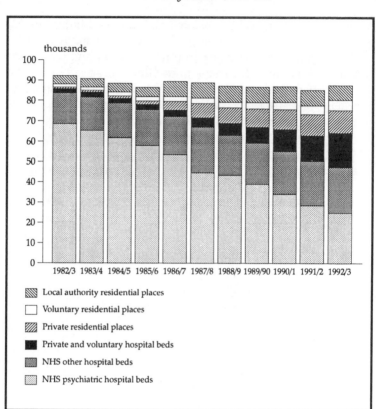

Figure 7.1 Mental health hospital beds and residential places, England, 1982-92

Source: Davidge et al. (1994).

distinguish them from private providers, but the sector maintained its share of (registered) *community* accommodation ("homes and hostels") at around 23 percent of the total until 1990. Since then it appears to have grown perhaps to as much as 35 percent (Department of Health, 1994), stimulated by joint or consortium initiatives between voluntary agencies (including housing associations) and the NHS (Wertheimer, 1991).[18] These national averages hide wide variations; for example, market share in community residential accommodation ranged from 9 to 54 percent in one recent survey of eight districts (Audini et al., 1996).

Total community provision increased threefold between 1975 and 1990, and growth has continued. As with residential care for elderly people, the growth of independent mental health provision was directly linked to the liberal social security environment of the 1980s, although in this case the demand was fed by hospital rundown and NHS placements rather than an ageing population and self-referral. That private mental health care residential provision did not achieve the same market dominance as in care of elderly people is due to the different nature of this demand (particularly its funding). In a north London study it was found that 49 percent of the funding of voluntary residential accommodation came from the NHS and 38 percent from social security payments, compared to 12 and 84 percent for private sector facilities (Knapp et al., 1997). The former were much more likely — in the pre-1990 reform period, at least — to receive contracted-out placements from the NHS. Interestingly, analysis of data collected in the same study suggests that voluntary sector facilities were less costly and achieved better resident outcomes than their statutory sector counterparts.

In addition to residential accommodation, the voluntary sector is an active and increasingly important provider of day care. There are no national statistics on total numbers of centres or places, but voluntary day centres which received some financial support from local authorities numbered 600 in 1992 and 1,180 in 1994 (49,000 and 76,500 places), representing 14 percent of total local authority purchases in the latter year (Department of Health, 1995). This is an increase on the share of total provision that was evident in the 1970s (Edwards and Carter, 1979).

7.5 The "contract culture"

In the four service areas just discussed, as elsewhere in health and social care, many changes in the external environment have left their mark on the voluntary sector. For many people working in the sector, or commentating upon it, none is currently more threatening than the so-called "contract culture". What is usually, if implicitly, meant by this term is not merely the substitution of formal contracts or service agreements for grant aid, but also the promotion of competition for state funding. Neither contracting nor competition is peculiar to the 1990s, but both have been encouraged enormously by recent health and social care legislation and by wider trends in public administration, particularly the move towards "enabling, not providing" (Ridley, 1988; and see Clarke and Stewart, 1990; Walsh, 1991; Wistow et al., 1994, ch. 2).

The growing use of formal contracts (or their near relatives) by local and health authorities during the 1980s, and particularly since 1990, was noted in section 7.3, and the service areas described in section 7.4 illustrate that the spirit of competition is certainly abroad. Preliminary indications from evidence gathered in early 1996 point to further growth in both contracting and competition.[19] However, the 1990 legislation was phased in over a three-year period, and — on the social care side — left sufficient local discretion to allow, for example, many Labour authorities to delay the introduction of formal contracting mechanisms (Wistow et al., 1994, ch. 5). Consequently, little time has elapsed for evidence to accumulate on the effects of the new "contract culture". What evidence there is appears to be fairly consistent with some of the US experiences (see Smith and Lipsky, 1993, and Kramer, 1994, for recent evidence), even though the historical positions of health and social care voluntary bodies, and their links with the state, are different in salient respects between the two countries (Gutch, 1992; Lewis, 1993; Richardson, 1993).

In organizing the discussion of these effects, we return to a previously developed categorization of hypotheses, which suggested that the effects of contracts might be seen in five areas: bureaucratization or formalization of voluntary organizations, inappropriate regulations, threats to autonomy and goal diversion, financial insecurity, and the erosion of the social and economic advantages which voluntary agencies are often claimed to confer (Knapp et al., 1990). In what follows, we use the term "contract" to include any *significant* departure from grant aid with no (obvious) strings attached (Judge, 1982) — and thus include service agreements which may technically not be contracts because they lack legal enforceability — although it is important to remember that different arrangements can have rather different impacts (Wistow et al., 1996, ch. 8). We marshall existing UK evidence on the consequences of a contract culture, although it should be remembered that it comes mainly from small-sample research.

Formalization

A common concern is that contract funding will lead to the bureaucratization of voluntary bodies, with concomitant increases in management costs. By its very nature, a contract (or documented service agreement) requires the formalization of a relationship between two parties. Previously spoken agreements will need to be written down, and previously informal arrangements will need to be codified. Authorities may want to demonstrate that they are operating fairly by having open competition for funds, at the same time hoping that competition will drive down prices. They may want to audit a provider's income and expenditure, and to decide who should receive services. They may impose certain service orientations or qualities. Generally, trust may be replaced with more formal linkages between the sectors, characterized by closer monitoring and reduced discretion for providers.

Some British studies have documented the administrative burden of competing for public funding, receiving it and accounting for how it has been spent (Kramer, 1981; Leat et al., 1986; Hedley and Rochester, 1992; Lewis, 1993; Mocroft and Thomason, 1993). Contracts are more demanding than grants in each respect. Moreover, the contract revenue may not fully compensate for the administrative burden, risking the diversion of resources away from direct service provision and reducing operational flexibility. Smaller organizations may be especially vulnerable. Professionalization of management and formalization of decision-making processes are other consequences — "running a contract requires both new and more skills" (Lewis, 1993, p.186; and see Meadows, 1992) — which could be inconsistent with the values of voluntarism, mutual aid and informal democracy. Hedley and Davis Smith (1994) found few contracts which made explicit reference to volunteers. To what extent this formalization will push out volunteers or crowd out donations is unclear, for the effects would depend on many things, including the organization's activities and the funding route: quantitative evidence for the UK has yet to unearth any marked effects (Kendall and Knapp, 1991; Leat, 1995; Richardson, 1995; Knapp et al., 1996). In time, voluntary organizations could find it hard to sell themselves to potential donors, and indeed to government purchasers, as alternatives to an over-bureaucratized, unresponsive public sector if they themselves are administratively cumbersome.

However, looking outside the UK, Salamon noted a tendency among US voluntary agency managers to exaggerate the extent to which bureaucratization effects were attributable to government funding:

the pressures for improved agency management, tighter financial control, and use of professionals in service delivery do not, after all, come solely from government (1987, p.115).

Richardson (1995) is just one of a number of people to point out that the movement towards the "new managerialism" in the UK sector cannot be attributed solely to contracting or to competition, but was part of a bigger, cross-sectoral trend of the 1980s which had some explicit encouragement from within the sector, such as the NCVO's commissioning of Charles Handy's (1988) report (Deakin, 1995). The formalization of management is clearly not bad *per se*, and will have led, in many voluntary bodies, to improved clarity of purpose and standards of care. The changes it brought on the local authority side should also have made it easier for independent sector providers to understand purchasers' intentions. Whether inflexibility is the sequela of clarity, as Deakin (1996) posits, is an empirical question yet to be answered.

Inappropriate regulations

To the extent that contracts are enforced, each party would be expected to change in ways consistent with fulfilling the requisite terms and conditions. But the amount of change need not be equal. Many voluntary bodies express concerns that health and local authorities wield considerable purchasing power, and that they may be forced to alter their objectives, processes or clientele.

Contractual regulations may govern input ratios, input prices, service outputs and their prices, access to and distribution of the product, financial probity and even governance. Contracts obviously need to be worded in ways which generate criteria for monitoring, giving rise to the danger that they become dominated by input or process indicators, rather than quality or user outcome measures. This runs the danger of creating inappropriate incentives. If the former *do* predominate, then voluntary sector providers may perform better in global efficiency terms, in spite of an apparent tendency to do less well on measured criteria. The classic study of Wisconsin nursing homes by Weisbrod and Schlesinger (1986) demonstrated how for-profit facilities complied better with input and process regulations than their non-profit counterparts, but had a greater frequency of resident complaints about (unmonitored) aspects of service quality.

The danger of perverse incentives is widely recognized — across all sectors — but the challenge is to make contract regulations or criteria simultaneously manageable and constructive. The problem is compounded when a voluntary body is regulated by more than one public agency, or when a single purchaser is contracting with many providers. The management structures in some voluntary bodies militate against performance-based incentives (Young, 1987; Billis and Harris, 1992, 1996), so that contracts might encourage not only the formalization of voluntary agency management, but also a change of direction. They might represent a "shift of emphasis away from accountability to the user and towards accountability to the purchaser" (Rochester, 1995, p.198; Leat, 1990), when in fact two authoritative reviews of the sector a decade earlier found that accountability of *any* kind was rare (Hatch, 1980; Judge, 1982).

The effects could be more fundamental. As Taylor and Lewis (1993) pointed out, the government's initial hopes that constructive purchaser-provider partnerships would emerge in the new mixed economy (DH/Price Waterhouse, 1991) now look unrealistic.[20] It is true that many local authorities have yet to exercise fully their new purchasing and market-shaping powers,[21] but they are facing financial constraints, many have uncovered high levels of need, and various other forces are pushing them to tighten up their regulation of provision (Leat, 1995). These and other trends could increase the likelihood that authorities will come to view voluntary bodies simply as cheap alternatives to in-house provision, or that resentment will build up because the advantageous tax and social security treatment of voluntary agencies perpetuates the "uneven playing field". (Lewis, 1993, p.186 writes of the exposure of "hidden subsidies".)

There might emerge within a public authority the attitude that something must be done, in Taylor and Lewis's words, to tackle the sector's "apparent reluctance to buckle down to the harsh realities of the new marketplace" (1993). There are certainly examples from across the country of voluntary bodies struggling to gain the status of "approved providers".

Threats to autonomy and goal distortion

It is but a short step from formalization and inappropriate regulation to the dangers that voluntary organizations will lose their autonomy or independence. Contracts may offer security, and the opportunity to compete for public funding may offer the chance to increase organizational revenue, but associated threats to autonomy and independently-set goals have long worried people in the social care sector (Mencher, 1958; Judge, 1982; Leat, 1995). There are, of course, similar worries in other fields where tighter links have also been a cause for concern, even if not dubbed "contracts" at the time (cf. Chapters 5 and 6). Are voluntary organizations in danger of "becoming alternative, rather than autonomous providers of welfare"? (Lewis, 1995a, p.6)

One concern is simply perceived or actual loss of independence,[22] with an organization coming to be seen as an agent of the state — or certainly not supplying a sufficiently distinctive service (Forder and Knapp, 1993) — perhaps leaving volunteers and donors less enthusiastic to offer their support, stifling innovation, marginalizing certain groups in the population, or limiting user choice. The label "voluntary" may itself come to be questioned (see Chapter 8). Loss of independence could then be associated with mission or goal "distortion", where compliance with the state appears to compromise the spirit, if not the letter, of organizations' constitutions. Mencher (1958) cites the early post-war growth of some specialized children's services and community services for elderly people as examples of goal distortion, and Judge (1982) notes that some child care bodies organized their activities so as to avoid such an eventuality. More recent evidence in services for elderly people is offered by Lewis (1993). On the other hand, Richardson's (1995) postal survey revealed no evidence of mission distortion (in terms of who wrote the service specification, changing the nature of the service, changes in client group or introducing user charges), although his methodology was not ideal for answering questions about such fundamental effects.

Contracts may also make it harder for organizations to remain critics of government. Campaigning, lobbying and advocacy work may be reduced, either as a condition of receiving a contract, or via self-censorship prompted by political expedience, or simply because senior staff have less time to devote to these activities when they are busy negotiating contracts. This is a common fear (Flynn and Common, 1990; Gutch, 1992; Lewis, 1993), but again Richardson could find no evidence in his small sample: "contracting has [not] undermined voluntary organiz-ations' ability to engage in campaigning or advocacy" (1995, p.7).

Financial insecurity

Block contracts of reasonable duration clearly bring some financial security to social and health care providers, or at least to those awarded them who previously received no statutory funding or who relied on the relatively unpredictable annual grants cycle. Indeed, the 1989 White Paper, *Caring for People*, suggested that contracts will give voluntary organizations "a sounder financial base and allow them a greater degree of certainty in planning for the future" (Secretaries of State, 1989b, para. 3.4.12). But, perhaps paradoxically, contracts — and certainly competition — might actually engender *in*security. After all, it is the fear of failure, the very existence of insecurity, which gives a market its energy.

As noted earlier, the level of public contractual funding may, like grants, cover only a proportion of the total cost of provision. Voluntary organizations have found themselves having to use their donative or other income to cover deficits. Richardson (1995) found widespread evidence of top-up funding of this kind, as did Knapp (1986) when looking at residential child care some ten years earlier, and Mencher (1958) in the early post-war years. Their other activities, including their advocacy and com-munity development roles, may suffer. Payments may be delayed, a strategy for public sector purchasers given surprising credibility by some government ministers recently, or reim-bursement rates may be pegged at inappropriate levels despite inflated costs, due in turn to salary inflation or — more commonly today — because of changes in the needs of users (Davies and Edwards, 1990). Heightened cost awareness among purchasers leaves some specialist providers — for example, people with challenging behaviours or multiple disabilities — feeling exposed because of the necessarily high costs of their services.

Break clauses undermine the security of many contracts (Richardson, 1995). A rather different problem is the risk of over-investment encouraged by secure financing. It is certainly hoped by purchasers that providers funded under long-term block contracts will invest in quality provision, but they might over-extend themselves, finding themselves having to direct hard-won revenues into maintaining their capital stock (Vladeck, 1976), or they may simply find themselves investing in a service area which is no longer a priority for the purchaser, or a preference for the user. A further difficulty is that many local authorities are still preferring to rely quite heavily on spot rather than block contracts. While the former give flexibility to purchasers (and users, perhaps), they may leave providers vulnerable, especially when they are tied contractually to a multiplicity of authorities (Wistow et al., 1994, ch. 5; 1996, ch. 8).[23]

The transaction costs of learning about, competing for, receiving and accounting for public support can be burdensome (Leat et al., 1986; Davies and Edwards, 1990; Hedley and Rochester, 1992; Lewis, 1993; Mocroft and Thomason 1993; Taylor et al., 1995). Stipulations in the contract — to increase staff/user ratios, to extend night cover, or whatever — may push costs well above previous levels. Just dealing with contract bidding, negotiation and management can increase operating costs without necessarily increasing service level or quality. The transaction costs burden tends to be greater when an organization receives funding from more than one public sector agency (Hartogs and Weber, 1978), although, on the other hand, a multiplicity of funding sources is usually less threatening to an organization's autonomy. If the formalization of the organization's decision-making causes a drop in volunteer involvement, costs will rise even further. Another source of cost inflation could be reductions in statutory sector professional support for voluntary bodies as local authorities' former developmental budgets are transferred to monitoring and control (Taylor and Lewis, 1993). Voluntary bodies will have to do more from their own budgets if they are to maintain service quality.

Eroding the comparative advantage?

Many of the potential or actual effects of contracts run the risk of eroding key and desirable attributes of voluntary bodies. As we have seen, contract negotiations and compliance may inflate costs. Increased bureaucratization and professionalization can be antagonistic to the participative mode of working of many bodies, and may inhibit innovation or constrain flexibility. Contracting may narrow the choice available to individual purchasers if funding is contingent upon satisfaction of certain standards and conformity with certain operational criteria. When we consider the sector's advocacy role, it is clearly important that financial assistance for organizations which criticize either government or private sector producers should not interfere with their independence.

The "contract culture" might therefore threaten the very comparative advantages which local and health authorities often most appreciate when looking to support or purchase from the voluntary sector (Knapp et al., 1990; Flynn and Common, 1992; Walby, 1993; Deakin, 1996). Every major report on the voluntary sector since the early years of the century has emphasized these putative advantages — flexibility, innovative potential, specialist provider, promoter of user choice, cost-effective alternative to the state, participative body, advocate. Paradoxically, seeking to secure these benefits by purchasing them under contract or by giving voluntary bodies the chance to compete for "new money" could potentially undermine them.

7.6 Conclusion

Members of the public recognize the voluntary sector as a key provider of treatment and support for people with a range of health and welfare problems, particularly with physical, sensory or learning disabilities, age-related needs, family problems, or difficulties in childhood and adolescence. Family and other carers of these people are often supported by the voluntary sector, which also acts as an energetic advocate for change, a supporter of disadvantaged groups, and a vehicle for self-help. The general public will be familiar with many of the larger charities with national reputations, and they will probably know of many small groups in their areas offering a range of services.[24]

As we have seen, many of the defining characteristics of modern-day voluntary health and social care were set in place during the 19th century. However, at least as great an influence was the 1940s legislation. Social care remained a relatively low priority in the post-war construction of the welfare state, but the establishment of the NHS was one of the main successes of the period. Many in the Labour government of 1945 frowned on charity as the mainstay of welfare provision, regarding voluntary organizations with suspicion or worse, although perhaps expecting many of them to wither away. However, it was also recognized that it was not politically expedient to attack philanthropy, nor to allow voluntary provision to disappear before something at least as good could be put in its place. It was also regarded as important not to ignore the accumulated expertise of many organizations and individuals in the sector.

Increasing statutory responsibility has not necessarily signified the elimination of voluntary services. The trend has been rather, when possible, to incorporate voluntary effort into total welfare planning (Mencher, 1958, p.138).

Nevertheless, "taken together, the effect of the Labour reforms was to change the size and shape of the space within which the voluntary sector had to operate" (Deakin, 1995, p.43).

A number of traditional voluntary organizations initially struggled to find new roles after the 1940s reforms, particularly those previously most active in providing hospital or other health care. But sectoral fortunes change and, by the late 1960s, many of these organizations were caught up in a new wave of voluntary activity and took on new roles as "sources of information, centres of excellence and means of responsible pressure" (Younghusband, 1978, p.270; and see Deakin, 1995). In fact, throughout the 20th century, the state has recognized that the voluntary organization has distinctive contributions to make: as innovator, specialist, protector of particular interests, supplier to meet certain preferences, vehicle for participative social action, campaigner, and cost-effective alternative to a dominant, even monopolistic, public sector. These features were given particular emphasis around the time of Wolfenden (1978), and have regularly resurfaced as rationales for public sector support in national and local policy debates.

Although it is now the smallest of the three "formal" care sectors in the provision of hospital beds and residential care places for elderly people, the voluntary sector is the largest provider of staffed residential care for adults with physical or sensory disabilities, learning disabilities, and alcohol or drug problems; and of hospice care; and is a substantial provider of mental health services and many specialist child welfare services. Compared to the public sector, it is a relatively modest provider of many non-residential social care services and of most health services, but it dominates pre-school day care and youth development activity.

While considerably less dramatic in its intentions or its impacts than the 1940s legislation, the legislation of 1989 and 1990 is considerably reshaping the policy environments in which many voluntary health and social services bodies operate. Small, local groups may not be greatly affected — at least not directly — but any organization which is funded in more than an incidental way by a local or health authority, or perhaps by central government, is now caught in a maelstrom of fiscal, managerial and competition-induced change. As Lewis comments, "the process of creating the mixed economy has profound implications for relationships between different types of providers and between purchasers and providers." Within the new contract culture, will voluntary organizations emerge as "partners, competitors or also-rans in the provision of care?" (1993, p.191). It is too early to know how voluntary organizations have been affected by the new legislation and subsequent related developments.

The opportunities and challenges for health and social care organizations discussed above are closely mirrored by those confronting the voluntary sector more widely, and it is to these that we turn in the final chapter.

Notes

1 These are self-governing trusts within the public sector. They

are not charitable or independent of the state in law, and we have not included them in our mapping of the voluntary sector.

2 More radical were proposals from the right of the Conservative Party to broaden the base of health care provision, and to encourage private health insurance (e.g. Brittan, 1988; Redwood, 1988). These proposals were not implemented.

3 The statistical profiling of these parts of the voluntary sector was particularly complex, but was made possible by the excellent work of Jason Pinner, assisted at times and in some subfields by Michelle Asbury, Julien Forder, Diane French, Chris Ring and Phil Shore.

4 We do not have access to exactly equivalent data for Scottish regions, Welsh authorities or Northern Irish boards.

5 The CAF annual surveys provide estimates of *all* local authority expenditure (see Chapter 5), but these figures are not directly comparable due to differences in definition and coverage.

6 This decline during the course of the 1980s was primarily due to a fall in social services department "payments" as reliance was placed increasingly on central government's user subsidies to pay for residential care for elderly people, thus allowing local government to shift costs onto central government; see section 7.4, and Wright (1992).

7 According to Sia, the intermediary body for ethnic minority voluntary organizations, at least 2,000 ethnic minority organizations existed in the UK in the early 1990s, concentrated in Greater London and the Midlands, reflecting the large ethnic minority populations in those locales. Unpublished survey research by Sia in 1991, analysed at PSSRU, gives some impression of the huge range of activities undertaken by these groups. Thirty-seven percent of the 139 ethnic minority voluntary organizations which responded to the survey appeared to be primarily concerned with providing social services. The next most frequent primary activity was the provision of multipurpose community facilities, accounting for 28 percent of respondents. Many of the respondents were funded by local government, including social services departments, with far fewer funded under central government schemes. The most frequent central government funding sources cited were the Urban Programme (see Chapter 5), for 11 percent of respondents.

8 The latter's inclusion in Laing and Buisson's statistics as part of "the voluntary sector" is controversial. It can be argued that they do not satisfy the "independence" and "voluntarism" criteria of the structural operational definition (see Kendall and Knapp, 1993, 1995).

9 People who were accepted for admission to private or voluntary homes on the grounds of need — and there were no formal assessment procedures and no public sector monitoring of homes' admission criteria or decisions — were eligible for supplementary benefit support if their financial means prevented them from paying the fees. Although a ceiling was eventually put on the weekly rate of user subsidy, there was a virtually unchecked supply of social security money, and so a virtually unchecked stimulus to the growth of publicly-financed independent provision. The social security bill for these placements, roughly £10 million in 1979, eventually reached over £2 billion by 1993.

10 This preference was of course consistent with the government's stated policy goals. A central objective of the 1990 Act was to encourage greater reliance on care in people's own homes, restating an earlier view that "the primary sources of support and care for elderly people are informal and voluntary. These spring from the personal ties of kinship, friendship and neighbourhood" (DHSS, 1981, para. 1.9). Since 1992, new series of statistical data from the Department of Health show that there has been growth in both private and voluntary domiciliary and day care provision, and a greater willingness on the part of local authorities to contract out these services. The number of contracted-out hours of home help delivered by the voluntary sector increased ninefold in just two years (1992-94), but still represents less than 3 percent of total *registered* provision in England (Department of Health, 1995). The private sector's contracted-out business grew slightly faster and was six times larger than the voluntary sector's in 1994. In the provision and delivery of meals the voluntary sector is a more important contractor to local authorities (36 percent of all publicly-funded meals in 1994), as it is in the provision of day care for elderly people (28 percent of all places funded by authorities in 1994, up from 21 percent in 1992).

11 This "trust" differential probably reflects a mix of historic familiarity with voluntary sector providers, and *perceptions* of motivational differences between sectors. Whether *actual* motivations differ systematically between sectors is a complex question. For example, a study of the motivations and behaviours of independent sector homes, based in part on interviews with proprietors and managers in 1994, found that voluntary sector providers professed to be less likely than their private sector counterparts to see monetary rewards as important, and to be *more* likely to be motivated by a duty or responsibility to particular sections of society (Wistow et al., 1996, ch. 6; see also Wistow et al., 1992, and Common

and Flynn, 1992).Of course, *stated* motivations may diverge from *actual* motivations. Furthermore, both Wistow et al. (1996) and Taylor et al. (1995) point out that the motivational and other boundaries between private and voluntary organizations are blurred in community care, and factors such as size and provider background may be better motivational discriminators between suppliers.

12 For example, the committee of the Church of England Central Home for Waifs and Strays "more and more felt the necessity ... of leaving to the law (except under special circumstances) all cases capable of being relieved by it" (1884, p.12). A hundred years later, the Senior Director of Barnardo's echoed this view: "It is no part of a voluntary agency's task today to run ordinary homes for ordinary children. That is the responsibility of the local authorities and, in any case, ordinary children should not be in residential care at all" (Joynson, 1982, p.5).

13 Child care also had an oppressive side. Many voluntary organizations were active in the enforced emigration of children to Canada, Australia, South Africa and other far-flung parts of the British Empire (Wagner, 1987; Bean and Melville, 1989), a well-meant but quite awful practice which continued even until 1967. In earlier periods some children were taken away from Catholic families to be brought up in the "religiously more favourable" environment of an Anglican home.

14 Home Office Circular 65 in 1954 suggested that public sector payments should meet three-quarters of the cost.

15 The extent of the fall in local authority demand is hard to gauge *precisely* because central government statistics have altered over the post-war period and because they variously included and excluded what became known — after the 1969 Children and Young Person's Act — as controlled and assisted community homes and voluntary homes. All were in the voluntary sector, but had different proportions of their management boards appointed by local authorities.

16 We have not discussed here the contribution of the vast mainstream youth (development) subsector, but this should also be recognized in any discussion of the sector's contribution to young people's welfare. It includes the uniformed groups (including scouts, guides, sea cadets and boys brigades established towards the end of the 19th century), denominational groupings (including the YMCA and YWCA), and a myriad of "independent" youth clubs. Membership of 75 national youth organizations alone has been estimated at well over 6 million young people, with more than half a million volunteers involved at various levels, but there is

also an enormous range of fragmented and entirely local activity without a supporting national infrastructure. Overall, the youth development sector in 1990 was estimated to employ over 12,000 people and involve more than 1.1 million volunteers. Total income amounted to £1.4 billion, 55 percent of it from donations.

17 A feature of the post-war period has been the increasingly common and increasingly successful charitable fundraising activity by NHS hospitals or health authorities to fund core services. Income from this source amounted to £198 million in 1989/90 and £220 million in 1990/91 (Lattimer and Holly, 1992). The trust fund assets of the NHS were valued at £609 million in 1987/88, generating an annual income of £130 million (Fitzherbert, 1990). Prochaska (1992, ch. 9) gives an account of what he calls the "charitable revival" of the 1980s.

18 For people with learning disabilities, the voluntary sector's share of residential accommodation places grew as follows: in England from 20 percent (1985/86) to 28 percent (1990/91) and 36 percent (1993/94); in Scotland from 45 percent to 54 percent and 63 percent in the same years; and in Wales from 10 percent to 15 percent and 28 percent (Kavanagh and Opit, 1996).

19 Data are being gathered from the same 25 local authorities as were sampled in the work reported by Wistow et al. (1994, 1996), and will be published later in 1996.

20 "Partnership" was also a frequently used term in discussions between government and voluntary child care organizations in the run-up to the 1989 Children Act, as well as often being used in a more general rhetorical sense by government (see Chapter 5).

21 See the evidence in Wistow et al. (1994, 1996). In an earlier period, some commentators saw public sector regulation of voluntary bodies as little more than minimal (Home Office statement in Wolfenden, 1978; Hatch, 1980; Kramer, 1981, Judge, 1982). However, this marginal influence was probably correctly explained by Brenton as due to "the diminutive nature of the amounts involved from the government's point of view" (1985, p.93), the wish by public agencies not to counter the autonomy and flexibility of recipient bodies, and because close monitoring was simply impracticable.

22 The definition of independence is not as straightforward as some accounts of the sector have suggested (see 6, 1992).

23 There are many more arguments for and against spot and block contracts than space permits us to explore here. In social services contexts, see Flynn and Common (1990) and Wistow et al. (1996, ch. 8).

24 The variety can be considerable. For example, a survey of organizations in the Canterbury area, conducted as part of our research, found that 44 local social welfare organizations listed almost as many different social care activities, even before distinguishing user groups (French, 1992). Canterbury is not atypical in this regard.

Chapter 8

CONCLUSION

8.1 Introduction

In the opening chapter, we set out a number of reasons for the growth of interest in the role of voluntary organizations in UK society. We argued that this had not, however, been matched by an understanding of the nature of the sector's current, recent and historical economic contribution, nor of its social and political features. The research described in this book has addressed some of the needs for more systematic evidence on how and why the UK voluntary sector has developed historically (Chapter 2), noted the major features of the legal environment in which it operates (Chapter 3), and identified the basic parameters of voluntary organizations as they existed in 1990 (Chapter 4). In Chapters 5 to 7 we went beyond this snapshot to analyse how and why the sector has developed in a number of major fields of activity. Here we begin by making some tentative *ex post* links between our most important findings, and the theoretical perspectives that we described in Chapter 1. However, our main concern in this chapter is to identify and discuss a number of current policy challenges facing the voluntary sector in the UK.

8.2 Theoretical perspectives

An important contribution of this study has been to generate the first complete economic map of the sector, in terms of the key variables of paid employment, expenditures and revenues, as described in Chapter 4. We showed that overall, under both a broad and narrow definition, in 1990 the sector was a significant player as measured by these conventional economic indicators. Education and research, and social services were identified as the largest "industries" under each definition respectively. We charted the basic characteristics of these and other fields of activity, and compared their scale and scope, both with each other,

243

and with their counterparts in other countries participating in the study. It is significant to note that the outputs of the providers in the largest fields of activity under both definitions are usually thought of as quasi-public or collective goods, which is broadly consistent with the role of the sector posited in the theories of Weisbrod and other economists.[1]

These data also show that, in these and other fields, the voluntary sector is, to varying degrees, dependent upon the state for financial support. We have noted in a number of chapters that this typically represents the culmination of a long history of joint effort between the two sectors — involving not just a financial relationship, but also an important regulatory one. In as much as existing economic theories fail to attend to the intimacy of the relationship between the state and the voluntary sector, and are interpreted as implying that the two sectors are always likely to be in conflict and competition, then the critiques of Salamon (1987) and Kuhnle and Selle (1992) of economic approaches appear valid. The dominant economic theories are also partial in the more general sense that they are undergirded with an essentially rationalist, contractarian model — yet we have seen historically, as well as in the more recent past, that there are ideological and political factors, implicitly treated as epiphenomenal in these arguments, which have been critical in shaping the sector's role (cf. Badelt, 1990).

However, while recognizing that, in many cases, the relationships between the sectors appear to have been cooperative, this does not imply that conflict and competition have been unimportant in the UK — an analysis which might tempt us to characterize the relationship between the state and the voluntary sector as "corporatist" or "neo-corporatist". We suggested in Chapter 6 that this may have some purchase — with certain important qualifications — when thinking about the relationship that emerged between the state and maintained voluntary schools in the post-war era, and prior to the recent radical reforms. However, to suggest that this type of partnership, or variants of it, are *necessarily* of general applicability in other contexts would be to generate expectations of stability and balance in the relationship between the sectors. This would be just as misleading as those arising from a model which analysed relationships purely in competitive terms. Historically, the nationalization of the voluntary hospitals, for example, reminds us that the state has not been afraid to treat the sector with rather less respect than the label "partnership" perhaps implies when this has made ideological and political sense (Chapter 7).

More recently, we have argued that Wilson and Butler's (1985) model of "hybrid neo-corporatism" in the mid-1980s tended to overstate the power and influence of voluntary sector inter-mediaries (Kendall and 6, 1994). In Chapter 5, we also saw that some of the major beneficiaries of state largesse in recent years — providers of training under special employment schemes, and groups supported under the Urban Programme — found them-selves relatively powerless when the government decided that their services were no longer required as the economic and pol-itical climate changed. There are a number of good reasons why voluntary organizations, in many contexts, *can* hope to aspire to a more balanced relationship as government comes increasingly to rely upon them, even in the apparently *dirigiste* and competitive climate of the early 1990s (see section 8.3 below). But the factors conducive to a more balanced partnership need to be both theor-ized and charted empirically, rather than simply assumed.

The evidence gathered in this study also allows us to comment on the two major "structural" theoretical themes that we identified in the introductory chapter. As far as the first theme is concerned — the relative importance of legal tradition, the presence of an urban middle class emergent through economic development and political centralization — some observations on the first two of these can be made, using the evidence we have collected in this study.

We concluded Chapter 2 by noting that, at the most general level, the English common law tradition of tolerance has resulted in an absence of obvious legal barriers to the formation of voluntary organizations, obstacles which may exist in civil law countries (see Salamon and Anheier, 1994). However, as we noted in Chapter 3, voluntary organizations are not treated equally under existing law; those recognized as having exclusive-ly charitable purposes have certain special privileges and respon-sibilities, which do not apply to organizations without charitable status. Critics of the legal *status quo* would therefore argue that to treat the freedom of association supported by common law that exists in the UK as broadly supportive of voluntary action may be strictly true, but rather misses the point. The most important feature of the current legal system is how it differentiates *between* voluntary organizations, not how the sector in its entirety is treated.

What of the importance of a middle-class presence for the voluntary sector's development? In the UK, the middle ranks or classes emerged to political and economic power faster than in other countries in part because of the relative openness of the elite (Perkin, 1969), and Chapters 2, 6 and 7 all showed that they have been well represented historically in the formation and running of voluntary organizations. Indeed, the continued apparent dominance of the middle classes in charities in more recent times remains an issue of concern for some modern commentators who have wished to see those from lower socio-economic groups more involved in the late 1980s and early 1990s (for example, Brenton, 1985; Knight, 1993).

However, historically it is important to recall the part played by the long tradition of philanthropy among the aristocratic-church elite in pre-industrial society. Not only was this a mainstay of voluntary action prior to middle-class expansion, but it was this very model which often inspired the new philanthropists to act as they sought to acquire social status. Furthermore, we have also noted that working-class voluntary action also has a healthy tradition, particularly from the 19th century onwards — an aspect of UK voluntary sector activity neglected until relatively recently by historians (Davis Smith, 1995). In the UK at least, the apparent dominance of the middle classes in the world of philanthropy may therefore in part result from a bias in research towards exploring the contribution of the middle, as opposed to both upper and working, classes. Finally, another word of caution is apposite. The middle classes have themselves been an important force behind the expansion of the state (Perkin, 1989). This growth has sometimes been at the expense of voluntary provision, another important reason for being cautious about a positive link between the existence of a significant middle-class presence, and a thriving voluntary sector.

Our final structural theme was the extent to which philanthropy in particular has been an expression of social control exercised by dominant status groups. A ready historical example in the education field is the growth of Sunday schools in the

18th century. Their growth has been characterized as part of a "social control" strategy pursued by newly emerging capitalists keen to create a disciplined and docile workforce, and working in concert with the existing elite's objective to stifle social unrest in the turbulent political climate of that era. Most famously, Marxist historian E.P. Thompson (1980) mounted virulent attacks on the Methodist schools that emerged at that time, accusing them, *inter alia*, of "direct indoctrination", "psychological atrocities", and "religious terrorism". Similar motives characterized some of the other types of schooling which the sector has historically delivered, as well as many of the philanthropic initiatives in health, social services and housing, particularly in the 19th century and in the first half of the 20th century.

Such an emphasis, however, fails to do justice to the full range of motives involved, and certainly oversimplifies the realities of social control. Most obviously, the significance of non-capitalist and non-economic middle-class motives, and the working classes themselves are underplayed in this analysis. For example, Owen (1964) reminds us that mercantilist labour market concerns were joined with genuine humanitarian impulses in motivating support for charity schools, and anti-Catholic prejudice was another factor. These motives cannot easily be explained as narrowly economic, or functional for capital. Furthermore, some historians have correctly questioned the extent to which the notion of "social control" can be dealt with straightforwardly for any given set of motives. Sunday schools, for example, while initially conduits of middle-class values through their sponsors and teachers, may often have been effectively absorbed into working-class culture. As mutual aid social functions were established alongside them, and as working-class tutors replaced middle-class ones, these schools themselves helped to create a self-reliant working-class culture.[2]

8.3 Current policy issues

A diverse, not to say confusing, array of policy issues currently confronts the UK voluntary sector. In pulling these issues together we can structure the discussion around eight broad themes (Box 8.1), some of which have emerged from, and been suggested by,

---

Box 8.1   Current policy issues

- Out of the shadows
- Managing conflict
- The challenges of formalization
- Riding the tiger of competition
- Fostering voluntarism
- Promoting trust and confidence
- Beating the bounds?
- Of maps, means and ends

---

the wider international study (Salamon and Anheier, 1996a).

While pitching some analysis at this level is undoubtedly helpful, it is clear that generalization also has its dangers. "The" voluntary sector (like "the" business sector and "the" public sector) is obviously a shorthand term for many different types of organization. As we have seen, there is huge diversity in terms of size, field of activity, societal function, financial and control structures, organizing principles, ideologies and orientations. By no means every policy issue will therefore be relevant to every organization, or even necessarily to a majority of organizations. By providing this broad overview, therefore, we do not mean to imply that these issues are universal; rather, that the issues are sufficiently pervasive, and certainly sufficiently important to those they affect, to warrant emphasis.

Out of the shadows

Voluntary organizations were the dominant mode for the formal delivery of social welfare up until the early 20th century. We have seen (Chapter 2) that, despite the expansion of the state during this century, and — more recently — the increasing penetration into many of its traditional fields by private enterprise (Chapters 5 and 7), the sector has remained an influential social and economic player. What is clear from this research is increasing awareness of this resilience, with the sector's existing and potential efforts becoming more widely recognized for the reasons we spelt out in Chapter 1.

Conclusion

Although the public profile of voluntary organizations has risen steadily in recent years, a "two sector model" still largely dominates both public discourse and official statistics. The general public still thinks first or mainly of the distinction between public and private, and between the "state" and the "market". And the sector's activities and contributions are usually not separately identified in statistical collections, or are tucked away in some obscure place — a consideration that made the statistical mapping described in Chapter 4 particularly challenging. Perhaps this is understandable given the enormous size of government and the scale and presence of private sector entities, but it means that the voluntary sector and its considerable contributions are frequently overlooked.

There will be exceptions, but we would argue that generally voluntary organizations ought to be able to benefit from a collectively higher profile. They should be able to act as more effective advocates, participative bodies, or instruments of community development. "Transparency" may also be an appropriate *quid pro quo* for their favourable treatment by the tax authorities. Organizations can choose to assume a low profile, but they may then have more difficulty in raising voluntary funds, recruiting volunteers, or offering a realistic and accessible alternative either to government or to the private sector. This is an argument for the production of regular, reliable statistics about the voluntary sector, and for further illumination through research: the sector should not be in the shadows.

Managing conflict

We should not lose sight of the fact that most voluntary bodies do not receive any direct funding from the state, although charities automatically enjoy indirect support through tax advantages. Nevertheless, an imperative facing many organizations is the need for better collaborative links with government. A number of significant tensions or flashpoints arise in this context. For example, differing views exist about the tax advantages extended to charities. Are these government resources which have "escaped from the Treasury" and which are extended to charities in recognition of their activities and social contributions? Or are they charities' resources legitimately kept away or won back from the clutches of a burgeoning state? That is, are they fundamentally public resources or private resources?

Conflict may manifest itself in the development of direct public funding (through grants and contracts) and the concomitant demand for public accountability. The ways in which accountability requirements are pitched and put into practice are likely to be contested by funders and recipients. Measures interpreted as interfering and insensitive by voluntary bodies may be seen as entirely appropriate by their government funders. There are also the tensions which arise when a charity's campaigning is deemed to be inconsistent with the Charity Commission's stipulations on political activity (see Chapter 3), or — more generally — is at odds with government policy or preferences.

In general, some parts of the voluntary sector face the challenge of establishing links with government which are close enough to gain influence and tangible support, but not so close as to lose, or *appear* to lose, operational autonomy or collective identity. The £12 billion question is whether voluntary organizations can sustain the resource and organizational security which can come with statutory funding, while at the same time retaining sufficient ideological integrity and independence to preserve their chosen modes of participation and control. In addition, they must ensure that the public perception of them as recipients of government funding does not dampen volunteering or monetary donations.

The voluntary sector's relations with the public sector will often be tense. Conflict of this kind is the *raison d'être* of some pressure groups. Cosy relationships with central or local government are not necessarily in anyone's long-term interests, but neither is destructive conflict.

The challenges of formalization

Recent policy initiatives have sought to formalize and extend direct forms of government support for the sector, giving rise to a set of developments sometimes referred to as "the contract culture". The highest profile example in the late 1990s is the encouragement of contractual relationships between local government and the sector in the social services field, as we described in Chapter 7. These developments create both opportunities and threats, and certainly pull some of the tensions noted earlier into sharper focus.

The tension currently abroad in the UK about the "contract culture" has not developed because organizations in the voluntary sector have never before faced monitoring restrictions or experienced the mixed blessings of formalized contractual or quasi-contractual links: the job creation, training and child care fields, in relations with central and local government respectively, are obvious precedents (cf. Chapters 5 and 7). Looking further back, 19th century grants in education and early 20th century agency payments all came with strings attached, as we noted in Chapter 6. Rather, the tensions stem from the scale and speed of the changes and the political, social and economic contexts in which they have been introduced. The climate of policy and public opinion in the 1990s is now more strongly interventionist as public sector funders (purchasers) have begun to accumulate the experience, information and confidence to enable them to be more *dirigiste* in their dealings with (funded) providers.

As funding links between voluntary and government agencies become more formal, they impose on all parties various monitoring conditions and duties, as well as penalties for non-compliance. Contract monitoring requires "relevant accurate and complete information ... to judge costs, performance and effectiveness" (De-Hoog, 1984, p.244) and this imposes burdens and constraints on voluntary groups, as we have already noted. From a normative standpoint, society has a right and a duty to exercise some control over how public funds are spent, while from a positive perspective, "politicians have the power to demand a *quid pro quo*, and they use this power to establish rules and standards that gain them goodwill from diverse constituencies" (James, 1987, p.409).

The challenge of formalization, therefore, is that voluntary bodies may find they cannot afford to refuse government money, but in accepting it they may have to acquiesce "too much" with concomitant risks to organizational culture, and to the values and operational principles to which members, users and staff adhere. In the mid-1980s, this was a major dilemma which challenged recipients of central government funding under the job creation and training programmes (see Chapter 5). Today the dilemma is more widely experienced within the voluntary sector in social welfare fields and beyond.

The rules and regulations inherent in contracts, and increasingly common in grant aid, could drive a wedge between the "helper" and the "helped" when many organizations are trying hard not to make the distinction. Indeed, few contracts appear to mention or make allowances for volunteers, a state of affairs which could be interpreted as symptomatic of state agencies' insensitivity to voluntarism (Hedley and Davis Smith, 1994).

For many organizations in the UK voluntary sector, contracts may therefore be seen as potentially threatening. Yet there may also be benefits in terms of clarity, security and income generation (Richardson, 1995). And several commentators have alerted us to reasons why organizational autonomy and integrity may be sustainable in the face of these developments. The cross-national comparative work of Ralph Kramer and colleagues — which has included analysis of social services in England — is of particular relevance in this context. His research concluded that fears about loss of autonomy have often been exaggerated, drawing attention to a number of factors that, taken together, may help to preserve autonomy. This includes organizations' access to a multiplicity of funding sources, the protection of traditional values and practices afforded by some contractual forms, providers' countervailing oligopsony power, and recognition by state agencies that their autonomy should be respected (Kramer, 1981; Kramer et al., 1993). Furthermore, state agencies may (legitimately or otherwise) simply trust voluntary agencies to get on with the job. And even if state agencies may *intend* to implement potentially stifling controls and monitoring procedures, their *ability* to do so in practice may be limited by the pervasiveness of transaction costs (Kendall, 1992). There may also be considerable *political* benefits to be reaped by voluntary organizations from close relations with the state. Being seen to be involved in public service delivery can allow agencies to gain recognition, confirming their legitimacy. In addition, they may also be better positioned to keep abreast of policy developments and to exercise leverage and influence over state officials, shaping public policy priorities and service-delivery structures (Grønbjerg, 1993).

At a broad strategic level, the UK situation has been contrasted with the German "corporatist" model and the "interest group" (lobbying) model in the US, between which it has been located on the grounds that it is not as formal, conservative and elitist as the former, but is more centralized and coherent and less *ad hoc* than the latter (Salamon and Anheier, 1996a). Such generalizations about the relationship between the sectors across all industries and contexts obviously should be treated with caution for the reasons we have already identified. For example, the education field, at least until the recent reforms, appears rather closer to the German model than other fields (cf. Chapter 6). But it is noteworthy that the broad principle of putting an onus on government departments and agencies to clarify both their own goals and the expectations of the voluntary organizations they fund — as set out in the recent Efficiency Scrutiny of government funding of the sector (Home Office, 1990) — have been broadly welcomed by the sector's umbrella body. While there have been teething problems associated with the report's implementation, these are still early days. It remains to be seen whether the various tensions at stake can be satisfactorily resolved from the perspective of both government and voluntary organizations.[3]

Riding the tiger of competition

In many chapters of this book, we have described how the new climate of competition is generating some difficult challenges. In many fields, voluntary organizations are facing increasing competition from private sector and government providers in the emerging "quasi-markets" of British public policy. Moreover, there is often tough competition *between* voluntary organizations for government support or market share. In making purchasing decisions, public sector bodies often find themselves increasingly hamstrung by budget constraints and the requirements of auditors. In such situations, the qualities and contributions of well-respected voluntary sector providers might not easily be couched in terms or measures which are consistent with the demands of the new competitive environment. Furthermore, developmental support for new and innovative organizations may be even harder to justify under the pressures of short-term fiscal austerity.

Existing legal and fiscal arrangements give voluntary organizations in general, and charities in particular, both advantages and disadvantages when compared to private sector operators.

For example, while they have favoured tax treatment, their inability to offer returns to shareholders (because they cannot distribute profit) may also limit their access to capital, and make them relatively less responsive than their "for-profit" (private) counterparts. Their constitutions may limit the scope for diversification. Acute hospital care, residential and nursing home care, and government programmes in the fields of training and urban regeneration, are all examples of areas where voluntary bodies have conspicuously lost market share to private sector competitors in recent years (Chapters 5 and 7).

Even if they are able to respond (and some may simply not *wish* to), perhaps through fundraising or capital support from government (housing is a particularly good example of the latter), the dilemma confronting many organizations is whether and how to be competitive (in terms of prices) without jeopardizing quality, compromising ideologies, "distorting mission" or destroying well-honed collaborative links with other voluntary bodies. Any of the latter outcomes could undermine the rationale for special treatment by society, threatening monetary donations, volunteering and tax advantages. Commercial and other pressures on voluntary bodies may require significant internal restructuring and the professionalization of management. In turn, these may destroy valued aspects of organizational culture or ethos.

Fostering voluntarism

How are voluntary organizations to survive, to resist the potential loss of autonomy associated with government funding and simultaneously to improve competitiveness in the face of various other challenges? One possible solution is to expand commercial income earned from activities related or unrelated to organizational mission (from fees and sales, respectively). Another is to expand the scale of donations of money and time. We have already discussed some of the dangers and tensions associated with the first option. What are the prospects for success with the second? Increasing the supply of volunteers — either the number of people participating or the number of hours they work — could be made more difficult by changes in demography, labour markets and marital patterns. Volunteering is more common in middle age and then declines,

while many services and activities for older people rely on volunteer support. Women are more likely than men to volunteer for
some activities and in some fields, for example in health and social
welfare, but not if they are in full-time employment. And volunteering is less common among single people than among married
couples (Knapp et al., 1995). On the other hand, many voluntary
organizations are getting better at recruiting, training and keeping
volunteers, through careful targeting on different groups within
the population, by encouraging the view of volunteering as a social
activity rather than a duty, and by offering to pay expenses where
needed.

Turning to monetary donations, the broad UK voluntary sector
currently gets a comparatively large proportion of its total
revenue from private giving, around 12 percent, making it one
of the best-resourced within the thirteen-country comparative
study. The narrower voluntary sector (by our definition) gets a
considerably higher proportion of income — nearly a quarter —
from private donations. Yet this probably represents a lower
proportion of the sector's total income than ever before. Diverse
data sets and definitions make comparisons over time extremely
difficult, but donations as a *proportion* of total income almost
certainly witnessed a steady decline between the 1940s and the
late 1970s (Chesterman, 1979), and this trend seems likely to
have continued (Kendall, 1996).

With commercial income and public funding continuing to
rise, and the *proportion* of income attributable to individual donations declining, what about other sources of private giving?
We have seen that companies and grant-making trusts also make
significant contributions. Nevertheless, the most important
source of private donative income is still the public at large.
Voluntary organizations (in the broad voluntary sector) received
some £1.9 billion from individual donors in 1990, while in the
same year under a much broader definition from the givers'
side — which includes a variety of forms of support that we
have treated as commercial, and includes gifts for sacramental
purposes and to statutory bodies — total donations may have
been somewhere in the range £3.4 to £5 billion (Halfpenny and
Pettipher, 1991).

Yet most people give only small amounts — the typical
(median) respondent in the 1993 Individual Giving Survey

(Halfpenny and Lowe, 1994) gave just £2.50 per month. More-over, the national lottery may further reduce voluntary sector income by "diverting" individuals' donations — creating the most acute problems for organizations which cannot turn to the lottery itself for funding as they lie outside its priority areas. The National Council for Voluntary Organisations has expressed concern that the lottery may provide an excuse for government to decrease its direct funding of the sector, and that it may adversely affect existing small lotteries which are important to the financial health of some organizations.

Should government be offering more and better fiscal or tax incentives to aid the sector? In recent years, tax advantages to charities have been progressively expanded, particularly in the Chancellor of the Exchequer's budgets over the period 1986 to 1990, in part to compensate organizations for an increased indirect tax burden through higher rates of value added tax (London Economics, 1995). There certainly remains scope for expansion, as Britain's tax system still offers fewer inducements to donate to charity than are to be found in some other countries, noticeably the US. The voluntary sector would of course itself argue that tax advantages should be protected and enhanced, yet such calls are unlikely to remain unchallenged over the coming years. In particular, following in the footsteps of their US counterparts (US Small Business Administration, 1984), there are signs that some private sector organizations are not happy with the *status quo*, let alone any further extension of tax advantages. Do tax advantages give charities an "unfair" advantage? Or are they legitimate recognition of special qualities inherent in their activities? If it is the latter, is it appropriate for this support to be "unselective" and "indiscriminate", linked merely to legal objects as at present; or should it be more closely related to the proven meeting of individual or social need? Or would the latter necessitate the building of a stifling bureaucracy? We do not have the answers to these questions — although we would obviously have our own views — but they are sure to be asked with increasing frequency over the coming years (see Chesterman, 1979, ch. 17, for an interesting early discussion; more recently, see Knight, 1993; Windsor, 1994; Mulgan and Landry, 1995).

It must be stressed that enhancing tax incentives does not,

of course, *guarantee* increased charitable giving. The Individual Giving Surveys reveal that only 9 percent of individual donations reach organizations through tax-efficient routes, and much of this appears to be channelled to sacramental religious organizations (Halfpenny and Lowe, 1994). Moreover, it is certainly not obvious from recent UK evidence that improvements in tax incentives to individual and corporate donors would increase donations by an amount which is larger than the loss in tax revenue to government.

The fact that the direction and volume of donations of money and time are — by definition — largely determined by individuals' preferences (constrained by income), within the framework of wider norms, values and social expectations, and not by tax treatment alone should not be overlooked. In these circumstances, if greater levels of donative income are desired, it may be more important to change individual and corporate attitudes and interpretations of responsibility and citizenship than to tinker with fiscal privileges. Yet recent experience suggests that this, too, may be difficult to engineer. The apparent failure of the concept of "active citizenship" to take off in the early 1990s confirms that rhetoric and exhortations in isolation are unlikely to yield results. The cultivation of an ethos of giving is likely to require substantial long-term commitment and fundamental cultural change.

Promoting trust and confidence

Voluntary organizations depend heavily on public trust. They need to exude competence and inspire confidence if they are to be first-preference providers for users of services, reliable contractors to government agencies, and responsible recipients of donations. The "bad apple" problem could be serious: a single scandal involving a voluntary organization and its misuse of donations can have repercussions for other organizations working in the same field or even for the sector as a whole. Even seemingly "excessive" expenditure on organizational management and administration, apparently diverting donated funds from mission-related activities, could affect the public's willingness to give (Saxon-Harrold, 1993). In the last two or three years, the "sleaze spotlight" has lingered longest on central and local government and on the newly-privatized industries, with less attention paid to the voluntary sector (although there have certainly been examples of scandals). Thus far it would appear that the voluntary sector has remained *relatively* unscathed (Chapter 1). But as voluntary organizations shoulder more public responsibilities, and so come under greater public scrutiny, any perceived weaknesses, insufficiencies or misjudgements could make them easy targets for criticism.

Coming "out of the shadows" is obviously important for engendering trust and confidence, but accountability — including the effective monitoring of the non-distribution constraint — is also critical. The role of law is pivotal in generating trust among potential donors, and the importance for charities of an effective Charity Commission "watchdog" has been widely recognized. The Commission came in for a fair amount of criticism in the 1980s because of its failure to implement effective monitoring policies, and there has been widespread support for the recent reforms which give it more authority. There is, however, still considerable scope for improvement in the operation of these reforms, for example, in enhancing the usefulness of the register and clarifying inter-agency procedures in the handling of allegations of fraud.[4]

The voluntary sector can itself contribute to the drive for greater trust and confidence. This may have to be earned proactively, and should certainly not be taken for granted. A common aim is to indicate to the general public that donations are appropriately and efficiently used for charitable purposes, and that impropriety will not be tolerated. There already exist some voluntary codes of practice to assure quality and probity in fundraising. Making actual and potential donors aware of the arrangements for accreditation and self-regulation is an important complement to the external regulation from government, their appointees or the courts.

Beating the bounds?

Towards the new millennium, the voluntary sector — and more especially the charitable sector with its automatic and wide-ranging tax advantages — may well be forced to generate more substantive evidence than currently exists as to its exceptional character in order to legitimize its claim for special treatment from the state. At the same time, however, it has little room for man-oeuvre to preserve or enhance a distinct identity because of the various resource constraints it faces. This raises fundamental questions about the meaning of "the voluntary sector", and its distinctive features, on which the debate has only just begun — and a debate to which, it is hoped, this book will contribute.

The boundaries around the voluntary sector have never been clear in the UK. Moreover, some of the pressures and develop-ments identified in this book — both within the sector and out-side it — are making sectoral distinctions harder to sustain. Many such developments are "putting the squeeze" on voluntary org-anizations. These include the formalization of links between government funders and voluntary sector contractors, the com-petitive pressures from government and private businesses in newly developing quasi-markets, and the threats to donations from the national lottery. Other trends could also be seen as dissolving the integrity of the "voluntary sector" concept, in-cluding increased fundraising by or on behalf of statutory bodies, such as NHS trusts and local authority schools, the lowering of the barriers between paid workers and volunteers, and the creation of hybrid "not-for-profit" entities, including grant main-tained schools (Chapter 6) and quasi-businesses floated off from local authorities in social care (Chapter 7).

Further confusing those who value the notion of a distinctive "third sector" has been the government's dismissal of calls for clarification of the allocation of responsibilities between the state and voluntary sector (as recommended by the Commission on Citizenship, 1990, set up by the Speaker of the House of Com-mons) as "neither feasible nor desirable", and potentially stultify-ing. Similarly, a recent commentary on the sector's resource base concluded:

Those who search for certainty in demarcation will not find it in legislation, nor in statements of government policy, nor in departmental practice. The world is simply not that neat and tidy a place and the players strenuously resisted being placed in neatly labelled com-partments (Hazell and Whybrew, 1993, p.29).

Inappropriate and insensitive "pigeon-holing" may not be the answer, and the "voluntary" label is clearly but one dimension of identity for the organizations we have discussed in this book. But although the "voluntary" label provides only a partial description, it does not automatically follow that the concept of the voluntary sector is no longer a useful one. Nor does it imply that some of the confusion which currently appears to be prevalent in the sector cannot be removed. After all, the government, business and informal sectors are characterized by a confusing variety of organizational forms which often appear to have little in common. Yet few have suggested that these sectoral labels be jettisoned or replaced. We should be aware of the limitations of such labels, and continuously seek to assess and re-assess the taken-for-granted assumptions that underpin their deployment. But the case that they are no longer useful "islands of meaning" with which we can communicate and by which we can economically make sense of reality (Zerubavel, 1991) has yet to be convincingly made.

While the search for absolute unifying principles underpinning voluntary action would almost certainly prove fruitless, the sector might stand to gain from "beating the bounds" — tracing out more clearly its territory in terms of its goals and expectations, its priorities and interests, its values and strengths. The fact that these vary by field of activity and policy community makes the task all the more important. It is plausible to suggest that, as government builds on the important first steps of implementation of its major 1990 Efficiency Scrutiny and becomes increasingly explicit about its funding priorities and expectations, those parts of the voluntary sector which continue to engage directly with the state could themselves benefit from making clearer what they can and cannot realistically achieve.

Of maps, means and ends

Nearly fifty years ago, William Beveridge abandoned his attempt to map "voluntary action" or the philanthropic motive, and counselled others to do likewise. At the start of a chapter which described his classification of organizations and gave a few summary indicators, he wrote:

There is thus no possibility of making a numerical estimate of the total scale of philanthropic action. Nor indeed would much be gained by attempting this. Individual philanthropic agencies differ from one another so widely that they cannot be made the subject of useful statistical summary. They are so numerous that they cannot be described in any reasonable limit of space. They are liable to rapid change and development (Beveridge, 1948, p.121).

The inherent variability within the voluntary sector — variability of size, governance structures, orientation, goals, resources, constraints, ideologies and many other things — necessarily makes any mapping of statistical characteristics all the more difficult to complete. The same variability has made it extremely hard to summarize general policy issues facing the sector and its main stakeholders. But it is precisely because of this variability that such endeavours are so important. The voluntary sector's contributions to the UK economy, polity and society are so many and so various that its distinguishing features and its distinctive contributions need to be charted accurately and appreciated widely.

Notes

1 On the public good and externality characteristics of education, see, for example, Barr (1993, pp.341, 345); on social services, see Knapp (1984, ch.6).
2 Davis Smith (1995, pp.17-19) provides references supporting and refuting the "social control" thesis.
3 Mabbott (1992a) notes complaints about a lack of opportunity to influence programme aims and objectives, failure to provide information about application procedures, and problems of timeliness.
4 We are grateful to Perri 6 for this observation.

APPENDIX 1

A1.1 Applying the ICNPO in the UK

Table A.1 summarizes the three-digit level categories used in applying the ICNPO to the UK, and identifies which elements of the GUSTO approach were used in the mapping in each case (see page 104 for an explanation of GUSTO). Table A.2 provides details of the response rates where there was almost exclusive reliance on targeted surveys and the subsectors turned out to be economically significant; while Table A.3 reports on the coverage and response rates to our territorial surveys.

Establishments or groups in the sector were in principle always divided between those which were primarily grant-making, and those whose resources were used internally: that is, in-house, within the organization. "Primarily" meant the activity in which most operating (current) expenditures were incurred: i.e. primarily grant-making organizations were defined as those for which external grants to other organizations exceeded 50 percent of total expenditure. Organizations which were primarily grant-making were then allocated to Group 8 as "philanthropic intermediaries", regardless of the field of operation of their fundees. As is demonstrated in Table A.1, Group 8 as interpreted in the UK therefore included traditional grant-making trusts and foundations relying heavily on endowment or property income. But it also included fundraising organizations at the local and national level whose principal activity was making cash or in-kind grants to other bodies (voluntary or statutory), and which might rely largely on donations, subscriptions and membership fees for their income.

Primarily *non*-grant-making organizations (for which grants to other organizations totalled less than 50 percent of total expenditure) were allocated to their appropriate subgroup. This involved identifying the ICNPO category in which the majority of operating expenditure was incurred. If this could not be separately identified, then the name of the organization and any other available information was used as an indicator (for example, activities described in the Annual Report, if available). The only case where this rule was not applied was that of certain "types" of organization specifically identified in Table A.1 which were always all kept in the same group, even if some appeared to be more active in other ICNPO subgroups. For example, all *Councils for Voluntary Service* were allocated to Group 8, even if individual CVSs appeared to use most of their resources under Group 4 or Group 6. Similarly, all *village halls* were classified in group 6 100, even if they appeared to be primarily recreational. This was to ensure consistency when umbrella group survey data were used.

A1.2 Specific data sources deployed by mapping strategy for ICNPO group

Table A.1 summarizes which elements of the GUSTO approach were used at the three-digit UK-specific version of the ICNPO. In the remainder of this appendix, we simply identify the relevant data sources that were most important in mapping the most substantive components in each ICNPO group.

Group 1 Culture and recreation

The *culture and arts* subsector was mapped using financial information contained in the annual reports and other documentation supplied by arts-funding quangos (including Arts Councils and Regional Arts Boards); information extracted from research by the Policy Studies Institute on amateur arts, arts centres, arts festivals; and data available from government and independent research on national and independent museums. In addition, we employed data collated by the Chartered Institute of Public Finance and Accountancy (CIPFA), the Association for Business Sponsorship of the Arts, and the Department of Employment's Census of Employment. A small survey of zoos and aquaria was undertaken. For *recreation*, the Henley Centre for Forecasting's surveys of amateur sports clubs were utilised, and our own small survey of non-profit, non-sports social clubs was conducted and combined with information from, *inter alia*, the Clubs and Institutes Union. *Service clubs* (including Rotary, Lions, Inner Wheel, etc.) were mapped with a small targeted survey.

Group 2 Education and research

In *primary and secondary education,* charitable independent schools were charted using data extracted from Department for Education (DfE) annual surveys, the Independent School Information Service and work undertaken for the Charities Aid Foundation in the mid-1980s (Posnett and Chase, 1985); maintained voluntary schools were mapped using published data from the DfE for paid employment and by combining CIPFA data with unpublished DfE data using regression analysis to generate financial estimates (Kendall, 1993a). We surveyed voluntary sector special schools. *Higher education* estimates drew on published information collated by the Universities Statistical Record for the Universities Funding Council (as was), and published and unpublished data from the Polytechnics and Colleges Funding Council (as was). *Other education* relied, *inter alia*, on our own targeted surveys of Workers' Educational Association Districts, Women's Institutes, and Residential Colleges. Estimates for *research* were constructed by combining survey data reported annually by the Central Statistical Office with intermediary body data.

Group 3 Health

Data for *acute hospitals* came from umbrella body information and our own targeted survey. *Nursing homes* were mapped as part of the Group 4 stream of work (see below). *Mental health providers* were covered by means of another targeted survey (Schneider, 1993); and this strategy was also adopted in the case of *other health*, with the exception of hospices and terminal care, where existing survey information from umbrella bodies and others was deployed.

Group 4 Social services

Personal social services were mapped partly by means of a postal survey of voluntary organizations listed in the *Social Services Yearbook 1990/91*, requesting annual reports and accounts. We chose random samples of organizations in some heavily-populated fields, and contacted all listed organizations in other fields. We also deployed data used to compile the CAF "top 400 fund-raising charities" in 1991 (Charities Aid Foundation, 1991), and we approached many of these bodies for supplementary information. A separate postal survey was also undertaken of social services exclusively for women (or men) not covered by other service categories.

Our estimates were cross-checked by examining Revenue Outturn (RO3) returns by local authorities to central government, detailing payments to voluntary organizations by client group and service type (available on databases held at PSSRU); and by checking NCVO and CAF data on local and health authority funding of the sector. With knowledge of receipts by larger voluntary organizations coming from our other mapping activities, we could treat the residual as an approximation to the receipts of local government and NHS funds by smaller bodies, which we were only able to map on a sample locality basis. *Youth development* was mapped using annual reports and accounts data held by the National Association of Voluntary Youth Services (as was), supplemented by experts' guestimates for bodies not so covered.

Other components of group 4, *emergency and relief* and *income maintenance*, were mapped by combining umbrella body information and a small targeted survey, and data available in Hemmington Scott and CAF publications on larger organizations, respectively.

Group 5 Environment

A large targeted survey was undertaken for environmental bodies, sampling from the Environmental Information Service database, and these estimates were combined with information collected by a number of generalist and specialist intermediary bodies (see Pinner et al., 1993).

Group 6 Development and housing

Community development was mapped using information already collated or available from Action with Communities in Rural England and the British Association of Settlements and Social Action Centres on village halls and settlements respectively. A special survey of community associations was undertaken with the cooperation of the National Federation of Community Organisations (now renamed Community Matters). Data also came from the Commission for Racial Equality on Race Equality Councils. *Economic development* relied on, *inter alia*, information on credit unions from independent surveys, business support agencies from Business in the Community and Open University surveys, estimates and guestimates supplied by Community Enterprise UK on community businesses and Loughborough University Department of Transport Technology on community transport, and information from the Association of Technical Aid Centres. *Housing* was charted using data supplied by the Housing Corporation on housing associations and the National Federation of Housing Associations. The profile of *training and employment providers* drew on NCVO's databases on Employment Training, Youth Training and the European Social Fund, and sheltered employment data from the Employment Department's Disability Services Branch.

Group 7 Civic and advocacy organizations

A small survey was undertaken of national *pressure groups not elsewhere classified* (see Chapter 4) drawing on a number of directories, primarily the CBD Directory of British Associations. *Law and legal services* were charted using data supplied by the National Association of Citizens Advice Bureaux, the Federation of Independent Advice Centres and the Law Centres Federation. Data supplied by the relevant national and umbrella bodies were used to map the remainder of this field.

Group 8 Philanthropic intermediaries

Statistics on national endowed and fundraising *grant-making trusts* were extracted from the directories of various intermediary bodies, the Hemmington Scott directory and the Association of Medical Research Charities. Local estimates drew on the work undertaken for the Community Council for Wiltshire's parochial charities database, while information on charitable government-funded quangos was extracted from annual reports and accounts. National *voluntarism promotion and support* were mapped using targeted survey data, while local groups were covered using existing survey data from the National Association of Councils for Voluntary Service, the National Association for Volunteer Bureaux, and an Aston Business School survey of Rural Community Councils.

Group 9 International activities

A small targeted survey was conducted and combined the data with national intermediary body information, including the Yearbook of International Organisations and the Third World Directory (Giles, 1990).

Group 11 Trade unions, professional, business associations and trade associations

Employment data were used from the Department of Employment's Census of Employment. In the case of trade unions and employers' associations, the financial information came from the Certification Officer for Trade Unions and Employers' Associations. Financial estimates for professional associations and trade associations were generated using surveys based upon the CBD Directory of British Associations, while umbrella body data (including figures supplied by the Association of British Chambers of Commerce) were used to map chambers of commerce.

Table A.1

Three digit-level data: UK specific codes and data collection strategies

	G	U	S	T	O
GROUP 1: CULTURE & RECREATION					
1 100 Culture and Arts					
1 110 Professional arts organization	✓	✓	✓	✓	
1 120 Arts festival	✓				
1 130 Arts centre or youth theatre NEC	✓				
1 140 Other amateur arts or media organization, etc.		✓		✓	
1 150 Museum, gallery or related body	✓	✓			
1 160 Zoo or aquarium					✓
1 200 Recreation					
1 210 Amateur sports club	✓	✓			
1 220 Other recreation/leisure organization				✓	
1 230 Ex-servicemen's social club		✓			
1 240 Other social club		✓		✓	
1 300 Service Club				✓	
GROUP 2: EDUCATION & RESEARCH					
2 100 Primary and Secondary Education					
2 110 Charitable independent school	✓	✓	✓		
2 120 Aided or special agreement voluntary school	✓		✓		
2 130 Voluntary special school	✓				✓
2 140 Grant maintained (opted out) school	✓	✓			
2 150 City technology college	✓	✓			
2 160 Intermediary or umbrella body				✓	
2 200 Higher Education					
2 210 University funded by UFC	✓		✓		
2 220 Oxbridge college		✓	✓		
2 230 Polytechnic or college funded by PCFC	✓				
2 240 Higher education not funded by UFC or PCFC					✓
2 300 Other Education					
2 310 WEA (incl. branches, districts)		✓		✓	
2 320 Women's Institute		✓		✓	
	G	U	S	T	O

Table A.1 (continued)

		G	U	S	T	0
2 325	Townswomen's Guild*					
2 330	Residential adult education					✓
2 340	Urban studies centre					
2 350	Development education centre					✓
2 360	Culture and/or language association*					
2 370	Other adult/continuing education (incl. primarily educational recreation/leisure organization)*					
2 380	Vocational and technical education NEC*					
2 390	Intermediary or umbrella body					✓
2 400	**Research**					
2 410	In-house medical research body		✓			
2 420	Other in-house research body	✓				

GROUP 3: HEALTH						
3 100	**Hospitals and Rehabilitation**					✓
3 200	**Nursing Homes**	✓	✓			
3 300	**Mental Health and Crisis Intervention**					✓
3 400	**Other Health Services**					
3 410	Hospice or other terminal care		✓	✓		
3 420	Emergency medical services		✓			✓
3 430	Complementary medicine/alternative health		✓		✓	✓
3 440	HIV or AIDS-related organization		✓		✓	✓
3 450	Alcohol and addiction services		✓		✓	✓
3 460	Health education and promotion NEC				✓	✓
3 470	Other health services NEC				✓	✓

GROUP 4: SOCIAL SERVICES						
4 100 Social Services, excl. temporary housing, emergency & refugees, income support, etc.						
4 110	Social services for children and families (not pre-school playgroups, etc.)		✓		✓	✓
4 120	Social services for elderly people	✓	✓		✓	✓
4 130	Social services for people with learning difficulties/disabilities		✓		✓	✓

		G	U	S	T	0

Table A.1 (continued)

			G	U	S	T	0
4 140	Social services for people with physical disabilities		✓			✓	✓
4 150	Social services for women			✓		✓	✓
4 160	Carers' organizations					✓	✓
4 170	Pre-school day care organization			✓			
4 180	Mainstream youth development organization			✓			
4 190	Social services NEC, incl. multiple client groups					✓	✓
4 200	**Emergency and Relief**						
4 210	Refugee and immigrant social services					✓	✓
4 220	Disaster/emergency prevention and control					✓	✓
4 300	**Income Support and Maintenance**		✓			✓	
GROUP 5: ENVIRONMENT							
5 100	Environment			✓			✓
5 200	Animals			✓			✓
GROUP 6: DEVELOPMENT AND HOUSING							
6 100	**Economic, Social & Community Development**						
6 110	Multipurpose community association/centre						✓
6 120	Village hall			✓	✓		
6 140	Settlement or social action centre			✓	✓		
6 150	Other multipurpose community organization, committee or council, incl. residents' and tenants' association*						
6 160	Business support agency			✓			
6 170	Community business NEC			✓			
6 180	Community transport association NEC			✓			
6 190	Economic development intermediary or umbrella body NEC (incl. credit unions)			✓			✓
6 200	**Housing**						
6 210	Housing association		✓	✓	✓		
6 240	Housing organization other than housing association			✓			✓
6 300	**Employment and Training**						

			G	U	S	T	0

Table A.1 (continued)

	G	U	S	T	0
6 310 Primarily ET or YT provider	✓			✓	✓
6 320 Primarily ESF funded provider	✓			✓	✓
6 350 Provider not funded by the above				✓	✓

GROUP 7: LAW, ADVOCACY, AND POLITICS
7 100 Civic and Advocacy Organisation

	G	U	S	T	0
7 110 Pressure/interest/campaigning group other than civil rights NEC					✓
7 120 Civil rights organization					✓
7 200 Law and Legal Services					
7 210 Citizens' advice bureau		✓			
7 220 Law centre		✓			
7 230 Generalist independent advice centre		✓			
7 240 Crime prevention NEC		✓		✓	
7 250 Victim support scheme		✓		✓	
7 260 Rape crisis/support		✓		✓	
7 270 Women's refuge		✓		✓	
7 280 Care and resettlement of offenders, intermediate treatment		✓		✓	
7 290 Consumers' association NEC		✓		✓	

GROUP 8: PHILANTHROPIC INTERMEDIARIES AND VOLUNTARISM PROMOTION
8 100 Philanthropic Intermediaries

	G	U	S	T	0
8 110 Endowed grant-making trust (not medical research)	✓		✓		
8 120 Fundraising grant-making trust (not medical research)	✓		✓		
8 130 Grant-making medical research charity	✓		✓		
8 140 Federated fundraising organization					✓
8 180 Grant-making government-funded charitable quango (incl. Arts Councils, Boards)					✓
8 190 Voluntarism promotion: local generalist (multi-ICNPO, sector-wide)	✓				
8 195 Voluntarism promotion: national generalist (multi-ICNPO, sector-wide)					✓

	G	U	S	T	0

Table A.1 (continued)

	G	U	S	T	0
GROUP 9: INTERNATIONAL ACTIVITIES		✓			✓
GROUP 11: BUSINESS, PROFESSIONAL ASSOCIATIONS AND UNIONS					
11 100 Business, Professional Associations and Unions					
11 110 Trade unions		✓			
11 120 Employers' association		✓			
11 130 Business association					✓
11 140 Professional or trade association					✓
11 150 Chamber of Commerce			✓		
	G	U	S	T	0

Groups 7 300 (political parties) and 10 (religious congregations) were not included in the statistical mapping.

* Field where no feasible mapping strategy was identified. These were areas assumed to be small in financial and paid employment terms.

Abbreviations: NEC Not elsewhere classified; UFC Universities Funding Council; PCFC Polytechnic and Colleges Funding Council; WEA Workers' Educational Association; ET Employment training; YT Youth training; ESF European Social Fund.

Table A.2

Response rates to major organizational surveys[a]

ICNPO code and field	Total identified	Sampling population	No. of usable responses	Effective response rate (%)
1 260 Zoos and aquaria	21	21	11	52.4
2 130 Special schools[b]	230	230	53	23.0
3 100 Acute hospitals	83	83	46	56.0
3 300 Mental health[c]	40	40	20	50.0
5 100 5 200 Environment[d]	5,247	783	151	19.3
6 130 Community associations	770[e]	384	99	25.8
11 130 Trade/business associations	1,509	200	63	31.5
11 140 Professional associations	1,180	788	102	12.9

a   We do not report *all* survey response rates: in total some 50 surveys were undertaken as part of the organizational survey component of the GUSTO strategy, some with very small identified populations. Rather, we have chosen the nine areas which are both economically significant — with a total estimated income in excess of 0.25 per cent of the estimated total operating income of the broad voluntary sector in 1990 (greater than £74 million) — and where we relied exclusively, or almost exclusively on targeted ICNPO top-down surveys to generate our estimates. Some of these surveys are available in report form from the PSSRU or elsewhere:

b   See Kendall (1993b).

c   See Schneider (1993).

d   See Pinner et al. (1993).

e   This figure refers to the number of organizations in membership of the umbrella body from which the sample was drawn (then the National Federation of Community Organisations, now renamed Community Matters). This was known to represent only a fraction of the total number of multipurpose community halls throughout the UK, and for the purposes of estimation it was assumed that 5,000 such facilities existed (a figure based on anecdotal evidence, but verified by experts in the area).

Table A.3

Territorial (locality) surveys

Locale	Auspices	Population	No. of usable responses	Effective response rate (%)
Liverpool[a]	PSSRU	1,046	298	28
Staffordshire[b]	Staffs TEC[d]	1,000	322	32
Canterbury & Thanet[c]	PSSRU	275	44	16
Camden[c]	PSSRU/NISW	116	31	27

Note: Primary data generated in the CENTRIS study local mappings (Knight, 1993, Chapter 6) were also deployed and used to identify potential gaps in coverage.

ICNPO coverage:

a Broad voluntary sector *less* groups 2, 3100, 3200, 11.
b Approximate (implicitly) to narrow voluntary sector.
c Groups 3 and 4 only.
d Survey originally undertaken and analysed by CAG consultants. Data re-analysed for the Comparative Nonprofit Sector Project, UK leg, by PSSRU.

Table A.4

Broad voluntary sector employment and operating
expenditures by ICNPO groups and subgroup, 1990

ICNPO major group and subgroup	FTE employment		Operating expenditures	
	N	%	£m	%
1 CULTURE & RECREATION	**262,401**	**27.7**	**5,394**	**20.4**
1 100 Culture	56,011	5.9	1,503	5.7
1 200 Recreation	206,357	21.8	3,877	14.7
1 300 Service clubs	33	0.0	14	0.0
2 EDUCATION & RESEARCH	**330,307**	**34.9**	**11,182**	**42.4**
2 100 Primary & secondary education	133,622	14.1	4,672	17.7
2 200 Higher education	180,891	19.1	5,941	22.5
2 300 Other education	4,599	0.5	26	0.1
2 400 Research	11,195	1.2	543	2.1
3 HEALTH	**43,338**	**4.6**	**926**	**3.5**
3 100 Hospitals & rehabilitation	12,928	1.4	303	1.1
3 200 Nursing homes	8,925	0.9	146	0.6
3 300 Mental health	3,317	0.4	70	0.3
3 400 Other health services	18,168	1.9	407	1.5
4 SOCIAL SERVICES	**146,028**	**15.4**	**3,029**	**11.5**
4 100 Social services	143,534	15.2	2,955	11.2
4 200 Emergency & refugees	1,000	0.1	42	0.1
4 300 Income support & maintenance	1,494	0.2	31	0.1
5 ENVIRONMENT[a]	**16,668**	**1.8**	**570**	**2.2**
6 DEVELOPMENT & HOUSING	**73,551**	**7.8**	**2,057**	**7.8**
6 100 Community development	13,331	1.4	475	1.8
6 200 Housing	39,792	4.2	1,107	4.2
6 300 Employment & training	20,428	2.2	476	1.8
7 CIVIC ADVOCACY	**9,037**	**1.0**	**177**	**0.7**
7 100 Civic & advocacy	454	0.0	12	0.0
7 200 Law & legal services	8,583	0.9	166	0.6

Table A.4 (continued)

ICNPO major group and subgroup	FTE employment		Operating expenditures	
	N	%	£m	%
8 PHILANTHROPIC INTERMEDIARIES	**7,203**	**0.8**	**191**	**0.7**
8 110 Grant-making body	4,961	0.5	148	0.6
8 120 Voluntarism promotion	2,242	0.2	43	0.1
9 INTERNATIONAL ACTIVITIES	**22,550**	**2.4**	**975**	**3.7**
11 BUSINESS ASSOCIATIONS, ETC.	**34,800**	**3.7**	**1,871**	**7.1**
TOTAL	**945,907**	**100**	**26,370**	**100**

a Data not separable between subgroups 5 100 (environment) and 5 200 (animals).

Table A.5

Broad voluntary sector revenue sources by ICNPO groups and subgroups, 1990, £ millions

ICNPO major group and subgroup	Income from government				Private giving					Private earned income						Total revenue
	Central gov't	Local gov't	User sub's, other gov't	Sub-total	Found-ations	Busi-ness	Direct indiv-idual	Feder-ated cam-paigns	Sub-total	Fees	Sales	Dues	Invest-ment income	Other revenue	Sub-total	
1 CULTURE & RECREATION	535	131	–	666	47	234	150	4	435	703	2,664	822	71	502	4,762	5,863
1 100 Culture	488	116	–	604	14	56	78	–	148	703	–	20	10	130	862	1,613
1 200 Recreation	47	14	–	61	33	178	60	–	271	–	2,657	800	61	361	3,879	4,211
1 300 Service clubs	–	1	–	1	–	–	12	4	16	–	7	2	1	12	21	39
2 EDUCATION & RESEARCH	4,050	3,229	101	7,381	263	156	109	0	528	2,577	384	2	363	301	3,626	11,535
2 100 Prim. & sec. ed.	323	2,814	–	3,138	34	23	56	0	113	1,565	33	2	113	1	1,714	4,964
2 200 Higher education	3,599	412	87	4,097	201	133	11	–	344	932	163	–	164	272	1530	5972
2 300 Other education	12	3	0	15	1	1	2	–	3	9	4	1	2	1	17	36
2 400 Research	116	–	14	130	27	0	41	–	68	71	183	–	84	27	365	564
3 HEALTH	92	72	71	236	41	15	210	4	270	414	8	–	40	59	521	1,026
3 100 Hospitals	–	–	–	0[a]	2	–	24	–	26	277	0	–	6	34	317	343
3 200 Nursing homes	8	–	50	58	11	–	–	–	11	80	0	–	2	10	92	161
3 300 Mental health	27	14	3	43	5	2	11	1	18	7	1	–	2	2	13	75
3 400 Other health	58	58	18	134	23	13	174	4	215	50	7	–	29	13	99	447
4 SOCIAL SERVICES	270	445	137	853	181	270	836	28	1,314	359	113	264	343	64	1,143	3,309
4 100 Social services	265	439	137	842	154	270	754	28	1,205	352	109	264	238	51	1,015	3,062
4 200 Emergency & r'gees	5	3	–	8	2	0	38	–	40	3	3	–	5	12	24	71
4 300 Income support	–	3	–	3	25	44	44	–	70	4	0	–	100	0	104	176

5 ENVIRONMENT[b]	120	—	—	120	14	39	173	3	228	39	34	—	88	121	283	631
6 DEVELOPMENT & HOUSING	1,056	202	559	1,817	39	36	47	4	126	687	174	0	122	228	1,211	2,954
6 100 Comm. dev't	96	137	3	236	21	30	30	4	85	97	61	0	23	24	205	527
6 200 Housing	665	4	542	1,212	2	—	8	—	11	579	47	—	88	4	719	1,941
6 300 Empl't & training	294	61	13	368	15	5	9	0	30	10	66	0	10	0	87	485
7 CIVIC ADVOCACY	37	62	5	104	6	3	4	0	13	41	8	—	4	13	65	183
7 100 Civic & advocacy	1	0	—	1	1	2	2	—	4	0	3	—	1	3	8	12
7 200 Law & legal serv.	36	62	5	103	5	2	3	0	9	41	5	—	2	9	58	170
8 PHILANTHROPY	296	23	19	337	35	26	184	0	245	38	4	—	581	10	633	1,215
8 100 Grant-making	284	5	19	307	32	25	184	0	241	36	3	—	577	6	622	1,170
8 120 Voluntarism prom.	12	18	—	30	3	1	0	0	4	2	1	—	4	4	11	45
9 INTERNATIONAL ACTIVITIES	402	402	—	402	85	59	222	57	422	93	42	—	23	90	247	1,072
11 BUSINESS ASSOCIATIONS	22	—	—	22	14	11	6	—	32	380	190	815	140	427	1,952	2,006
UNADJUSTED TOTAL[c]	6,854	4,164	919	11,937	724	848	1,942	99	3,613	5,331	3,620	1,904	1,773	1,614	14,242	29,792
ADJUSTED TOTAL[d]	6,512	4,218	900	11,630	724	848	1,942	99	3,613	5,331	3,620	1,904	1,773	1,614	14,242	29,485

a Note that this figure is not zero but is all included in user fees.

b Data not separable between subgroups 5 100 (environment) and 5 200 (animals).

c *Unadjusted total.* These totals are as reported in the statistical supplement containing data on each country in the international study (Salamon et al., 1996, p.34, table 8.2), with two exceptions. First, income of recreational organizations (group 1 200) treated as fee income for the purposes of aggregation in that publication has been reallocated as sales income here. Second, the "other income" total for subgroup 6 100 reported there is incorrect; this table gives the correct figure.

d *Adjusted total.* These are the figures that underpin the charts and figures presented in Chapter 4. These differ in aggregation from those contained in Salamon et al. (1996, p.34, table 8.2) because (a) income from government not attributable by tier (to environmental and international organizations) has been treated slightly differently in the sector-wide aggregation; and (b) an adjustment has been made to avoid double-counting of charitable quango funding of arts organizations, which appears twice in the unadjusted figures.

APPENDIX 2

A2.1 Data sources for market share estimates

General

Information on market share (Table 4.5, page 128) was variously available either for England only, for England & Wales only, for Great Britain (England, Scotland and Wales) or for the United Kingdom (England, Scotland, Wales and Northern Ireland). Where possible, we have aimed to provide UK-wide data for 1990 for consistency with the data described in Chapter 4 and Appendix 1, but this has not always proved possible. Country coverage and year are noted adjacent to the industry, in italics below.

Primary/secondary education, England, 1990

For the purposes of the structural operational definition, the voluntary sector includes voluntary aided/special agreement establishments, primarily run by religious foundations, which are almost fully funded by the state and usually regarded in the UK as "state schools". The *non-public sector* breakdown is as follows: 1.13 million pupils in charitable voluntary aided/special agreement (local state-funded) schools; 0.49 million in charitable independent (private fee-funded) schools; 0.07 million in for-profit independent (private fee-funded) schools (this figure is an estimate only, but based on reasonable assumptions; see Kendall, 1993a); 0.06 million in non-maintained (local state-funded) special schools; 0.03 million in grant-maintained (central state-funded) schools. The size of the latter category has expanded significantly in size since 1990, as schools formerly funded by the local state have "opted out" of this status to become grant-maintained charities.

Sources: Department of Education and Science (1991a, Table A13/90, p.133; 1991b, Table 1, p.1); Kendall (1993a).

Appendix 2

Health, England, 1990/91

Acute hospitals. Activity data were available in the NHS (public) sector, but not in the voluntary and for-profit sectors. The only readily available indicator across all sectors in 1990/91 was simply numbers of non-psychiatric (in-patient) beds available. This has been multiplied by occupancy data for 1986, the latest available across the sectors, to give the closest indicator we can get to "activity". Note that another indicator (not used in the table) is consistent with our estimate of the scale of NHS versus other provision: 95.5 percent of whole-time equivalent registered and enrolled nursing and midwifery staff in England were employed in NHS hospitals in 1990, leaving a residual of just 4.5 percent employed in for-profit and voluntary hospitals (these data were not separable by sector).

Nursing homes. The figures refer to the number of staffed residential places for the main adult client groups: elderly people and younger (16+) physically disabled people, people with mental health problems and people with learning disabilities. Note that psychogeriatric residents are included in the elderly persons' client group.

Sources: Department of Health (1992, Table 4.3, p.77); Laing & Buisson (1992, Figure 2.7, p.96 and Table 2.7, p.92); Nicholl et al. (1989).

Social services, England, 1990

Residential homes. The figures refer to the number of staffed residential places for the main adult client groups: elderly people and younger (16+) physically disabled people, people with mental health problems and people with learning disabilities.

Pre-school day care. Data were available on places available for children under five, in public and "other" facilities, but the latter are not split into for-profit and voluntary sectors. The figures relate to registered facilities only. An estimate of this split was available for the number of facilities and groups only for each of full-time and part-time provision (see below), based on information supplied by the Pre-school Playgroups

Association, and this ratio has been applied to give a rough indication of children in each sector (the average size of groups and facilities in each sector is unknown, so it has not been possible to adjust for this). The sectoral shares are sensitive to the definition employed. Two measures have therefore been provided. The top row relates to children in full-time day nurseries only; the bottom row covers children in both full-time and part-time groups, covering playgroups, parent and toddler groups, under-5 groups and other groups operating on a part-time basis, as well as full-time day nurseries.

Sources: Department of Health (1992, Table 4.3, p.77); Laing & Buisson (1992, Figure 2.7, p.96 and Table 2.7, p.92); Department of Health (1991, Table 2, p.8).

Housing, Great Britain, 1990

Number of completions. Data were available across sectors for permanent dwellings started, under construction at the end of the year, and completed. The table relates only to completions. 1990 was the first year ever that there were more completions in the voluntary than the public sector.

Data on percentages were available from the General Household Survey of individuals aged 16 and over (rather than organizations), which asks about housing tenure. Information on the size of the GB population from the 1991 census, and the proportion of that population aged under 16, was used as the total to which these percentages have been applied.

Two sets of figures are shown. The penultimate row relates to market share if owner-occupiers are *included* as part of the for-profit sector. The bottom row relates to market share if these are excluded. The effect is large because 66 percent of people aged over 16 were owner-occupiers, and the private rented sector is relatively small, at 8 percent. Note that the voluntary sector figures include cooperatives, some of which, strictly speaking, should not be in the sector under the structural operational definition, but were not separable in the data.

Sources: Department of the Environment et al. (1991, Table 6.1, p.64); Office of Population Censuses and Surveys Social Survey Division (1992, Table 3.1, p.56); Central Statistical Office (1994).

References

Abel Smith, B. (1964) *The Hospitals, 1800-1948*, London.

Acheson, D. and Williamson, A. (1989) *Voluntary Action and Social Policy in Northern Ireland*, Avebury, Aldershot.

Addy, T. and Scott, D. (1987) *Fatal Impacts? The MSC and Voluntary Action*, William Temple Foundation, Manchester.

Alexander, K. (1975) *Adult Education: The Challenge of Change*, HMSO, London.

Allan, S. (1993) *A Contemporary Oregon Trail*, NCVO Publications, London.

Anheier, H.K. (1995) Theories of the nonprofit sector: three issues, *Nonprofit and Voluntary Sector Quarterly*, 24, 1, 15-23.

Anheier, H.K. and Seibel, W. (eds) (1990) *The Third Sector: Comparative Studies of Nonprofit Organizations*, de Gruyter, Berlin.

Anheier, H.K., Knapp, M.R.J. and Salamon, L.M. (1993) No numbers, no policy: Can EUROSTAT count the nonprofit sector, in S. Saxon-Harrold and J. Kendall (eds) *Researching the Voluntary Sector*, vol. 1, Charities Aid Foundation, Tonbridge.

Arthur, J. (1993) Catholic responses to the 1988 Education Reform Act: problems of authority and ethos, in L. Francis and D. Lankshear (eds) *Christian Perspectives on Church Schools*, Gracewing, Leominster.

Ashworth, M. (1984) Employment in the voluntary sector, unpublished paper, Institute for Fiscal Studies, London.

Audini, B., Lelliott, P., Chisholm, D., Knapp, M.R.J. and Astin, J. (1996) Mental health residential care in eight services: description of residents and facilities, working paper, Royal College of Psychiatrists, London.

Aves, G.M. (1969) *The Voluntary Worker in the Social Services*, Allen and Unwin, London.

Badelt, C. (1990) Institutional choice and the nonprofit sector, in H.K. Anheier and W. Seibel (eds), *The Nonprofit Sector: International and Comparative Perspectives*, de Gruyter, Berlin and New York.

Bamford, T.W. (1967) *Rise of the Public Schools: A Study of Boys' Public Boarding Schools in England and Wales from 1837 to the Present Day*, Thomas Nelson & Sons, London.

Barclay, P. (1982) *Social Workers: Their Role and Tasks (The Barclay Report)*, NISW/NCVO, London.

Barker, C.R., Elliot, R.C. and Moody, S.R. (1994) The impact of the new regulatory framework on Scottish charities, [1994] S.L.T. (News), 331.

Barr, N. (1993) *The Economics of the Welfare State*, Weidenfeld and Nicholson, London.

Batsleer, J., Cornforth, C. and Paton, R. (eds) (1992) *Issues in Voluntary and Non-profit Management*, Addison Wesley, Wokingham.

Batsleer, J. (1995) Management and organisation, in J. Davis Smith, C. Rochester and R. Hedley (eds) *An Introduction to the Voluntary Sector*, Routledge, London.

Batsleer, J. and Paton, R. (1993) Managing voluntary organisations in the contract culture: continuity or change?, Paper presented at conference on *Contracting — Selling or Shrinking?*, South Bank University, July.

Bayley, M. (1973) *Mental Handicap and Community Care*, Routledge and Kegan Paul, London.

Bean, P. and Melville, J. (1989) *Lost Children of the Empire*, Unwin Hyman, London.

Beckford, J. (1991) Great Britain: voluntarism and sectoral interests, in R. Wuthnow (ed.) *Between States and Markets: The Voluntary Sector in Comparative Perspective*, Princeton University Press, Princeton, New Jersey.

Ben-Ner, A. and Van Hoomissen, J. (1993) Nonprofit organizations in the mixed economy: a demand and supply analysis, in A. Ben-Ner and B. Gui (eds) *The Nonprofit Sector in the Mixed Economy*, University of Michigan Press, Michigan.

Beresford, P. and Croft, S. (1983) Welfare pluralism: the new face of Fabianism, *Critical Social Policy*, 9, Spring, 19-39.

Beveridge, W. (1948) *Voluntary Action*, George Allen and Unwin, London.

Billis, D. and Harris, M. (1992) Taking the strain of change: UK local voluntary agencies enter the post-Thatcher period, *Nonprofit and Voluntary Sector Quarterly*, 21, 211-25.

Billis, D. and Harris, M. (eds) (1996) *Voluntary Agencies: Challenges of Organisation and Management*, Macmillan, London.

Black, A. (1984) *Guilds and Civil Society in European Political Thought from the Twelfth Century to the Present*, Methuen, London.

Bradshaw, J. (1988) Financing private care for the elderly, in S. Baldwin, G. Parker and R. Walker (eds) *Social Security and Community Care*, Avebury, Aldershot.

Brenton, M. (1985) *The Voluntary Sector in British Social Services*, Longman, Harlow.

Bridge Group (1991) Contracts for success or failure, Bridge Group memorandum, Liverpool.

Briggs, A. (1994) *A Social History of England*, 2nd edition, Weidenfield and Nicolson, London. Citations from 1994 Book Club Association edition.

References

Briggs, A. and Macartney, A. (1984) *Toynbee Hall: The First 100 Years*, Routledge and Kegan Paul, London.

Brittan, L. (1988) *A New Deal for Health Care*, Conservative Political Centre, London.

Brown, A. (1993) Aided schools: help, hindrance, anachronism or trailblazer, in L.J. Francis and D. Lankshear (eds) *Christian Perspectives on Church Schools*, Gracewing, Leominster.

Brown, R. (1991a) *Society and Economy of Modern Britain 1700-1850*, London, Routledge.

Brown, R. (1991b) *Church and State in Modern Britain*, Routledge, London.

Burnell, P. (1992) Charity law and pressure politics in Britain: after the Oxfam inquiry, *Voluntas*, 3, 3, 311-34.

Cahill, M. and Jowitt, T. (1980) The new philanthropy: the emergence of the Bradford City Guild of Help, *Journal of Social Policy*, 9, 3, 359-82.

Carter, C. and John, P. (1992) *A New Accord: Promoting Constructive Relations Between Central and Local Government*, Joseph Rowntree Foundation, York.

Catholic Bishops' Conference of England and Wales (1987) *Education Reform Bill: A Commentary for Catholics*, Catholic Bishops' Conference of England and Wales, London.

Catholic Education Service (1992) *A Response to the DfE White Paper "Choice and Diversity: A New Framework for Schools"*, Catholic Education Service, London.

Central Statistical Office (1994) *Social Trends 24*, HMSO, London.

Central Statistical Office (1995) *Social Trends 25*, HMSO, London.

Challis, L., Fuller, S., Henwood, M., Klein, R., Plowden, W., Webb, A., Whittingham, P. and Wistow, G. (1988) *Joint Approaches to Social Policy*, Cambridge University Press, Cambridge.

Charities Aid Foundation (1991) *Charity Trends*, Charities Aid Foundation, Tonbridge.

Charity Commissioners (various years) *Annual Report*, HMSO, London.

Chesterman, M. (1979) *Charities, Trusts and Social Welfare*, Weidenfeld and Nicolson, London.

Chitty, C. (1992) *The Education System Transformed*, Baseline Books, Chorlton.

Church of England Central Home for Waifs and Strays (1884) *Third Annual Report*, London.

Clark, A. (1993) *Diaries*, Weidenfeld and Nicolson, London.

Clarke, M. and Stewart, J.D. (1990) *General Management in Local Government: Getting the Balance Right*, Longman, Harlow.

Cm 2021 (1992) *Choice and Diversity: A New Framework for Schools*, HMSO, London.

Cmd 6458 (1943) *Educational Reconstruction*, HMSO, London.

Cmd 7910 (1949) *Annual Report for 1948-9*, Ministry of Health, HMSO, London.

Cmnd 9474 (1955) *Taxation of Profits and Income*, The Radcliffe Commission, HMSO, London.

Cmnd 8710 (1952) *Report of the Law and Practice Relating to Charitable Trusts (The "Nathan Report")*, HMSO, London.

Cochrane, A. (1993) *Whatever Happened to Local Government?*, Open University Press, Buckingham.

Cole, G.D.H. (1948) *A Short History of the Working Class*, Allen and Unwin, London.

Cole, G.D.H. (1945) A retrospect of the history of voluntary social service, in A.F.C. Bourdillon (ed.) *Voluntary Social Services: Their Place in the Modern State*, Methuen, London.

Coman, P. (1977) *Catholics and the Welfare State*, Longman, Harlow and New York.

Commission on Citizenship (1990) *Encouraging Citizenship: Report of the Commission*, HMSO, London.

Common, R. and Flynn, N. (1992) *Contracting for Care*, Joseph Rowntree Foundation, York.

Dancy, J. (1984) Independent schools, in J. Sutcliffe (ed.) *A Dictionary of Religious Education*, SCM, London.

Darton, R.A. and Wright, K.G. (1988) PSSRU/CHE survey of residential and nursing homes, Discussion Paper 563, Personal Social Services Research Unit, University of Kent at Canterbury.

Darton, R.A. and Wright, K.G. (1991) PSSRU/CHE survey of private and voluntary residential care and nursing homes, *PSSRU Bulletin*, 8, 10-11.

Davies, C. (1985) Government and politics in England 1450-1553, in C. Haigh (ed.) *The Cambridge Historical Encyclopedia of Great Britain and Ireland*, Cambridge University Press, Cambridge.

Davies, A. and Edwards, K. (1990) *Twelve Charity Contracts*, Directory of Social Change, London.

Davies, B.P. (1968) *Social Needs and Resources in Local Services*, Michael Joseph, London.

Davies, B.P. and Challis, D.J. (1986) *Matching Resources to Needs in Community Care*, Gower, Aldershot.

Davies, B.P., Barton, A. and McMillan, I. (1972) *Variations in Children's Services among British Urban Authorities*, Bell, London.

Davis Smith, J. (1995) The voluntary tradition: philanthropy and self-help in Britain 1500-1945, in J. Davis Smith, C. Rochester and R. Hedley (eds) *An Introduction to the Voluntary Sector*, Routledge, London.

Davison, R. (1992) *Good Neighbours: An ISIS Survey of Independent Schools' Involvement with their Local Communities*, Independent Schools Information Service, London.

Day, P. (1992) Accountability, paper for Rowntree symposium, University of Birmingham, November.

Deacon, D., Fenton, N. and Walker, B. (1995) Communicating philanthropy: the media and the voluntary sector, *Voluntas*, 6, 2, 119-39.

Deakin, N. (1994) *The Politics of Welfare: Continuities and Change*, Harvester Wheatsheaf, Hemel Hempstead.

Deakin, N. (1995) The perils of partnership, in J. Davis Smith, C. Rochester and R. Hedley (eds) *An Introduction to the Voluntary Sector*, Routledge, London.

Deakin, N. (1996) What does contracting do to users?, in D. Billis and M. Harris (eds) *Voluntary Agencies: Challenges of Organisation and Management*, Macmillan, Basingstoke.

Deakin, N. and Edwards, J. (1993) *The Enterprise Culture and the Inner Cities*, Routledge, London.

Dean, M. (1991) *The Constitution of Poverty: Toward a Genealogy of Liberal Governance*, Routledge, London.

Dearlove, J. and Saunders, P. (1991) *An Introduction to British Politics*, Polity Press in association with Blackwell, Oxford.

DeHoog, R. (1984) Theoretical perspectives on contracting out for services: implementation problems and possibilities of privatising public services, in G.C. Edwards III (ed.) *Public Policy Implementation*, JAI Press, Greenwich, Connecticut.

Department for Education (DfE) (1994a) Statistical bulletin 8/24 statistics of schools in England, January 1993, Department for Education, Darlington.

Department for Education (DfE) (1994b) *Statistics of Education: Schools 1993*, Department for Education, Darlington.

Department of Education and Science (DES) (1982) *Statistics of Education: Schools 1981*, Department of Education and Science, Darlington.

Department of Education and Science (DES) (1987) *Statistics of Education: Schools 1986*, Department of Education and Science, Darlington.

Department of Education and Science (DES) (1991a) *Statistics of Education: Schools 1990*, Department of Education and Science, Darlington.

Department of Education and Science (1991b) Statistics of schools in England — January 1990, Department of Education and Science, London.

Department of Employment (1991) *Employment Gazette*, April.

Department of Health/Price Waterhouse (1991) *Purchaser, Commissioner and Provider Roles*, Department of Health, London.

Department of Health (1992) *Health and Personal Social Services Statistics in England, 1992 Edition*, HMSO, London.

Department of the Environment, Scottish Development Department and Welsh Office (1991) *Housing and Construction Statistics 1981-1991*, HMSO, London.

Department of Health (1991) *Children's Day Care Facilities at 31 March 1991, England, A/F91/6*, Department of Health, London.

Department of Health (1994) *Personal Social Services Statistics: Residential Accommodation in England 1993*, Statistical Bulletin 1994/2, Department of Health, London.

Department of Health (1995) *Children Looked After by Local Authorities, 14 October 1991 to 31 March 1993, England, A/F 93/12*, Department of Health, London.

Department of Health and Social Security (1981) *Care in the Community: A Consultative Document on Moving Resources for Care in England*, DHSS, London.

Devlin, T. (1984) *Choosing your Independent School*, Arrow Books, London.

DiMaggio, P.J. and Anheier, H.K. (1990) The sociology of nonprofit organizations and sectors, *Annual Review of Sociology*, 16, 137-59.

Diocese of Westminster (1988) *Our Catholic Schools: Safeguarding and Developing their Catholic Identity*, Education Service, Diocese of Westminster, London.

Driscoll, L. and Phelps, B. (1992) *The Charities Act 1992: A Guide for Charities and other Voluntary Organisations*, National Council for Voluntary Organisations, London.

Dunleavy, P. and O'Leary, B. (1987) *Theories of the State: The Politics of Liberal Democracy*, Macmillan, London.

Edwards, C. and Carter, J. (1979) Day services and the mentally ill, in J.K. Wing and R. Olsen (eds) *Community Care for the Mentally Disordered*, Oxford University Press, Oxford.

Ernst and Whinney, Management Consultants (1986) *Survey of Private and Voluntary Residential and Nursing Homes for the DHSS*, London.

Evers, A. (1993) The welfare mix approach. Understanding welfare pluralism systems, in A. Evers and I. Svetlik (eds) *Balancing Pluralism. New Welfare Mixes in Care for the Elderly*, Avebury, Aldershot.

Fenton, N., Golding, P. and Radley, A. (1993) Charities, media and public opinion: a research report, Loughborough University of Technology.

Finlayson, G.H. (1990) Moving frontiers: voluntarism and the state in British social welfare 1911-1949, *Twentieth Century British History*, 1, 2, 183-206.

References

Fitzherbert, L. (1990) *Charity and the National Health: A Report on the Extent and Potential of Charitable Funds within the NHS*, Directory of Social Change, London.

Fleming, A. (1988) Employment in the public and private sectors 1982-1988, *Economic Trends*, 422, December.

Flynn, N. and Common, R. (1990) *Contracts for Community Care*, Community Care Implementation Documents, CCI 14, HMSO, London.

Flynn, N. and Common, R. (1292) *Contracting for Care*, Joseph Rowntree Foundation, York.

Fogarty, M. and Christie, I. (1991) *Companies and Communities: Promoting Business Involvement in the Community*, Policy Studies Institute, London.

Forder, J. and Knapp, M.R.J. (1993) Social care markets: the voluntary sector and residential care for elderly people in England, in S. Saxon-Harrold and J. Kendall (eds) *Researching the Voluntary Sector*, vol. 1, Charities Aid Foundation, Tonbridge.

Francis, L.J. (1993) Church and state, in L.J. Francis and D. Lankshear (eds) *Christian Perspectives on Church Schools*, Gracewing, Leominster.

Francis, L.J. and Lankshear, D. (eds) (1993) *Christian Perspectives on Church Schools*, Gracewing, Leominster.

French, D. (1992) The voluntary social welfare sector in Canterbury and Thanet, Discussion Paper 896, Personal Social Services Research Unit, University of Kent at Canterbury.

Garfield, L. (1994) *Efficiency Scrutiny: Have They Listened?*, No. 3 Report Services, Wales Council for Voluntary Action, Caerphilly.

Gash, N. (1965) *Reaction and Reconstruction in British Politics, 1832-1852*, Clarendon Press, Oxford.

Gassler, R. (1990) Nonprofit and voluntary sector economics: a critical survey, *Nonprofit and Voluntary Sector Quarterly*, 19, 2, 137-49.

Gay, B. (1985) *The Church of England and the Independent Schools*, Culham Monograph, Culham Educational Foundation, Abingdon.

General Synod of the Church of England Board of Education (nd) *Response to the DfE White Paper "Choice and Diversity"*, General Synod of the Church of England Board of Education, London.

Gerard, D. (1983) *Charities in Britain: Conservatism or Change?*, Bedford Square Press, London.

Giles, S. (1990) *The Third World Directory: A Guide to Organisations Working for Third World Development*, Directory of Social Change, London.

Gladstone, F. (1979) *Voluntary Action in a Changing World*, Bedford Square Press, London.

Gladstone, F. (1982) *Charity Law and Social Justice*, Bedford Square Press, London.

Glennerster, H. (1992) *Paying for Welfare: The 1990s*, Harvester Wheatsheaf, Hemel Hempstead.

Glennerster, H. (1995) *British Social Policy Since 1945*, Blackwell, Oxford.

Glennerster, H. and Low, W. (1990) Education and the welfare state: does it add up?, in J. Hills (ed.) *The State of Welfare: The Welfare State in Britain Since 1974*, Clarendon Press, Oxford.

Glennerster, H. and Wilson, G. (1970) *Paying for Private Schools*, Allen Lane, London.

Golding, P. and Middleton, S. (1982) *Images of Welfare: Press and Public Attitudes to Poverty*, Robertson, Oxford.

Goodin, R.E. and Le Grand, J. (1987) *Not Only the Poor*, Allen and Unwin, London.

Goodman, Lord (1976) *Report on Charity Law and Voluntary Organisations*, HMSO, London.

Gosden, P. (1973) *Voluntary Associations in Nineteenth Century Britain*, Batsford, London.

Gray, C. (1994) *Government Beyond the Centre: Sub-national Politics in Britain*, Macmillan, London.

Grønbjerg, K. (1993) Transaction costs in social service contracting: lessons from the USA, paper presented at a NCVO/South Bank University conference on *Contracting — Selling or Shrinking*, July, London.

Gutch, R. (1992) *Contracting Lessons from the US*, NCVO Publications, London.

Gutch, R. (1994) Unpublished discussant's comments at a seminar organised by the Centre for Voluntary Organisation, London School of Economics, London.

Gyford, J. (1985) *The Politics of Local Socialism*, Allen and Unwin, London.

Hadley, R. and Hatch, S. (1981) *Social Welfare and the Failure of the State*, Allen and Unwin, London.

Haigh, C. (1985) Reformation and inflation 1450-1625: overview in C. Haigh (ed.) *The Cambridge Historical Encyclopedia of Great Britain and Ireland*, Cambridge University Press, Cambridge.

Hain, L. (1980) *Neighbourhood Participation*, Temple Smith, location unknown.

Halfpenny, P. and Lowe, C. (1994) *The 1993 Individual Giving Survey*, Charities Aid Foundation, Tonbridge.

Halfpenny, P. and Pettipher, C. (1991) *Individual Giving and Volunteering in Britain: Who Gives What and Why?*, 5th edition, Charities Aid Foundation, Tonbridge.

Ham, C. (1992) *Health Policy in Britain*, Macmillan, London.

References

Ham, C. and Hill, M. (1993) *The Policy Process in the Modern Capitalist State*, Harvester Wheatsheaf, Hemel Hempstead.

Hampton, W. (1991) *Local Government and Urban Politics*, Longman, Harlow.

Handy, C. (1988) *Understanding Voluntary Organisations*, Penguin, Harmondsworth.

Hansmann, H.B. (1980) The role of nonprofit enterprise, *Yale Law Journal*, 89, 835-98.

Hansmann, H.B. (1987) The effect of tax exemption and other factors on the market share of nonprofit versus for-profit firms, *National Tax Journal*, 40, 71–82.

Harris, J. (1990) Society and the state in twentieth century Britain, in F.M.L. Thompson (ed.) *The Cambridge Social History of Britain, 1750-1950. Volume 3: Social Agencies and Institutions*, Cambridge University Press, Cambridge.

Harrison, B. (1987) Historical perspectives, in National Council for Voluntary Organisations, *Voluntary Organisations and Democracy*, NCVO, London.

Hartogs, N. and Weber, J. (1978) *Impact of Government Funding on the Management of Voluntary Agencies*, Greater New York Fund/United Way, New York.

Hatch, S. (1980) *Outside the State*, Croom Helm, London.

Hatch, S. and Mocroft, I. (1977) The relative costs of services provided by voluntary and statutory organisations, *Public Administration*, 57, 397-405.

Haughton, G., Hurst, T., Strange, I. and Thomas, K. (1995) TECs and their non-employer stakeholders, Employment Department Research Series No. 46, Research Strategy Branch, Sheffield.

Hazell, R. and Whybrew, E. (1993) *Resourcing the Voluntary Sector*, Nuffield Foundation in association with the Association of Charitable Foundations, London.

Health Care Information Services (1990) *Fitzhugh Directory of Independent Hospitals and Provident Associations*, Health Care Information Services, London.

Hedley, R. and Davis Smith, J. (1994) *Volunteers and the Contract Culture*, Volunteer Centre UK, Berkhamsted.

Hedley, R. and Rochester, C. (1992) *Understanding Management Committees*, Volunteer Centre UK, Berkhamsted.

Hems, L. and Osborne, S. edited by Passey, A. (1995) A survey of the income and expenditure of UK charities and the contribution to gross domestic product, in S. Saxon-Harrold and J. Kendall (eds) *Dimensions of the Voluntary Sector*, vol. 1, Charities Aid Foundation, Tonbridge.

Hems, L. and Passey, A. (1996) The development of a new classification system for registered charities in England and Wales, unpublished paper, National Council for Voluntary Organisations, London.

Hibbert, C. (1987) *The English: A Social History of 1066-1945*, Harper Collins, London.

Hill, C.P. (1970) *British Economic and Social History, 1700-1964*, 3rd edition, Edward Arnold, London.

Hills, J. (1989) The voluntary sector in housing: the role of British housing associations, in E. James (ed.) *The Nonprofit Sector in International Perspective*, Oxford University Press, Oxford.

Hills, J. and Mullings, B. (1990) Housing: a decent home for all at a price within their means?, in J. Hills (ed.) *The State of Welfare: The Welfare State in Britain since 1974*, Clarendon Press, Oxford.

Hobsbawm, E. (1968) *Industry and Empire: An Economic History of Britain Since 1750*, Weidenfeld and Nicholson, London.

Hodgkinson, V. and Weitzman, M. (1993) Measuring the non-profit sector in the U.S. economy: conceptual framework and methodology, *Voluntas*, 4, 2, 141-62.

Hodgkinson, V., Weitzman, M., Murray, S., Toppe, C., and Noga, S. (1992) *Nonprofit Almanac: Dimensions of the Independent Sector, 1992-93*, Jossey-Bass, San Francisco.

Hodson, P. (1984) The urban programme in England, *Charity Trends 1984*, Charities Aid Foundation, Tonbridge.

Hollingsworth, J.R. and Hollingsworth, E.J. (1989) Public organizations: the behaviour of hospitals in England and Wales, in E. James (ed.) *The Nonprofit Sector in International Perspective*, Oxford University Press, Oxford.

Holmwood, M. (1993) Social justice and equality, in R. Bellamy (ed.) *Theories and Concepts of Politics: An Introduction*, Manchester University Press, Manchester.

Home Office (1990) *Efficiency Scrutiny of Government Funding of the Voluntary Sector*, Home Office, London.

House of Commons (1975) *10th Report from the Expenditure Committee of the House of Commons*, HMSO, London.

Howard, A. (1987) *RAB: The Life of R.A. Butler*, Jonathan Cape, London.

Jacobs, B. (1989) Charities and community development in Britain, in A. Ware (ed.) *Charities and Government*, Manchester University Press, Manchester.

James, E. (1987) The nonprofit sector in comparative perspective, in W.W. Powell (ed.) *The Nonprofit Sector: A Research Handbook*, Yale University Press, New Haven, Connecticut.

References

James, E. and Rose-Ackerman, S. (1986) *The Nonprofit Enterprise in Market Economies*, Harwood, New York.

Jeffries, A. (1993) Freedom, in R. Bellamy (ed.) *Theories and Concepts of Politics: An Introduction*, Manchester University Press, Manchester.

Johnson, D. (1987) *Private Schools or State Schools: Two Systems or One?*, Open University Press, Buckingham.

Johnson, N. (1981) *Voluntary Social Services*, Martin Robertson, Oxford.

Johnson, N. (1987) *The Welfare State in Transition: The Theory and Practice of Welfare Pluralism*, University of Massachusetts Press, Amherst, Massachusetts.

Jordan, W.K. (1959) *Philanthropy in England: 1480-1660*, George Allen and Unwin, London.

Joynson, M. (1982) A perspective on child care, in *Partnership in Child Care*, National Council for Voluntary Child Care Organisations, London.

Judge, K. (1982) The public purchase of social care: British confirmation of the American experience, *Policy and Politics*, 10, 397-416.

Judge, K. and Smith, J. (1983) Purchase of services in England, *Social Service Review*, 57, 209-33.

Kavanagh, S. and Opit, L. (1996) The prevalence, balance, costs and cost-effectiveness of care for people with learning disabilities in Great Britain, Report to the Mental Health Foundation, Personal Social Services Research Unit, University of Kent at Canterbury.

Keeton, G.W. and Sheridan, L.A. (1992) *The Modern Law of Charities*, 4th edition, Barry Rose Law Publishers, Chichester.

Kemp, P. (1992) Housing, in D. Marsh and R. Rhodes (eds) *Implementing Thatcherite Policies: Audit of an Era*, Open University Press, Buckingham.

Kendall, J. (1992) Review of Jennifer R. Wolch, *The Shadow State: Government and Voluntary Sector in Transition*, *Voluntas*, 3, 2, 247-56.

Kendall, J. (1993a) Voluntary/nonprofit primary and secondary education in the UK, Discussion Paper 988, Personal Social Services Research Unit, University of Kent at Canterbury.

Kendall, J. (1993b) Voluntary sector special schools in the UK, 1990, Discussion Paper 1009, Personal Social Services Research Unit, University of Kent at Canterbury.

Kendall, J. (1995) An initial comparison of key recent estimates of the size of the UK voluntary sector, in S. Saxon-Harrold and J. Kendall (eds) *Dimensions of the Voluntary Sector*, Charities Aid Foundation, Tonbridge.

Kendall, J. (1996) United Kingdom, in L.P. Doyle (ed.) *Funding Europe's Solidarity: Resourcing Foundations, Associations, Voluntary Organisations and NGOs in the Member States of the European Union*, Association for Innovation Cooperation in Europe, Brussels.

Kendall, J. and Knapp, M.R.J. (1990) The UK voluntary sector: terminology, definitions and data, Discussion Paper 712/4, Personal Social Services Research Unit, University of Kent at Canterbury.

Kendall, J. and Knapp, M.R.J. (1991) Barriers to giving, report to the Windsor Group of Charities, Discussion Paper 741/3, Personal Social Services Research Unit, University of Kent at Canterbury.

Kendall, J. and Knapp, M.R.J. (1992) *Charity Statistics in a European Context*, RSU Occasional Paper 2, Charities Aid Foundation, London.

Kendall, J. and Knapp, M.R.J. (1993) Defining the nonprofit sector: the United Kingdom, working paper no. 5, Institute for Policy Studies, Johns Hopkins University, Baltimore, Maryland.

Kendall, J. and Knapp, M.R.J. (1995) A loose and baggy monster: boundaries, definitions and typologies, in J. Davis Smith and R. Hedley (eds) *Introduction to the Voluntary Sector*, Routledge, London.

Kendall, J. and 6, P. (1994) Government and the voluntary sector in the United Kingdom, in S. Saxon-Harrold and J. Kendall (eds) *Researching the Voluntary Sector*, vol. 2, Charities Aid Foundation Tonbridge.

Knapp, M.R.J. (1977) The design of residential homes for the elderly, *Socio-Economic Planning Sciences*, 11, 202-12.

Knapp, M.R.J. (1984) *The Economics of Social Care*, Macmillan, London.

Knapp, M.R.J. (1986) The relative cost-effectiveness of public, voluntary and private providers of residential child care, in A.J. Culyer and B. Jönsson (eds) *Public and Private Health Services*, Blackwell, Oxford. Reprinted in E. James (ed.) *The Nonprofit Sector in International Perspective*, Oxford University Press, Oxford.

Knapp, M.R.J. (1996) Are voluntary agencies really more effective?, in D. Billis and M. Harris (eds) *Voluntary Agencies: Organisation and Management in Theory and Practice*, Macmillan, London.

Knapp, M.R.J., Robertson, E. and Thomason, C. (1987) Public money, voluntary action, Discussion Paper 500, Personal Social Services Research Unit, University of Kent at Canterbury.

Knapp, M.R.J., Robertson, E. and Thomason, C. (1990) Public money, voluntary sector: whose welfare?, in H.K. Anheier and W. Seibel (eds), *The Nonprofit Sector: International and Comparative Perspectives*, de Gruyter, Berlin and New York.

Knapp, M.R.J., Cambridge, P., Thomason, C., Beecham, J.K., Allen, C. and Darton, R.A. (1992) *Care in the Community: Challenge and Demonstration*, Ashgate, Aldershot.

Knapp, M.R.J., Koutsogeorgopoulou, V. and Davis Smith, J. (1995) *Who*

Volunteers and Why? The Key Factors Which Determine Volunteering, Volunteer Centre UK, London.

Knapp, M.R.J., Davis Smith, J. and Koutsogeorgopoulou, V. (1996) Volunteer participation in community care, *Policy and Politics,* forthcoming.

Knapp, M.R.J., Beecham, J.K. and Hallam, A. (1997) The mixed economy of psychiatric reprovision, in J. Leff (ed.) *Caring in the Community,* John Wiley, Chichester, forthcoming.

Knight, B. (1993) *Voluntary Action,* HMSO, London.

Knott, J. (1986) *Popular Opposition to the Poor Law,* Croom Helm, London.

Korman, N. and Glennester, H. (1990) *Hospital Closure,* Open University Press, Buckingham.

Kramer, R.M. (1981) *Voluntary Agencies in the Welfare State,* University of California Press, Berkeley.

Kramer, R.M. (1990) Change and continuity in British voluntary organisations, 1976 to 1988, *Voluntas,* 1, 33–60.

Kramer, R.M. (1994) Voluntary agencies and the contract culture: "Dream or Nightmare", *Social Service Review,* March, 33-60.

Kramer, R.M., Lorentzen, H., Melief, W.B. and Pasquinelli, S. (1993) *Privatization in Four European Countries,* Sharpe, Armonk, New York.

Kuhnle, S. and Selle, P. (eds) (1992) *Government and Voluntary Organizations,* Avebury, Aldershot.

Labour Party (1922) *The Labour Movement and the Hospital Crisis,* Labour Party, London.

Laing and Buisson (1992) *Laing's Review of Private Health Care 1992,* Laing and Buisson, London.

Laing and Buisson (1995) Care of elderly and disabled people, in *Laing's Review of Private Health Care 1995,* Laing and Buisson, London.

Lane, J. (1994) Corporate support for the voluntary sector 1992/93, in S. Saxon-Harrold and J. Kendall (eds) *Researching the Voluntary Sector,* vol. 2, Charities Aid Foundation Tonbridge.

Lane, J. and Saxon-Harrold, S. (1993) Corporate philanthropy in Britain, in S. Saxon-Harrold and J. Kendall (eds) *Researching the Voluntary Sector,* vol. 1, Charities Aid Foundation, Tonbridge.

Lankshear, L. (1993) Church and state, in L. Francis and D. Lankshear (eds) *Christian Perspectives on Church Schools,* Gracewing, Leominster.

Lattimer, M. and Holly, K. (1992) *Charity and NHS Reform,* Directory of Social Change, London.

Lawless, P. (1990) British inner urban policy: a review, *Regional Studies,* 22, 6, 531-42.

Leat, D. (1990) Voluntary organisations and accountability, in H.K.

Anheier and W. Seibel (eds) *The Third Sector: Comparative Studies of Non-Profit Organisations*, de Gruyter, Berlin.

Leat, D. (1995) Funding matters, in J. Davis Smith, C. Rochester and R. Hedley (eds) *An Introduction to the Voluntary Sector*, Routledge, London.

Leat, D., Tester, S., and Unell, J. (1986) *A Price Worth Paying? A Study of the Effects of Government Grant Aid to Voluntary Organisations*, Policy Studies Institute, London.

Lee, N., Halfpenny, P., Jones, A. and Elliot, H. (1995) Data sources and estimates of charitable giving in Britain, *Voluntas*, 6, 1, 39-66.

Lester, A. and Pannick, D. (1991) *Independent Schools: The Legal Case*, Independent Schools Information Service, London.

Lewis, J. (1993) Developing the mixed economy of care: emerging issues for voluntary organisations, *Journal of Social Policy*, 22, 2, 173-92.

Lewis, J. (1994) Voluntary organizations in 'new partnership' with local authorities: the anatomy of a contract, *Social Policy and Administration*, 28, 3, 206-20.

Lewis, J. (1995a) *The Voluntary Sector, the State and Social Work in Britain*, Edward Elgar, Aldershot.

Lewis, J. (1995b) Welfare state or mixed economy of welfare?, *History Today*, 45, 2, 4-6.

Lewis, J. (1996) What does contracting do to voluntary agencies?, in D. Billis and M. Harris (eds) *Voluntary Agencies: Organisation and Management in Theory and Practice*, Macmillan, London.

London Economics (1995) *A Better VAT Deal for Charities*, London Economics, London.

Lynn, P. and Davis Smith, J. (1991) *The National Survey of Voluntary Activity in the UK*, Volunteer Centre UK, Berkhamsted.

Mabbott, J. (1992a) *Improving Government Funding: Report and Recommendations*, National Council for Voluntary Organisations, London.

Mabbott, J. (1992b) *Local Authority Funding for Voluntary Organisations: Report and Recommendations*, National Council for Voluntary Organisations, London.

Mabbott, J. (1993) *Local Authority Funding for Voluntary Organisations: Survey Report 1993*, National Council for Voluntary Organisations, London.

Maltby, R. (1993) *Canterbury*, David & Charles Publishers, Newton Abbot.

Marsh, D. and Rhodes, R.A.W. (eds) (1992) *Implementing Thatcherite Policies: Audit of an Era*, Open University Press, Buckingham.

McCree, B. (1993) Charity and gild solidarity in late Medieval England, *Journal of British Studies*, 32, 195-225.

Mayer, C. (1989) Discussant's comments, in N. Lee (ed.) *Sources of Charity Finance*, Charities Aid Foundation, Tonbridge.

Meadows, A. (1992) *Reaching Agreement: Wiltshire's Experience of Service Agreements*, NCVO Publications, London.

Means, R. (1976) Social work and the "undeserving" poor: the evolution of family advice centres in Birmingham, unpublished PhD thesis, University of Birmingham.

Mencher, S. (1958) Financial relationships between voluntary and statutory bodies in the British social services, *Social Service Review*, 32, 138-51.

Mocroft, I. (1989) Discussant's comments, in N. Lee (ed.) *Sources of Charity Finance*, Charities Aid Foundation, Tonbridge.

Mocroft, I. (1995) A survey of local authority payments to voluntary and charitable organisations 1992/93, in S. Saxon-Harrold and J. Kendall (eds) *Dimensions of the Voluntary Sector*, vol. 1, Charities Aid Foundation, Tonbridge.

Mocroft, I. and Thomason, C. (1993) The evolution of community care and voluntary organisations, in S. Saxon-Harrold and J. Kendall (eds) *Researching the Voluntary Sector*, vol. 1, Charities Aid Foundation, Tonbridge.

Moffat, G. (1989) Independent schools, charity and government, in A. Ware (ed.) *Charities and Government*, Manchester University Press, Manchester.

Moon, J. and Richardson, J. (1984) The unemployment industry, *Policy and Politics*, 12, 391-411.

Morrison, J. (1994a) Clearer guidelines but new restrictions, *NCVO News*, April, 53, 8.

Moyle, J. and Reid, D.J. (1975) Private non-profit-making bodies serving persons, *Economic Trends*, 78-86.

Mulgan, G. and Landry, C. (1995) *The Other Invisible Hand: Remaking Charity for the 21st Century*, Demos, London.

Mullard, M. (1993) *The Politics of Public Expenditure*, Routledge, London and New York.

Munt, I. (1991) Race, urban policy and urban problems: a critique of current UK practice, *Urban Studies*, 28, 2, 183-203.

Narendranatham, W. and Stoneman, P. (1989) The scale and determinants of large corporate donations to UK charities, 1979-86, in N. Lee (ed.) *Sources of Charity Finance*, Charities Aid Foundation, Tonbridge.

Nathan, Lord (1952) *Report of the Committee on the Law and Practice relating to Charitable Trusts* (Cmd 8710) HMSO, London.

National Audit Office (1989) *The NHS and Independent Hospitals*, HMSO, London.

National Council for Voluntary Organisations (1991) Half of ET special training needs places may be lost, *NCVO News*, February, 21.

National Council for Voluntary Organisations (1994) *Compromising on Quality. The 1994 NCVO Survey of Training Contractors: Report of Main Findings*, NCVO, London.

National Council for Voluntary Organisations (1995) Political guidelines revised, *NCVO News*, March, 62, 1.

National Old People's Welfare Committee (NOPWK) (1961) *Age is Opportunity*, National Council of Social Service, London.

Nice, D. (1992) *County and Voluntary Schools*, Longman, Harlow.

Nicholl, J.P., Beedy, N.R. and Williams, B.T. (1989) The role of the private sector in elective surgery in England and Wales, 1986, *British Medical Journal*, 298, January, 243-7.

Norman, E. (1985) *Roman Catholicism in England*, Oxford University Press, Oxford.

Northern Ireland Office (1993) *Strategy for the Support of the Voluntary Sector and for Community Development in Northern Ireland*, Northern Ireland Office, Belfast.

Nuffield Provincial Hospitals Trust (1946) *The Hospital Survey: The Domesday Book of the Hospital Service*, NPHT, London.

Obelkewich, J. (1990) Religion, in F.M.L. Thompson (ed.) *The Cambridge Social History of Britain, 1750-1950. Volume 3: Social Agencies and Institutions*, Cambridge University Press, Cambridge.

Office of Population Censuses and Surveys Social Survey Division (1992) *General Household Survey 1990*, HMSO, London.

O'Keefe, B. (1986) *Faith, Culture and the Dual System: A Comparative Study of Church and County Schools*, Falmer Press, Lewes.

Oliver, Q. (1992) The role of nonprofit organizations in a divided society: the case of Northern Ireland, in K. McCarthy, V. Hodgkinson, R. Sumariwalla et al. (eds) *The Nonprofit Sector in the Global Community: Voices from Many Nations*, Jossey-Bass, San Francisco, California.

Osborne, S. and Waterston, P. (1994) Defining contracts between the state and charitable organisations in national accounts: A perspective from the UK, *Voluntas*, 5, 3, 291-300.

Owen, D. (1964) *English Philanthropy: 1660-1960*, Harvard University Press, Cambridge, Massachusetts.

Packman, J. (1968) *Child Care: Needs and Numbers*, Allen and Unwin, London.

Packman, J. and Jordan, B. (1991) The Children Act: looking forward, looking back, *British Journal of Social Work*, 21, 4, 315-27.

Palmer, J. (1990) *Employment Training: The Decline of Care*, Scottish Council for Voluntary Organisations, Edinburgh.

References

Parker, R. (1990) Care and the private sector, in I. Sinclair, R. Parker, D. Leat and J. Williams, *The Kaleidoscope of Care: A Review of Research on Welfare Provision for Elderly People*, HMSO, London.

Passey, A. (1995) Corporate support of the UK voluntary sector 1993/94, in S. Saxon-Harrold and J. Kendall (eds) *Dimensions of the Voluntary Sector*, Charities Aid Foundation, Tonbridge.

Payne, P. (1985) The British economy: growth and structural change, in C. Haigh (ed.) *The Cambridge Historical Encyclopedia of Great Britain and Ireland*, Cambridge University Press, Cambridge.

Perkin, H. (1969) *The Origins of Modern English Society*, Routledge, London.

Perkin, H. (1989) *The Rise of Professional Society*, Routledge, London.

Picarda, H. (1995) *The Law and Practice Relating to Charities*, 2nd edition, Butterworth, London.

Pinker, R.A. (1966) *English Hospital Statistics 1861-1938*, Heinemann, London.

Pinner, J., Fenyo, A., Kendall, J., Knapp, M.R.J. and 6, P. (1993) *The Voluntary Sector and the Environment: Scope, Contributions, Issues*, RSU Occasional Paper No. 5, Charities Aid Foundation, Tonbridge.

Posnett, J. (1993) The resources of registered charities in England and Wales, in S. Saxon-Harrold and J. Kendall (eds) *Researching the Voluntary Sector*, vol. 1, Charities Aid Foundation, Tonbridge.

Posnett, J. and Chase, J. (1985) Independent schools in England and Wales, *Charity Trends 1984/85*, Charities Aid Foundation, Tonbridge.

Prochaska, F. (1988) *The Voluntary Impulse*, Faber and Faber, London.

Prochaska, F. (1990) Philanthropy, in F.M.L. Thompson (ed.) *The Cambridge Social History of Britain, 1750-1950. Volume 3: Social Agencies and Institutions*, Cambridge University Press, Cambridge.

Prochaska, F. (1992) *Philanthropy and the Hospitals of London: The King's Fund 1987-1990*, Clarendon Press, Oxford.

Pugh, M. (1993) *The Making of British Politics 1867-1939*, Blackwell, Oxford.

Pym, B. (1974) *Pressure Groups and the Permissive Society*, David and Charles, Newton Abbott.

Rae, J. (1981) *The Public School Revolution*, Faber & Faber, London.

Randon, A. and 6, P. (1994) Constraining campaigning: the legal treatment of non-profit policy advocacy across 24 countries, *Voluntas*, 5, 1, 27-58.

Rankin, M. (1987) *A Fistful of Tinsel: The Effects of the Community Programme on Local Voluntary Activity and some Proposals*, Volunteer Centre UK, Berkhamsted.

Redwood, J. (1988) *In Sickness and in Health: Managing Change in the NHS*, Centre for Policy Studies, London.

Rhodes, R.A.W. (1988) *Beyond Westminster and Whitehall: The Sub-central Governments of Britain*, Unwin Hyman, London.

Richardson, J. (1995) *Purchase of Service Contracting: Some Evidence on UK Implementation*, Inter-Agency Services Team of the National Council for Voluntary Organisations, London.

Ridley, N. (1988) *The Local Right: Enabling not Providing*, Policy Study No. 92, Centre for Policy Studies, London.

Robson, M.H. and Walford, G. (1989) Independent schools and tax policy under Mrs Thatcher, *Journal of Education Policy*, 4, 2, 149-62.

Rochester, C. (1995) Voluntary agencies and accountability, in J. Davis Smith, C. Rochester and R. Hedley (eds) *An Introduction to the Voluntary Sector*, Routledge, London.

Rodgers, B. (1949) *Cloak of Charity: Studies in Eighteenth Century Philanthropy*, Methuen, London.

Rooff, M. (1957) *Voluntary Societies and Social Policy*, Routledge and Kegan Paul, London.

Rose, M.E. (1981) Social change and the industrial revolution, in R. Flood and D. McCloskey (eds) *The Economic History of Britain since 1700, Vol I: 1780-1860*, Cambridge University Press, Cambridge.

Rose, M.E. (1982) *Understanding the United Kingdom*, Longman, Harlow.

Rosenthal, J.T. (1972) *The Purchase of Paradise: Gift-Giving and the Aristocracy, 1307-1435*, Routledge and Kegan Paul, London.

Rowntree, B.S. (1947) *The Nuffield Foundation Survey Committee on the Problems of Ageing and the Care of Old People*, Oxford University Press, London.

Rubin, M. (1988) *Charity and Community in Mediaeval Cambridge*, Cambridge University Press, Cambridge.

Russell, L., Scott, D. and Wilding, P. (1995) *Mixed Fortunes: The Funding of the Voluntary Sector*, Department of Social Policy and Social Work, Manchester University, Manchester.

Salamon, L.M. (1987) Partners in public service: toward a theory of government-nonprofit relations, in W.W. Powell (ed.) *The Nonprofit Sector: A Research Handbook*, Yale University Press, New Haven, Connecticut.

Salamon, L.M. (1994) The rise of the nonprofit sector, *Foreign Affairs*, 73, 4, 109-22.

Salamon, L.M. (1995) *Partners in Public Service: Government-Nonprofit Relations in the Modern Welfare State*, Johns Hopkins Press, Baltimore, Maryland.

Salamon, L.M. and Anheier, H.K. (1992a) In search of the non-profit sector. I: The question of definitions, *Voluntas*, 3, 2, 125-51.

References

Salamon, L.M. and Anheier, H.K. (1992b) In search of the non-profit sector. II: The problem of classification, *Voluntas*, 3, 3, 267-309.

Salamon, L.M. and Anheier, H.K. (1993) A comparative study of the non-profit sector: purpose, methodology, description and classification, in S. Saxon-Harrold and J. Kendall (eds) *Researching the Voluntary Sector*, vol. 1, Charities Aid Foundation, Tonbridge.

Salamon, L.M. and Anheier, H.K. (1994) The non-profit sector cross-nationally, in S. Saxon-Harrold and J. Kendall (eds) *Researching the Voluntary Sector*, vol. 2, Charities Aid Foundation, Tonbridge.

Salamon, L.M. and Anheier, H.K. (1996a) *The Emerging Nonprofit Sector: An Overview*, Manchester University Press, Manchester.

Salamon, L.M. and Anheier, H.K. (1996b) *Defining the Nonprofit Sector: A Cross-National Analysis*, Manchester University Press, Manchester.

Salamon, L.M., Anheier, H.K., Sokolowski, W. and associates (1996) *The Emerging Sector: A Statistical Supplement*, Institute for Policy Studies, Johns Hopkins University, Baltimore, Maryland.

Salter, B. and Tapper, T. (1985) *Power and Policy in Education. The Case of Independent Schooling*, Falmer Press, Lewes.

Salter, B. and Tapper, T. (1994) *The State and Higher Education*, Woburn Press, Ilford.

Saxon-Harrold, S. (1993) Attitudes to charities and government, in S. Saxon-Harrold and J. Kendall (eds) *Researching the Voluntary Sector*, vol. 1, Charities Aid Foundation, Tonbridge.

Schneider, J. (1993) Survey of voluntary organisations in mental health, Discussion Paper 1007, Personal Social Services Research Unit, University of Kent at Canterbury.

Schneider, J. (1994) Give and take, *Community Care*, 17 March, 22-3.

Schwarz, W (1989) *The New Dissenters: The Nonconformist Conscience in the Age of Thatcher*, Bedford Square Press, London.

Seibel, W. (1990) Organizational behavior and organizational function, in H.K. Anheier and W. Seibel (eds), *The Nonprofit Sector: International and Comparative Perspectives*, de Gruyter, Berlin.

Seibel, W. and Anheier, H.K. (1990) Sociological and political science approaches to the third sector, in H.K. Anheier and W. Seibel (eds), *The Nonprofit Sector: International and Comparative Perspectives*, de Gruyter, Berlin.

Shattock, M. (1989) The universities as charities, in A. Ware (ed.) *Charities and Government*, Manchester University Press, Manchester.

Sheard, J. (1992) Volunteering and society, 1960 to 1990, in R. Hedley and J. Davis Smith (eds) *Volunteering and Society: Principle and Practice*, Bedford Square Press, London.

Sheard, J. (1995) From Lady Bountiful to active citizen: volunteering and the voluntary sector, in J. Davis Smith, C. Rochester and R. Hedley (eds) *An Introduction to the Voluntary Sector*, Routledge, London.

Shepherd, M. (1989) Primary care of patients with mental disorder in the community, *British Medical Journal*, 9 September, 299, 666-9.

Shore, P., Knapp, M.R.J., Kendall, J., Fenyo, A. and Carter, S. (1994) The local voluntary sector in Liverpool, in S. Saxon-Harrold and J. Kendall (eds) *Researching the Voluntary Sector*, vol. 2, Charities Aid Foundation, Tonbridge.

Simey, M. (1951) *Charitable Effort in Liverpool*, Liverpool University Press, Liverpool.

Skeffington, Lord (1969) *People and Planning: Report of the Committee on Public Participation in Planning*, HMSO, London.

Smelser, N. (1991) *Social Paralysis and Social Change: British Working Class Education in the Nineteenth Century*, University of California Press, Berkeley, California.

Smith, F. (1936) The nation's schools, in H.J. Laski, W.I. Jennings and W.A. Robson (eds) *A Century of Municipal Progress: The Last Hundred Years*, Allen and Unwin, London.

Smith, S.R. and Lipsky, M. (1993) *Nonprofits for Hire: The Welfare State in the Age of Contracting*, Harvard University Press, London.

Social Services Yearbook 1991/92 (1991) Longman, Harlow.

Stedman Jones, G. (1971) *Outcast London: a Study in the Relationship between Classes in Victorian Society*, Clarendon Press Oxford. Citations from Penguin 1992 edition.

Stephen, Sir James (1849) *Essays in Ecclesiastical Biography*, 4th edition, publisher unknown, London.

Stevenson, P. (1994) Raising and utilisation of capital by housing associations for housing and care services for elderly people, paper presented at Laing and Buisson's seventh annual Elderly Care Conference, London.

Stoker, G. (1991) *The Politics of Local Government*, 2nd edition, Macmillan, London.

Sumner, G. and Smith, R. (1969) *Planning Local Authority Services for the Elderly*, Allen and Unwin, London.

Sutherland, G. (1990) Education, in F.M.L. Thompson (ed.) *The Cambridge Social History of Britain, 1750-1950. Volume 3: Social Agencies and Institutions*, Cambridge University Press, Cambridge.

Taylor, M. (1995) Voluntary action and the state, in D. Gladstone (ed.) *British Social Welfare: Past, Present and Future*, University College London Press, London.

Taylor M. and Lansley, J. (1992) Ideology and welfare in the UK: the implications for the voluntary sector, *Voluntas*, 3, 2, 153-74.

Taylor, M. and Lewis, J. (1993) Contracting: What does it do to voluntary and non-profit organisations?, paper presented at NCVO conference, London, July.

Taylor, M., Kendall, J. and Fenyo, A. (1993) The survey of local authority funding of the voluntary sector, in J. McQuillan (ed.) *Charity Trends 1993*, Charities Aid Foundation, Tonbridge.

Taylor, M., Langan, J. and Hoggett, P. (1995) *Encouraging Diversity: Voluntary and Private Organisations in Community Care*, Arena, Aldershot.

Thane, P. (1982) *The Foundations of the Welfare State*, Longman, Harlow.

Thomas, D. (1983) *The Making of Community Work*, George Allen and Unwin, London.

Thomas, E.G. (1980) The old Poor Law and medicine, *Medical History*, 24, 1-19.

Thompson, E.P. (1980) *The Making of the English Working Class*, Gollancz, London. First printed 1936; citations from 1980 Penguin edition.

Tinker, A. (1992) *Care for Elderly People in Modern Society*, Longman, Harlow.

Titmuss, R. (1958) *Essays on the Welfare State*, Unwin University Books, London.

Tudor (1995) *Tudor on Charities*, 8th edition, edited by J. Warburton and D. Morris, Sweet and Maxwell, London.

Underhill, A. and Hayton, D.J. (1995) *Law Relating to Trusts and Trustees*, 15th edition, Butterworth, London.

Unell, J. (1989) The changing pattern of public sector support for voluntary organisations, in N. Lee (ed.) *Sources of Charity Finance*, Charities Aid Foundation, Tonbridge.

US Small Business Administration (1984) *Unfair Competition by Nonprofit Organizations with Small Business: An Issue for the 1980s*, US Small Business Administration, Washington, DC.

Vincent, R. (1991) *Charity Accounting and Taxation*, Butterworth, London. A new edition is in preparation.

Vladeck, B.C. (1976) Why nonprofits go broke, *The Public Interest*, 42, 86-101.

Wagner, G. (1987) *The Chocolate Conscience*, Chatto and Windus, London.

Walby, C. (1993) The contract culture — mix or muddle?, speech to a conference organised by the ACC, AMA, and NCB, March.

Walford, G. (1990) *Privatisation and Privilege in Education*, Routledge, London.

Walford, G. (ed.) (1991) *Private Schooling: Tradition, Change and Diversity*, Paul Chapman, London.

Walsh, K. (1991) *Competitive Tendering for Local Authority Services: Initial Experiences*, HMSO, London.

Warburton, J. (1986) *Unincorporated Associations: Law and Practice*, Sweet and Maxwell, London.

Warburton, J. (1990) Charity corporations: the framework for the future? *The Conveyancer and Property Lawyer*, March-April, 95-105.

Warburton, J. (1993) Legal studies on voluntary and non-profit organisations in the United Kingdom: achievements and prospects, paper presented at SAUS/NCVO research symposium, Nonprofit studies: the state of the art.

Ware, A. (1989a) Introduction: the changing relations between charities and the state, in A. Ware (ed.) *Charities and Government*, Manchester University Press, Manchester.

Ware, A. (ed.) (1989b) Religion, charities and the state, in A. Ware (ed.) *Charities and Government*, Manchester University Press, Manchester.

Ware, A. (ed.) (1989c) *Between Profit and State*, Polity Press, Cambridge.

Webb, A. and Wistow, G. (1987) *Social Work, Social Care and Social Planning*, Longman, Harlow.

Webb, A., Day, L. and Weller, D. (1976) *Voluntary Social Services: Management Resources*, Personal Social Services Council, London.

Webb, S. and Webb, B. (1912) *The Prevention of Destitution*, Longmans Green, London.

Weisbrod, B.A. (1975) Towards a theory of the nonprofit sector, in E. Phelps (ed.) *Altruism, Morality and Economic Theory*, Russell Sage, New York.

Weisbrod, B.A. (1977) *The Voluntary Nonprofit Sector*, D.C. Heath, Lexington, Massachusetts.

Weisbrod, B.A. and Schlesinger, M. (1986) Public, private, nonprofit ownership and the response to asymmetric information: the case of nursing homes, in S. Rose-Ackerman (ed.) *The Economics of Nonprofit Institutions*, Oxford University Press, Oxford and New York.

Wertheimer, A. (1991) *Housing Consortia for Community Care*, National Federation of Housing Associations, London.

Whitaker, B. (1974) *The Foundations: An Anatomy of Philanthropy and Society*, Eyre Methuen, London.

Whiteman, P.G. (1988) *Whiteman on Income Tax*, Sweet and Maxwell, London.

Williams, I. (1989) *The Alms Trade*, Unwin Hyman, London.

Williams, L. (1984) Urban aid and voluntary organisations in Wales, 1978-84, *Charity Trends 1983/84*, Charities Aid Foundation, Tonbridge.

References

Wilson, D. and Butler, R. (1985) Corporatism in the British voluntary sector, in W. Streeck and P.C. Schmitter (eds) *Private Governments as Agents of Public Policy*, Sage, London.

Wilson, D. and Game, C. with Leach, S. and Stoker, G. (1994) *Local Government in the United Kingdom*, Macmillan, London.

Windsor (1994) 11th Arnold Goodman lecture, delivered by the Duke of Edinburgh, Charities Aid Foundation, London.

Wistow, G., Knapp, M.R.J., Hardy, B. and Allen, C. (1992) From providing to enabling: local authorities and the mixed economy of social care, *Public Administration*, 70, 24-45.

Wistow, G., Knapp, M.R.J., Hardy, B. and Allen, C. (1994) *Social Care in a Mixed Economy*, Open University Press, Buckingham.

Wistow, G., Knapp, M.R.J., Hardy, B., Forder, J. and Kendall, J. (1996) *Social Care Markets: Progress and Prospects*, Open University Press, Buckingham.

Wolch, J. (1990) *The Shadow State: Government and Voluntary Sector in Transition*, The Foundation Center, New York.

Wolfenden, Lord (1978) *The Future of Voluntary Organisations*, Report of the Wolfenden Committee, Croom Helm, London.

Woodfield, P., Binnes, G., Hirst, R. and Neal, D. (1987) *Efficiency Scrutiny of the Supervision of Charities*, HMSO, London.

Wright, F. (1992) *Fee Shortfalls in Residential and Nursing Homes: The Impact on the Voluntary Centre*, Age Concern Institute of Gerontology, London.

Wuthnow, R. (ed.) *Between States and Markets: The Voluntary Sector in Comparative Perspective*, Princeton University Press, Princeton, New Jersey.

Young, D.R. (1987) Executive leadership in nonprofit organizations, in W.W. Powell (ed.) *The Nonprofit Sector: A Research Handbook*, Yale University Press, New Haven, Connecticut.

Younghusband, E. (1978) *Social Work in Britain: 1950-1975, Volume 1*, George Allen and Unwin, London.

Zerubavel, E. (1991) *The Fine Line*, University of Chicago Press, Chicago, Illinois.

6, P. (1991) *What is a Voluntary Organisation? Defining the Voluntary and Non-profit Sectors*, National Council for Voluntary Organisations, London.

6, P. (1993) European competition law and the non-profit sector, *Voluntas*, 3, 2, 215-46.

6, P. (1994) *The Question of Independence*, Demos, London.

6, P. and Fieldgrass, J. (1992) *Snapshots of the Voluntary Sector*, National Council for Voluntary Organisations, London.

Name index

Abel Smith, B., 223
Acheson, D., 158
Addy, T., 145
Anheier, H.K., 14-15, 17, 21, 27, 103, 109-110, 124, 245, 248, 253
Arthur, J., 193
Ashworth, M., 104
Audini, B., 227
Aves, G.M., 135
Badelt, C., 244
Bamford, T.W., 178, 199
Barclay, P., 204
Barker, C.R., 97
Barr, N., 261
Batsleer, J., 134, 161
Bayley, M., 204
Bean, P., 240
Beckford, J., 15, 20, 134
Ben-Ner, A., 12-13
Beresford, P., 138
Billis, D., 231
Black, A., 30
Bradshaw, J., 216
Brenton, M., 7-8, 17, 20, 55, 134, 139, 204, 241, 246
Briggs, A., 31-32, 44
Brittan, L., 238
Brown, A., 188
Brown, R., 168, 172
Burnell, P., 91
Butler, R., 245
Cahill, M., 43-44
Carter, C., 152
Carter, J., 227
Challis, D.J., 204
Challis, L., 152, 209
Chase, J., 200, 265

Chesterman, M., 20, 29-30, 32, 34, 41, 47, 55, 62, 69-70, 255-256
Chitty, C., 189, 191
Christie, I., 127
Clark, A., 145
Clarke, M., 228
Cochrane, A., 151, 154
Coman, P., 177, 199
Common, R., 233, 235, 239, 241
Croft, S., 138
Dancy, J., 189
Darton, R.A., 214
Davies, A., 234
Davies, B.P., 204, 213, 220
Davies, C., 31
Davis Smith, J., 29, 33, 40, 53, 61, 107, 115, 205, 211, 229, 246, 252, 261
Davison, R., 88
Day, P., 142
Deacon, D., 6, 125
Deakin, N., 52-53, 135, 147, 203, 230, 235-236
Dean, M., 34, 38
Dearlove, J., 27
DeHoog, R., 251
Devlin, T., 189
DiMaggio, P.J., 27
Driscoll, L., 62
Dunleavy, P., 27
Edwards, C., 227
Edwards, J., 147
Edwards, K., 234
Evers, A., 162
Fenton, N., 4, 6, 125
Fieldgrass, J., 107
Finlayson, G.H., 54, 202

Subject index